CRYSTAL Love SECRETS

Also by Brett Bravo

CRYSTAL HEALING SECRETS

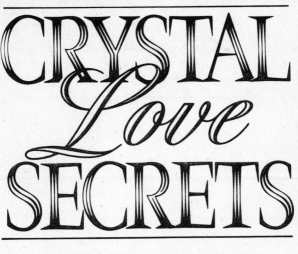

CRYSTAL Love SECRETS

BRETT BRAVO

WARNER BOOKS

A Time Warner Company

Warner Books, Inc., 666 Fifth Avenue, New York, NY 10103

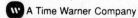 A Time Warner Company

Printed in the United States of America
First printing: July 1991
10 9 8 7 6 5 4 3 2 1

Library of Congress Cataloging-in-Publication Data

Bravo, Brett,
    Crystal love secrets / by Brett Bravo.
      p.   cm.
    Includes bibliographical references and indexes.
    ISBN 0-446-39169-7
    1. Crystals—Miscellanea.   2. Love—Miscellanea.   I. Title.
BF1442.C78B72   1991
133—dc20   90-44869
                                  CIP

Book design and illustrations by Giorgetta Bell McRee

To my sons, Lance Lindborg and Link Lindborg, to my adopted sons, Larry and Randy, to their fathers, and to my father, Carleton Wilson, who taught me so much about the masculine side of myself. That part which constantly amazes me and which I have finally learned to love—and . . .

"To all the boys I've loved before."

This is written for everyone who believes that we "fall into love" or that we "choose" love or that it is difficult to "find" love or that it is dishonest to say "I love you" unless you are "in" love or related by blood.

ACKNOWLEDGMENTS

Thank you, Nicki Monaco Clark, for knowing that I would write this book and planting the seeds. Thank you, Eva Shaw, for playing your role so perfectly, encouraging me to quit stalling and for helping me to get the proposal into action. Thank you, Pat Buc and Karen J. Stevenson, for patience, dedication, encouragement, and the true love that allowed me to write while you took care of my interests. Roseann Aud and Sheila Anderson have given me the great gifts of their energy beyond words to describe. I will always be "in love" with each one credited here.

Thank you, John Brockman and Katinka Matson, for representing me and being really good, efficient, and reliable agents in New York.

Thank you, Leslie Keenan, my editor at Warner Books, for believing in yourself and me.

My praise to and admiration for Lisa Karl who had to catch the pieces in midair and did it with agility, sensitivity and love.

Thank you, Warner Books, for fabulous distribution all over the world, and for a reasonably priced book.

This is also written for the Self because I want to love

my *Self* more clearly and more dearly every day of my life. I want you also to love, respect, and honor your "Self." The Spirit that we were millions of years ago, are now, and will be millions of years in the future is a *divine spark of the "stuff"* that we call love.

> The answer that I cannot find is known to my
>   unconscious mind
> I have no reason to despair because I am al-
>   ready there.

> —**W. H. Auden**

CONTENTS

INTRODUCTION

Brett Bravo has certainly done it again! Her unique trailblazing work and approaches to healing and relationships are reflected in her most recent gem, *Crystal Love Secrets*.

I remember quite vividly the first time I met Brett, several years ago at a national conference on crystals. In the midst of the excitement and controlled chaos of the movement she stood before me with a calm, gentle, and peaceful presence that was clear as a bell. In keeping with her unique being, she presented us with another extension of herself in 1988, when *Crystal Healing Secrets* emerged radiating the same clarity and calm in the midst of the accelerating chaos of our time. It is a beacon of wisdom and enlightenment that is relevant for us all.

This book, *Crystal Love Secrets*, stands out above the contemporary explosion of crystal books as a clear light, filled with clarity and insight, and imparting the wisdom of the ages in a manner that can be easily integrated into the reader's daily life. It is cogent, clear, and needed.

Because of Brett's gift of expression this book transcends the New Age genre and offers its readers, regardless of their outlook, practical information and guidance in the use of crystals and gemstones. These precious gifts possess the capacity to heal, enhance, and enrich our lives. This begins with the myriad of relationships that give substance and meaning to our world.

During the 1980s crystals became a mainstay of the New Age movement. They were subjected to a considerable amount of media hype and scrutiny. Away from the sensationalism, scientists have produced impressive results in a variety of settings. They have documented the healing powers of crystals and gem stones, unlocking the structural cell changes produced with controlled application. I have used them in my practice and found them to be wonderful agents in facilitating healing on both the physical and emotional levels.

Over the years Brett has been consistent in her work and insight, providing assistance to thousands afflicted with physical and emotional disease. She reminds us constantly that love is the source of healing, and that the path to healing begins first with loving the Self as an expression of divine love. Love is the energy that binds all things together. It is the consciousness guiding all of creation. Love is the prism through which all of life is reflected, including the rainbow of relationships we all possess.

Brett's message is profound in its depth, elegant in its simplicity, and paradoxical in its mystery. She provides us with great insight into the mysteries of the ages that have circumscribed life, love, and crystals. These are the mysteries that have prompted the search for a greater understanding of our relationships with one another, nature, and God.

Crystal Love Secrets spans the realm and covers a variety of love relationships: self-love, sexual, romantic, familial, filial, and unconditional. This book provides a much-needed contemporary insight into the wisdom of the ancients. It combines information about a variety of crystals that help to promote the expressions of love through harmonizing and healing the emotional and mental focus for each of us. Her writings demonstrate the importance of love and all of its expressions. It is not enough to say that love makes the world go round. In order to heal ourselves, we must become the embodiment of the living light of God that is love.

If we are to restore our planet, relieve ourselves of the divisive perspectives that separate us in so many ways, then it is vital for us to confront the separations and pain that reside within. This task can only be accomplished through love. Love is the greatest source of healing. It is the presence from which all healing flows. Love resolves the divisive nature of our world view— one that separates us from each other in our families, communities, nations, and the world—and binds us together to make us whole.

Crystal Love Secrets prompts us to re-evaluate our relationships in the light of a greater understanding, one that expresses not only the relationship with ourselves, but with the Cosmos. Brett's writings offer a balanced, evenhanded approach, acting as a bridge between the physical realms of life, the seen and unseen, the known and unknown, the masculine and feminine, the rational and intuitive.

Brett shows us how crystals reflect the vibrations of the Cosmos, expressions of God, and enable us to be all that we were intended to be. As scientists throughout the world continue to demonstrate the healing powers of crystals, Brett provides information that can be easily integrated into the daily life of anyone who reads it.

Crystal Love Secrets allows its readers the opportunity

to use crystals on a daily basis in an enriching and balanced manner. I am certain that readers will be excited and enlightened by the fund of knowledge she imparts. Her understanding and insight will assist our process of healing so we may live the abundant lives we were meant to live and contribute to the healing of our world. We are all indebted to Brett for sharing the light of her remarkable insight and clarity. May we continue to transform our lives and world into the prosperity of light and love that is available for us.

Elaine Ferguson, M.D.
Chicago, Illinois

Choosing a Crystal by Sight or Touch

This book was written for both you and me to use as a learning process. Please read the beginning chapters before you look up a specific crystal. I include these chapters to prepare a way for you to best experience the crystal energies.

Many readers worldwide have called or written me, asking that I prescribe a crystal for them. I want you to be able to decide on your own which crystal will help you—even before you see the crystal profiles.

Since you will not have my tray of healing and love crystals to see and hold, you will need to do some looking elsewhere. These are alternative ways to get in touch with your inner knowings of which crystal will help bring the love you want:

1. Find a museum of natural history. They usually have a mineral and gem display.
2. Find a local rock shop or gem and mineral club—every city has "rock hounds" who collect these things.
3. Go to jewelry stores and ask to see the gems you've never seen.
4. Go to the library and check out the best color photography of crystals and gems.

I suggest *Gemstones of the World* by Walter Schuman, published in Germany, or *Gems and Jewelry* by Joel Arem, Bantam Books. Neither of these books has the newer crystals. To find Larimar and Sugilite, get issues of *Lapidary Journal* from the library.

I have rough crystals and a price list if you cannot find them to buy (call 619-755-1530). Many metaphysical and New Age bookstores also sell crystals of many types.

Once you have done your homework, your heart (Spirit Body) and solar plexus (Emotional Body) will like one better than all the rest.

All of the crystals are love crystals, and all of them have healing vibrations. You cannot make a mistake if you follow your heart!

I Do Not Believe

Consciousness is woven implicitly into all matter, and matter is woven out of consciousness: matter and meaning affect each other. The assumption that we are separate atoms just doesn't work. To continue with that assumption could mean our extinction.

—David Bohm, Ph.D.
Physicist, author, metaphysician

In my first book, *Crystal Healing Secrets*, the first chapter began with a statement of what I believe, so readers could stop and decide for themselves whether to proceed.

This book begins with the personal biases of what I do not believe, therefore giving the reader the same option.

Contemplate these ideas; it is not necessary to agree, only to allow. Your own inner knowing will eventually sift and sort until there is a feeling of security that comes from the deep center of your being.

These are my personal biases:

. . . I do not believe the Designing Creative Force in the Universes, called God, is a masculine personality. For centuries children have gladly accepted the picture of Michelangelo's painting of an old man, with a great flowing beard, sitting on a throne somewhere "out there" in "heaven" as a subconscious substitute for an absent Earthly Father.

. . . I do not believe the Designing Creative Force in the Universe could possibly be a Goddess! Being a feminine force alone would never produce the explosion that scientists are calling the big bang, the creation of our particular Universe.

. . . I do not believe any thing, mineral, plant, animal, or human is composed of only one gender, that is, either masculine or feminine. The oriental symbol of the yin-yang represents the ancient wisdom of a circle divided into equal parts of black and white. In the center of the white there is a black dot. In the center of the black there is a white dot. The yin-yang indicates that separation is impossible.

In every human there are masculine and feminine glands that take special form in the embryo and remain after the chromosomes have decided the sexual preference/appearance of the developing baby.

. . . I do not believe that Homo sapiens on Earth can successfully separate themselves into sexes or warring sides of Masculine and Feminine Energy. The tension in human relationships of all types stems from the basic "war between the sexes."

Negativity can be subversive or just plain sneaky.

Worldwide television, carrying programs appearing to be situation comedies or soap operas, is subliminally teaching stereotypical attitudes of disgust between the sexes. Many a serious thought is planted within a joke.

. . . I do not believe we can love anyone else expertly until we can show total affection and acceptance to our own internal spirit, the male and female within ourselves, and to the body we have created for ourselves to inhabit!

To be dissatisfied, disappointed, even to hate our own body, causes a war inside. This would repress any real love energy that might develop to be given away.

Even though for two thousand years we have been taught differently, self-love, self-trust, self-kindness must be established before there is any reservoir to give away.

. . . I do not believe that Spirituality and Sexuality are opposites. For several thousand years, religions have attempted to separate these two energies into moral issues.

In esoteric writings the word *sexuality* has been designated as the masculine positive force. It is described as desire, brightness, action, visible, outgoing, mentally creative, flying-away, or uncontrolled energy that gets things moving.

The feminine energy is described as passive, grounded stillness, waiting, darkness, invisible, receptive, intuitive, nurturing, and physically creative.

These energies described as Masculine and Feminine energies (in the most positive sense) cannot be separated from Spiritual energies. They cannot be separated from sexual interaction on Earth.

On the highest level we are describing the Designing Creative Force in the Universe. On a different level we are describing sexual union between a man and a woman. On yet another level we are describing what takes place within a single being when a truly creative vision is born and made visible, usable. The two energies are united within.

The right side of our brain is devoted to the Feminine Energy, and the left side of our brain is using Masculine Energy. The right side sits quietly waiting, appreciating all the glories of the Universes, until it receives an insight, intuition, inspiration. This is relayed by the connecting cortex to the left side, which actively, logically gets to work and figures out a practical way to bring it into physical reality, with Masculine Energy.

. . . I do not believe the changeover from matriarchal to patriarchal power was an accident, nor was it harmful to Earth's evolution. It had happened before and is happening again, now. The pendulum swings back and forth at regular intervals to allow each of the two basic polarities of the Designing Creative Force to express itself. Neither energy is ever forsaken when one is operating in a predominant role on the Earth Plane.

. . . I do not believe this shift from male-female role-playing into a "person"-oriented society is easy for either sex. Personal, erotic, romantic relationships have been in such a state of flux for approximately a century, many have almost given up hope of ever accomplishing "relating" on a committed or long-term basis.

We contain within each of us Masculine, Feminine, Spiritual, and Sexual energies. How we choose to direct these energies makes all the difference in our ability to love and be loved.

. . . I do not believe there is only one way to evolve to spiritual understanding on Earth. Many different paths lead to the mountaintop. Some are shorter but may be more difficult. Others take longer but may be less stressful. Everyone eventually reaches the summit.

. . . I do not believe that any reader must believe what I have decided is true for me at this time. When I have more experiences, or acquire more information, I could change my mind. In the final scheme of things we are all left to our own choices. We do have total freedom to change and grow in any direction.

. . . I do not believe we can have total health without a good understanding of how love can be made into a formula and "acted out" until it becomes a natural response. Just to say "understand love" is to say understand Creation and All That Is! That becomes such a tall order, no one believes it possible.

On the level of scientific observation by wholistic medical healers and laboratory research, it has been found that more love means more health.

Crystallography as a science is only five hundred years old. We are learning new things every day. *The System of Mineralogy* (James D. Dana, 1837–1868) was published in 1906; the author identified two thousand crystals, gems, and minerals. Rock hounds, miners, geologists, petrologists, archaeologists, and tourists by accident have discovered another thousand new minerals and gems.

The crystals I am discussing here have all been pushed up by Mother Earth or have been exposed in the past few years. I feel she is acting in cycle to the new cosmic rays with perfect timing.

All crystals transmit a love quotient, because we are all involved in the radiation and "stuff" of the cosmos we call *love*.

PART I

LOVE'S CONNECTING
ENERGIES

The Four Facets
of Love

According to quantum mechanics, the physical world is not a structure built out of independently existing, unanalyzable entities, but rather, a web of relationships between elements whose meanings arise from their relationship to the whole.

—H. P. Stapp
Atomic Energy Commission

It may be that the search for the ultimate "stuff" of the universe is a crusade for an illusion. At the subatomic level, mass and energy change unceasingly into each other.

—Gary Zukav
The Dancing Wu Li Masters

Love is the most powerful, pure, and intense of all the energies in existence. Love is a dynamic, Universal Energy that changes every receptive thing it touches. It is not something that comes into being through the practice of attachment or togetherness.

Physicists have so far identified five forces in the Universe that comprise the sustaining flow of existence: Strong Force, Weak Force, Electric Force, Magnetic Force, and Unknown Force. All are components of the one great invisible light that we are. When we begin to take apart bit by bit anything that appears physically solid to us, at the last increment we find an atom, which we have never seen. Physicists can only speculate on the vibration atoms create. We have learned to manipulate this powerful, invisible energy into horrible explosions or into positive physical aids to our own health, warmth, and movement.

Radiation is the word we use to describe the natural "stuff" we have discovered, both inside the Earth and in the outside we call space. What does the word *radiate* mean? It derives from *radius*, a geometric term that is the measurement of a circle beginning at the center with a straight line to the circumference.

We speak of holy, religious, and mythological Earth personalities as radiant! Ancient artists have depicted a glow around the bodies or heads of persons who are reported by their peers as special in their display of kindness, sweetness, or power of a mystical source.

On some level all of us can sense this energy in a person, animal, or plant, even in rocks. Kirlian photography has now made it possible for us to see this radiation, or aura, of various colored lights around each thing. The word *radiant* suggests that we are each a circle with a center point, and the light of us begins in the center and shines outward. Radiation, so far as we know now, can only be called a dance of invisible energy!

Everything as we know it is permeated with this light. We are bodies who appear solid and yet we radiate to each other.

Our inner point sends out a light vibration that meshes with, entangles itself in, and is a part of everything that is! This is the latest discovery of quantum physics. Nothing is separate from anything. All is sustained, nurtured, changed, healed, recycled, and continually transformed within the Cosmic Circle—but never destroyed! The total energy of all the names we have called the parts can only be labeled as love. It sustains us. It is a light so brilliant we cannot see our own light. We are part of love and we are never separated from love.

Any one of us can recognize a sure sign of anything (person, animal, plant, crystal, or place) that is in harmony with the flow of the love energy because it radiates. From out of its center comes a glow! Even if we cannot see it, we can feel it.

Think back across your life, to the times when you felt this wonderful glow of joy coming to you from a puppy, a kitten, a bunny, your own favorite pet running to meet you! That is *Love Energy.*

Remember the times when you stood enthralled by our Mother Earth at some precious place where she is especially beautiful? Everyone has found a place like that. Even in the slums of a giant city, humans can feel the Radiant Love Energy in some special little corner of their world.

I have a friend who was born in Minneapolis, Minnesota, on the "wrong side of town" by the railroad tracks. The thing that he remembers about the Radiant Love Energy he felt there was going downtown to stay with his grandmother in her tiny old apartment. He found a place of joy, excitement, and safety in a small window seat. There he could curl up and see the stars at night, the neon signs in the street below, the people moving about, but was himself both protected and quietly involved. That is *Love Energy*.

I went skiing once in a remote area in Montana called Big Mountain. There were very few people there that day. I rode to the top of the ski lift, got off, and discovered myself totally alone! I moved away from the lift over to the edge of the downhill run. I turned slowly around and looked in a complete circle, 360 degrees of the largest expanse of Mother Earth I had ever seen. There were no other beings in sight, or any constructed things, only hundreds of miles of snow-covered peaks of purity below me. As I stood there in the clean, sparkling dazzle of sun on snow, I instantly recognized the Radiant Love Energy flowing through me. At that moment I was not alone! I was surrounded and engulfed in the *Life Force Energy*! Mother Earth was radiating and I saw her aura! The Sun was radiating and I felt his warmth. The snow was radiating and I felt its reflection, the crisp vibration of water transforming, in two states of life at once. The air was alive with electricity, ultraviolet, X rays, radio waves, infrared, gamma, and all the colors invisible to our eyes at this time. These feelings poured into me and out of me. I was breathing in the great Love Energy of the Universes. My heart was exploding with adoration, gratitude, and praise; my true Spirit recognized itself and its eternal connection to all that is.

Several years ago there was a Hollywood film about our space program, called *The Right Stuff*, which attempted to describe the mystical character and integrity of our Selves and our Universe. Each astronaut upon leaving Earth was psychologically and spiritually changed by discovering the "stuff" was even more powerful "out there." Edgar Mitchell, after walking on the Moon, returned to Earth so impressed that he founded The Institute for the Study of Noetic Sciences, an organization devoted to exploring the human mind and its ability to communicate and perceive through the "stuff" that permeates the Universes.

Albert Einstein, the most renowned mathematical scientist of our times, is famous for his recognition of the divine connection that we as humans have by using the "right stuff." He uses a special label for it in this quote: "Imagination is more important than knowledge." He acknowledged that his equations came to him from the Source of all thought, through his imagination. The right side of the brain receives the living helpful hints and humans call it insight, inspiration, or imagination.

You must be asking now, what does all of this "energy field" information have to do with crystals and/or love? You will be reading in simple terms how to translate this "right stuff," or Love Energy, into action in your own day-to-day living through the use of crystals in meditation. Once you open your mind and allow your Spirit to merge (or recognize that it is merged) with all that is, it will not be difficult to imagine your connections.

Crystals can work very effectively on the Emotional Body. The Emotional Body is a part of the aura, or radiation, from the physical body. It is much more powerful than the visible body and can perform at great distances. It is referred to in some esoteric writings as the Desire Body. It has a central attachment and energy source in the solar plexus of humans. It has a mind of its own and responds to all outside stimuli, then sends its messages to the brain (the Mental Body), which then directs our physical mechanisms.

The Emotional Body, being special in its survival tactics, makes decisions for or against love. It is a feeling in the solar plexus that signals the possibility of emotional attraction between two persons.

The majority of us monitor our fellow humans unconsciously by a mechanism we call feeling, but not with our hands in touching. We "feel" the energy or lack of it through different sensors, basically in our solar plexus.

Solar means "of the Sun." *Plexus* is a complexly interconnected arrangement of parts, a network. It comes from the Latin word that means to braid or intertwine. The *solar plexus* of the human is the physical area of the body that is intertwined with the Sun! The direct vibration of light to the solar plexus is as much a connection to the Universal Knowing as the connection we have from our Mental Body! The solar plexus is in the direct center of the human. This center is the most basic area of radiation that we project. It is also vulnerable and sensitive.

In astrology the Sun is designated as the *will* of a person. There are twelve groups of important stars grouped around the Sun called constellations. As the Earth rotates itself and circles around the Sun, different constellations are seen at the same time we see the Sun. When someone is born on Earth, we take note of the constellation that is visible with the Sun at that moment at that place on the globe. For example, for the person born on January 1, 1990, in North America the Sun was "in Capricorn." That means we could see the Sun in line with that group of stars we have named Capricorn. If the Sun equals the *will* of the baby born, there will be personal character traits developed by the baby according to the energies, in the form of light vibrations, coming from the stars and magnified by the Sun. The baby takes its first breath, full of those vibrations, and the rays from the Sun and stars penetrate all obstacles to enter the Sun center or solar plexus of the new human. This activates the *will to life.*

The grand passion is the indomitable Spirit of a person who loves life! This is not dictated by the circumstances of birth! Being poor, being crippled, being deserted or abandoned, being adopted by other parents, being abused, mistreated physically and/or emotionally, being sick or weakened by any physical cause cannot deter the unconquerable "Spirit" of a person with a strong will to live! This is also a "will to love."

I believe the "inner child" of each person is alive in the solar plexus or Emotional Body. In the final analysis of every human complaint, the basic Emotional Body (inner child) is crying out for love!

The first and most important area to treat with the placement of your chosen crystal is right on the solar plexus. The energy field of your Emotional Body will be expanded and healed.

The Spirit Body is located in the Heart. The Heart can also react and respond to other life forms. It makes judgments and decisions about situations in Earth life not based on logic. The physical body of a dying person loses several ounces within moments of the last breath. It is believed by ancient and present philosophies that this loss proves the Spirit Body has evacuated the Earth shell.

The Spirit Body never dies; it is eternal. It has a seed atom of memory that is present in every incarnation on every planet throughout all the Universes.

The Spirit Body is our channel and is connected by

an invisible silver thread to the Designing Creative Force in the Universes.

When the Spirit Body loses energy, we experience "the dark nights of the soul." This only occurs when we forget to recharge by receiving the *divine spark* by consciously connecting with the unconditional love always available to us in endless amounts.

All religions record this miracle—even the most primitive civilizations looked to the Great Spirit for love and protection.

As humanity moves into another level of understanding Earth life, the realization must dawn that we are all Spirit Body before we become physical body! Underneath our skin, muscle, and bones is the powerful force of the indomitable Spirit of the All That Is, the I Am that I Am, God, the Goddess, or the Great Spirit that moves across and through time, space, and the human heart.

The meanest, most violent, cruel, inhuman human is in fact a spirit connected to my spirit! And to the Great Spirit! And will *never* be disconnected from love! When we can accept this fact of physics, we can stop hating and cease our use of negative energy called revenge, fighting, killing, stealing, rape, and war.

When we hold our chosen crystal against our heart, it attracts the planetary colored ray of that crystal into the Spirit Body. This is energy and coded information designed by the Great Spirit to enlighten and enliven our Spirit Body when it needs recharging. There are many ways on Earth to recharge our Spirit Body. They are simple and logical—we all know how good we feel in nature's quiet spaces. We all know the lift we have from a tender embrace, or a comforting word.

The Crystal Love Secret is how we can give all of these

gifts to ourselves in an active meditation exercise every-day, without ever leaving home. This is not a substitute or a placebo for anything. It is a vitamin to the Spirit.

The Mental Body receives its energy from the brain. It lives there in a duplex apartment, called right and left. There is a bridge between the two called the cerebral cortex. There are canals, or electrical circuits, where thought travels throughout different neighborhoods or storage rooms to receive information in the right or retrieve information in the left.

When the Emotional Body has a very strong desire, it can send the Mental Body to the Spirit Body or any-where on Earth—possibly even into the void of space—for information, answers, and plans.

The Mental Body is the most free of all our bodies. It can travel at will.

Carl Jung, my teacher, and his friend Sigmund Freud explored the nocturnal activity of the Mental Body. They formulated opinions concerning the possibility of the Mental Body living another complete life for several hours of sleep each twenty-four-hour period. There are many dream analysis groups active worldwide whose purpose is learning from remembering and analyzing dreams.

Many humans dream the future or answers to current questions. The Mental Body seems to need very little inactive time.

Albert Einstein and many other inventive scientific minds have agreed upon the differing gifts and talents of right and left. The Mental Body must constantly cross the bridge back and forth between logic and intuition or image making and learning. There must be time spent in each apartment for a successful, creative, and balanced human.

When we hold our chosen crystal against our fore-head, we are directing the Cosmic Energy from specific planetary and unidentified rays through the crystal directly *into* our Mental Body. The brain is an energy-using machine and it fuels the Mental Body. It can be a more effective part of our overall Self if it gets a boost of the electromagnetic energies available and attracted in formulas contained in individual crystals.

Some humans are able to see the lights that are created by the various power centers in the human dynamo. While I was attending a beautiful and happy celebration, I picked up and admired a large Quartz crystal. From across the room, a stranger came directly over to me and said, "I have never experienced this before, but when I watched you pick up the crystal, there was a green glow all around your body!"

We frequently learn actions, judgments, ideas, and beliefs from others, by osmosis. We just absorb them without being conscious of choosing them ourselves. The Mental Body becomes impacted with false and in-congruent information files. The canals and electrical wiring systems of the brain become more deeply imbed-ded in unhealthy thought activity.

In order to de-program or re-route the pathways, we must demolish the old wagon trail and build new free-ways in the brain. Using a crystal introduces new fre-quencies and new vibrations to speed the reconstruction.

The Emotional Body must be felt and heard. The Spirit Body must be consulted for experience and ad-vice. The Mental Body must be constantly retrained, expanded, and balanced.

There are forty Earth crystals I have researched that seem to be the most effective in bringing special energies to accomplish change, healing, and love awareness.

Healing was the topic of my previous book, which explains twenty-nine of those crystals.

Love and the new crystals from Mother Earth are the topics of this book. Crystals can channel cosmic forces to increase our love-ability.

How can a crystal dug up from the Earth's crust possibly relate to living things? It appears to be inert, without power to move, without skill or art, idle. Scientifically we know this is not true. When the crystal is struck by light, it moves. When a plant is struck by light, it moves. When an animal or human is struck by light, it moves. Changes occur in the vibration of each, determined by which of the many different colors of light rays it absorbs or allows to pass through.

The earth crystals are being used in many different scientific ways at this time. Laboratories are learning to copy Mother Earth, to grow almost perfect duplicates. We are using them to direct their talents for focusing light to accomplish things we have imagined.

We know that some crystals can hold information and have the memory to retrieve it. We know that some have a molecular structure to increase or multiply the heat speed (energy force) when light is focused through their crystalline structure. We have learned to cooperate and even communicate with them. We accept this as science, never comprehending that vibration indicates life force is present.

This book is a presentation of both research and theory, based on the use of invisible energy to create a focus of power! If you the reader can be convinced of the scientific evidence of invisible energies at work in our health, you can also be convinced on how *love* can change your *energy* and how *energy* can change your *love*, because all of the *energy* in the universe is basically *love*. That is, the motive of the Designing Creative Force in the Universe is for us to be healthy, wealthy, happy, wise, and full of *love* (Universal Energy)!

The natural energy of Earth and the natural energies of space are for our benefit. It is only when we *do not* recognize the invisible (metaphysical, paranormal, esoteric, occult, unseen) influences of these energies that we ourselves *disrupt* the balance of the *Great Design*.

In his book, *Color Therapy*, Dr. Reuben Amber states, "Because of their permanent structure, cells tend to remain or return to normal if given the opportunity." Dr. William A. Tiller, chairman of the Department of Material Science at Stanford University, holds that "if the millions of new cells born into our bodies each day come into being in the presence of 'fields' polarized by the radionic (color ray waves of light) process, they tend to grow in healthier configuration."

The use of colored gem-crystals to transmit the invisible colored ray waves of light directly into the Emotional (Invisible Magnetic Energy) Body, Mental (Invisible Electric Energy) Body, and Spirit (Invisible Cosmic Energy) Body can *change* balance, polarity (direction of blood spin), and cell growth.

These gem crystals were used by our ancestors in ancient times with superknowledge lost by mankind due to Earth cataclysms. We will continue to rediscover these *Crystal Love Secrets* if we can overcome our false beliefs that it is unscientific or "the work of the devil" (how absurd) or in opposition or in competition to "God." The crystals are gifts from God, Goddess, Creator.

In a paper distributed by Environmental Polarity Research in San Diego, California, the work of Dr. Robert Becker is mentioned as foremost in healing fractured bones with low-level electricity. Dr. Becker also cautions us to be aware of the imbalance on Earth being caused by too much electricity. This interferes with basic levels of brain function.

Dr. Tyrone Denessy, a research biochemist, also agrees with the Rosicrucians about how electromagnetic imbalance in the body causes stress, which causes the pea-sized pineal gland in the brain to calcify.

Let us look at the pineal body, all but overlooked until recently even by the holistic health movement. This pea-sized, cone-shaped gland, sometimes called the third eye, is located at the base of the brain. Not only does it interact with other glandular functions such as [those of] the ovaries, testes, pituitary, and the adrenal glands, but it produces a number of very important hormones. One is serotonin, a powerful natural disinfectant. Serotonin abnormalities are found in most stress-related cancer cases. Another hormone is melatonin, which may function as a stress hormone as certain adrenal hormones do. Melatonin, serotonin, and melamin, another pineal hormone, also balance the *cosmic rays* through which we receive our life energy.

Continuing research indicates that when the pineal body is destroyed in animals, they become more susceptible to cancer, and malignant melanomas will grow larger and metastasize to more areas of the body than in animals with functioning pineal glands. When the pineal gland becomes calcified, its production of melatonin is reduced, which in turn stimulates the production of estrogen, causing an increased incidence of breast cancer. Research indicates that 60 percent of Americans over fifty have calcified pineal glands. The incidence of calcified pineal glands is much less in Japan and Africa than in North America and Europe. It seems to be a problem of "civilization"—too little sunlight and too much electromagnetic radiation.

This scientific research begins to sound strangely metaphysical when the pineal gland is mentioned. In my use of Earth crystals with clients in active meditation exercises, holding the crystal on the forehead puts it into direct position to transmit cosmic rays to the pineal. A description of this is complete in my previous book, *Crystal Healing Secrets* (Warner Books, 1988).

Please consider that scientific research, paranormal research, and religion are all based on the belief in things that are not (yet) visible to our physical eyes. And remember, electricity was not visible, X rays were not visible, the pictures in space we call television were not visible, and the music in space we call radio was not audible until we began to reexplore and rediscover *crystallography*.

The crystal kingdom is the original and oldest on Earth. The nervous system of our Mother Earth may be in her crystal veins. As science has discovered the nerves in the human body have a memory separate from the brain, so also may the crystal nerves of Earth have a memory. If this is found to be true in the Quartz crystal of a computer, telephone, and all electronic clocks and media, then how can we question the alive intelligence of a crystal?

If we know scientifically that a human nerve remembers, and we know through quantum physics and quantum logic that *everything* is interconnected, then memory is in everything.

The vibration of your chosen crystal will awaken the memory of your heart to the knowledge that you are loved, you are loving, you *are* made of love itself.

Since this book is about Crystal Love Secrets, the best thing for us to do now is to explore together the different aspects of practical day-to-day love situations we encounter or dream we can. For each crystal discussed, we will explain its applications to the three types of love we all encounter on Earth:

1. Family and platonic love
2. Erotic-romantic love
3. Unconditional spiritual love

FAMILIAL LOVE

Our first love is in the nest of our family. This type of love is called familial. How long has it been since you have told a brother or sister that you feel an interest in their welfare, health, and happiness? Maybe you've been gone from home or separated from your folks a long time. Maybe the entire family has drifted apart. We live in such a mobile world families can be spread apart by thousands of miles, even continents.

Write a postcard, pick up the phone. Let them know you love them, in any way you can manage. If you can't bring yourself to write it or say it, send a greeting card that says it for you, but begin to practice today.

Sure, people might be shocked . . . or maybe your love will come from you at the exact moment when they really need encouragement. They may not respond immediately, but I promise you, the Universe will respond; someone, somewhere, somehow will give *you* a sign of love.

There are many crystals to help you with this way of loving.

FRIENDSHIP LOVE

Familial love also includes your chosen family of friends. I sometimes refer to my close friends as my *divine family*. Has this happened to you? You meet someone and something just "clicks" between you. You have an unexplainable rapport. I often think there may be a recognition from a past life, or perhaps that "click" comes from being a part of a group soul that all reincarnated simultaneously. You might become buddies or simply exchange addresses, but you are friends. It's a love that needs to be expressed and it makes you both happier and stronger. So say it, or write it, if you feel it. You have nothing to lose and love to gain.

EROS LOVE

The second kind of love is *Eros*, the Greek word for romantic sexual love. Wars have been fought, murder and suicides committed, and courageous selfless acts of beauty have occurred in human history powered by the passion of Eros.

There are specific vibrations from the planets, transmitted by the Earth to bring crystals into your life and enhance this type of love, with others to help you evaluate your true feelings in romantic-Eros relationships.

Can you imagine the endless scores of music that have been inspired by Eros? Sculptures, paintings, books, and poetry all over our Earth in every civilization have been created by those experiencing romantic love or wishing they were experiencing it.

The green ray of the planet Saturn is trapped and reflected back to our eye through the Emerald crystal. The eye allows the green ray into the body through the opening of the pupil. In English, the word *pupil* can mean part of the human eye, or it can mean a student. We are all students under the tutelage of Saturn.

The green ray vibration is one of caution. Meditating with an Emerald crystal slows down the racing heart of infatuation. It brings our feet back onto solid Earth, helping us to investigate our true motives in the liaison. It will view all the facets of a purely sexual attraction.

"But I love that euphoria so much," you might be crying. "Why would I want to squelch the flames?" The endorphins produced by the brain in romantic love are equal to the costliest addictive drugs. Of course we crave that marvelous feeling! Romantic euphoria can be deadly.

Have you noticed that over 50 percent of the love songs are "brokenhearted, it's over, you did me wrong" type of songs? Why is romantic love often so painful? The crisis of breaking apart or having an unfulfilled sexual attraction is very often the result of a drunken blindness experienced and searched for from around the age of fourteen. We lust after excitement, and to be high on Eros love.

If you move from partner to partner, seeking the

thrill, you become crystallized in a repetitive action of nongrowth. The crystals help us examine our motives. Is this interaction taking place on the exact same level as your first stirrings of Eros (erotic) yearnings when you were fourteen? If the answer is yes but you haven't even asked yourself the question, each new love will be an old late-night movie, a rerun of your painful romantic past.

By deliberately meditating with an Emerald crystal, you choose to use the impersonal analysis of Saturn. Yes, it will expose the areas in your psyche that are not built on a firm foundation. If you wish to understand and work with Saturn, picture this:

Working with the Emerald, you will reach this understanding: Saturn rules your most solid physical parts, the bone-frame skeleton. Its rays affect the foundation and steel structures of every building. Saturn and Capricorn affect the solid crust or skeleton of our Mother Earth, all rocks, minerals, and crystals. Our psychological and mental structures are ruled by Saturn.

Saturn's rays working through Larimar, Azurite, Malachite, and Emerald crystals can help us on the love plane of Eros to judge ourselves and the action of the "other." Before you break your own heart, meditate for a clear motive.

No one else is ever responsible for our emotions. Saturn says, "Build your love on solid rock, reasoning as well as physical attraction and thrills. The glamour is an illusion; love is truth and trust nothing else."

UNCONDITIONAL LOVE

The energy that holds the Universes in perfect balance and order is unconditional love. It is the "stuff" we breathe, and it permeates every cell of our light, vibrational physical muscles, bone, and tissue. It begins at an unknown source. It is a Designing Creative Force that freely gives and provides cosmic rays, rain, and oxygen for all creatures on Earth and the elements for life anywhere else in the vast Universes.

We are totally accepted and loved by that force under any and all circumstances. The unconditional love is expressed without judgment, "the rain falls on the just and the unjust."

Unconditional love knows its own freedom, and as we are totally entwined in that love stuff, we are completely free to follow any script we choose to write, or any map we choose to draw.

Unconditional love gives us guidelines by speaking through the *actions* of loving humans we know or read of on Earth. We are always provided with a living example of love, but we must be alert, because it is usually quiet and not self-seeking.

When we look for ways to express this totally accepting "love without prejudged conditions" we usually need help to do it.

All times in the history of Earth, there have been evolving ways for communication between the Designing Creative Force and the so-called physical parts of itself. We have ancient generational stories eventually being drawn into pictures and written.

The terms we use for the invisible, nonphysical that we are integrated into are *spiritual* and *mystical*. We understand some are helpful, others seem dangerous. We are also coming to understand there is a balance and a need for both energies.

We read the words of the past and study the lives of the spiritual-mystical humans who made others feel better by their actions and words. Each time we see a pattern repeating itself. We are beginning to understand a tiny fraction of the "love stuff" within and without ourselves. The basic attitude appears to be: no judgment of the value of another person as better than, or lesser than, any other, anytime, anywhere.

Every major worshiping religious group that has ever written descriptions of unconditional love has described the method for us to use: accept each other person as part of ourselves.

It has been said and written in every language. This version is two thousand years old and has the same meaning forever:

> Though I speak with the tongues of men and angels, and have not love in my heart, I am become as sounding brass, or a tinkling cymbal.
>
> Though I have the gift of prophecy, and understand all mysteries, and all knowledge; and though I have all faith, so that I could remove mountains, and have not love in my heart, I am nothing.
>
> Love is long-suffering and kind, love does not envy, does not make a vain display of itself, does not boast.
>
> Does not behave itself unseemly, seeks not its own, is not easily provoked, thinks no evil.

Rejoices not over iniquity, but rejoices in the truth.

Bears all things, believes all things, hopes all things, endures all things.

Love never fails, but prophecies shall fail; where there are tongues, they shall cease; where there be knowledge, it shall vanish away.

And now abide faith, hope, love, these three; but the greatest of these is love."

—St. Paul's letters to the Corinthians
Chapter 13: 1–13, New Testament

We cannot own other persons' spirits or bodies. We do not know what their self-written scripts or maps are. Only they know. We cannot rescue other persons' spirits; only they can accomplish their own missions. We cannot decide their Universal value as humans. We cannot force love into them or take love out of them. We cannot take love away from anyone. We may be able to act as an example so another can discover how love pervades everything and is never withdrawn.

Our willingness to love and love and love again, and never to be fearful of loving, is using the unconditional emotion to its finest degree.

The flowers, the animals, and the crystals often send out vibrations of unconditional nonjudgmental loving, exactly as we did when we were babies.

All of the crystals that I have researched have in some manner expressed this "love stuff" directly to my heart and to all who have tried them. All of the crystals I have touched, researched, used for help, and given to my clients have sent unconditional love to us. They have transmitted by energy vibrations of cosmic light that everything is love. Love is constant throughout All That Is.

Any crystal you choose will give you that feeling. I have discovered some that are programed more strongly with that message; they are described in the section "Crystal Profiles."

When you have explored these ideas, my dream is that you will:

1. Have more of a feeling of belonging to the one great family of the living, breathing stuff we call love.
2. Love your "Self" completely as you are.
3. Feel more connected to your Mother Earth.
4. Feel more connected to those with whom you have had mutual problems.
5. Enjoy forgiving yourself and others for not satisfying you completely.
6. Be more open to *receiving* both from the Cosmic Data Bank and from all your neighbors in the Universes.
7. Understand that you cannot separate yourself from *love* or from anything! Love is constant in the Universe.
8. Be willing to forever risk (possible rejection) by being determined to love and love again, and love again!

Meditation Means "to Measure"!

What an interesting concept I found in Webster's dictionary! The root of the word *meditation* is the same Latin and Medieval French word *med*. What is perfect in this modern time is this root word refers to the word *medical*. To meditate is medical! Here are the other phrases to describe this healing practice:

1. to reflect upon
2. study, ponder
3. to plan or intend
4. think deeply and continuously
5. deep reflection on sacred matters as a devotional act

To describe *medical:*

1. to measure
2. to consider
3. wise counselor
4. doctor
5. connected with the study of medicine

The emotion connected with the word meditation that most of us feel inside is frustration. Somehow the Western mind has been so focused on the logic and action of the Masculine Energy in our left brain that when we are asked to meditate, we do not know what it means.

Because Eastern spiritual leaders have been coming to the Western countries more frequently in this century, we have heard the word *meditation* more. These yogis have established large corporations and physical complexes in many countries to teach a healing practice well-known in the East for centuries. It is in *divine order* that this melding of East and West take place now. The West is one extreme of *doing, doing, doing*, and the East is the other extreme of racial, national, and spiritual decay because of *not doing*.

The perfect evolutionary movement is occurring as the West teaches capitalism to the East, and East teaches meditation to the West.

Many of us have become frustrated and confused because when we sit down (possibly in a cross-legged, straight-backed position) to attempt this foreign practice, we feel our body complaining. Then our undisciplined, fidgety little "inner child" begins to rebel, and the "mind chatter" begins a senseless rundown of mundane, nonintellectual, nonspiritual thoughts. We become disgusted with our lack of focus, begin to criticize ourselves, and it goes downhill from there.

This is a normal reaction for the "action-oriented" Western mind. The logical intermediate practice for learning to use this healing time is to adapt an interlinking concept. The new phrase I have been using with my clients is *active meditation exercise*!

Yes, yes, I know it's a sneaky trick, but it's working, and who can argue with results?

After ten years of researching the reasons why people resist meditation, it seemed expedient to switch rather than fight! Just to give an idea of how perfectly in *divine order* everything is—it was an Eastern philosophy that eventually unlocked the secret of meditation in the West for me:

> The best way to manage anything is by making use of its own nature. A thing cannot function properly when its own nature has been disrupted.
>
> **—Tao Teh Ching**

Our nature is to be active, to be doing something (especially with the hands). The active meditation of using a crystal, placing it on a powerful point of energy circuits coursing through our bodies, speaking aloud positive sentences, is exactly how the Western mind can attune!

This practice is also called a *guided visualization*. I have made cassettes with background music for my clients who have difficulty sleeping or even relaxing. They include the visual description of certain gem-crystals. The invitation to the restless mind is to make pictures rather than worrisome thought.

Making pictures in the mind is very easy for the majority of us who have been seeing motion pictures, video, and TV most of our lives. Telling the restless mind that the vibrations of the crystal are changing something inside the meditator is true. It is also reassuring for the meditator to realize (1) we have Cosmic Energy at our disposal, and (2) the crystal is an antenna attracting specific rays.

While the left side of the brain is feeling good about being methodical, the right side of the brain is happily visualizing the changes taking place. Underneath the surface on another level of mind, the memory and subconscious is in a recall mode.

The three most powerful energy points on the body can be accessed by placing the crystal and hands over the areas. The affirmations can be repeated at each point, making an invisible change in the areas surrounding the whole body. This interruption or change in the amount of Cosmic Current taken in through our energy system has a noticeable effect on our ability to recall the past and anticipate future events!

When I ask clients who have already given themselves time alone what words they use to describe meditation, they reply with feelings such as quiet, peaceful, still, centered, etc.

If I ask them why they give themselves this quiet time alone, they have logical answers:

"I have to listen to my heart."

"It's the only way I can get in touch with what is right for me."

"I find that if I stop all distraction around me, my body will talk to me."

"I'm so busy most of the time, I have to do this every day just to ask myself, 'How am I really feeling?' "

"When I meditate long enough to get past the mind chatter, something really important that I've been shoving to the back of my mind appears on a screen."

"I know my blood pressure goes down because I've checked it before and after."

"When I take ten minutes a day just for myself sometimes, it makes the whole day worthwhile."

"Somehow I disconnect from everything on the physical level and I can fly."

"I can frequently get in touch with people I love who are far away from me."

"Sometimes I get insight into a person or a situation that I've been struggling over."

If there is one reason above all to practice a method of "measuring" what is happening, it would be to access the Cosmic Data Bank!

The purpose of these active meditation exercises is to:

A. *Release* old, unhealthy thought forms.
B. *Create* new, healthy thought forms.
C. *Receive* new feelings of self-love, out-going love, in-flowing love.

When we use the crystals, we are not only focusing on what the lesson inherent within it is, we are also using the energy from that crystal. Cosmic rays are floating all around us invisibly in the Universe. If we get into cycle and use these crystals that transmit certain specific energies, it's like receiving a gift from the Designing Creative Force.

These and any other (hidden) purposes will automatically be reflected back to ourselves. Universal law is as easy as A, B, C.

Reflecting means something is bounced back to us! When we look in the mirror, it reflects back our image—we see ourselves. When we send out our mind energy to the Cosmic Data Bank, we are in the process of having an image reflected back to us. The image is always there in the bank, but we have to go to the bank, call the bank, make contact and ask for what we want. When we have our radio or television turned off—

where are the pictures? Where are the sounds? They are in the ethers, awaiting contact!

If I have my radio and the television both turned on, each to a specific station, I'm getting a lot of sound and images. Maybe all this information is not really relevant to what I need or want. In order to be really tuned in to the right frequency, I must eliminate conflict, and excess stimulation.

In our busy, busy business we become totally distracted and/or sensorily overloaded. We are constantly dealing with what researchers call white noise. It is a combination of subliminal vibrations being cast out by electronic devices, including neon lights, computers, heating and cooling units, microwave ovens, telephone and electrical transformers, large power lines, traffic, street, and freeway movement and engine vibrations, air traffic, and all household appliances in use. Scientists are beginning to detect real physical reactions to this undercurrent of vibrations that are not healthful to humans. In our "high-tech" societies, as we develop even more electronic contraptions, how are we going to protect ourselves from an overdose?

To take the first step in protecting ourselves, we must plan our lives around a quiet time *alone* each and every day, for the rest of our lives!

In my previous book, *Crystal Healing Secrets*, and in the "Crystal Profiles" section of this book, you will find printed meditations for a total of fifty different crystals. These are easy and short vibrationally tested sentences and ways to use each crystal in an active meditation exercise.

When my clients choose a crystal from my healing tray to hold during our consultation, it is the perfect one for them to use for the next twenty-eight days. This is how I ask them to take a dedicated part in loving themselves. Only ten to twenty minutes a day is needed to be alone and quiet with the crystal. I ask them to hold it first on the solar plexus (between waist and ribs), say the printed sentence, then hold it on the heart, and last on the forehead, saying the printed sentence for each area. After this brief activity the invisible cosmic rays will be focused to vibrate the three invisible light bodies that will cause a physical molecular change. Then I ask my clients to write their thoughts or speak them into a cassette recorder, to be reviewed in a month.

Take a look around your home and find a comfortable place. Remember this is going to be your sanctuary, your haven, from all distraction. The spot you choose is going to be your healing temple. Look around and listen. Do you notice any electronic-devices' noise, any traffic vibrations? What can you do to clean this energy or yourself?

1. Remove clock radios and other electronic gadgets. Put them in other areas permanently.

2. Devise a thick roll-down covering for windows where commercial noises enter the room.

3. Choose a pillow or chair (unless you prefer the floor) that is inviting. Use a special piece of cloth that is large enough to throw over where you will be sitting. This cloth can be of any texture you desire. It could be a bed sheet, a towel, a tablecloth, a favorite bathrobe, a curtain, a small oriental carpet, or something purchased expressly for this purpose. The color is very important! The color has a vibration that will affect you. Please give yourself something special, let yourself have your favorite color. The very best you can do for yourself is to visit a fabric store and purchase at least one yard of the most desirable fabric you can afford! Keep this as a special "mood maker" for your healing temple. When you are ready each day, lay it over where you are going to sit. If you can afford more than one yard, give yourself another piece that you can wrap around your shoulders!

4. Use a candle in place of any electronic lighting. Use as many candles as you like; maybe you will even discover the number you choose will be significant! If you wish a maximum effect, purchase at least a two-inch-diameter candle that is scented and colored in your favorite shade.

5. Choose or devise a small table of some kind that will be convenient to keep in this special spot on which to place your candle safely. Buy a large box of wooden matches and keep it there also. This is a private personal altar, just for you! Make sure this area is cozy, convenient, private, comfortable, attractive, and inviting to you. You must be able to shut out distraction.

6. Place objects on the altar that are meaningful or precious to you. This is the perfect place for your crystals.

At this point, there are some rules that must be followed:

1. Use something physical to represent anyone in your exercise.
2. You cannot force your will upon another.
3. Replace and change *only your* feelings.
4. Speak your responsibilities and emotions aloud.
5. No accusations or attacks can be made.
6. Your meditations must be for the other person's highest and best good.
7. Examine your *real* motives.

An "active meditation exercise" that involves another person with whom you wish to communicate would be helped by having a photo or some item belonging to them on the altar. This brings their vibrations into your meditation and helps you to focus on them.

This practice must not become anything like black magic. It is merely a physical representation of the invisible energy that we call the spirit of a person or thing. The purpose of these meditations is to focus our own mind, body, and spirit vibrations on healing communications between ourselves and the one at a distance. Mental telepathy is a proven fact of our lives now! It takes place whether we know it or not, every day, when someone at a distance, without reasons, appears in our thoughts. . . . Minutes later the phone will ring or a letter arrives . . . from that person! It is a fact that we can send messages with mental energy.

When we have misunderstandings, old arguments, hurts, angers, and resentments still bubbling deep down under the surface of our Emotional Body, we are not healthy! Our negative feelings and thoughts are transmitted unconsciously to the other person(s) at any distance! They receive this negativity and have feelings that are uncomfortable, unhealthy, fearful, and eventually focus the energy back to us. It is the *reflecting effect* of Universal Law: "I get back what I give out."

In order to change this pattern of unhealthy chain reaction, it is necessary to replace the old feelings with new feelings. To eliminate the old feelings, we must get them out of the body where we have carried them in the cells. The most effective ways are through the voice or physically "acting them out."

In these active meditation exercises we do both! We

tell how we are feeling out loud to the other person (living or not), and we act out in our mind the motion picture of how we want to feel. We forgive ourselves for our bad feelings and we forgive the other(s) for any (imagined) blame. We say aloud how we understand our own choosing to react in the negative. To begin to acknowledge our own responsibility in any confrontation is an act of healing. To say these things with our own voice changes the vibrations around us and eventually around the other(s).

It must be very clear in the meditation of any sort that includes another person that the intention is for the "highest and best good" of yourself and the other(s). The reflecting effect will apply!

If the meditation is designed to attract another person to yourself for any reason, it must definitely be for clean, pure, and truthful love purposes. There must be no self-delusion concerning a hidden agenda. A purely sexual lust, a financial benefit, or wildly impossible hero/idol worship of a public figure would be unhealthy. We read of these unbalanced individuals in the news who become so obsessed with a personality who is unobtainable or inaccessible to them, their frustration causes violence.

The same can be true for any of us on a smaller scale with lost loves, imagined or real! So many clients have poured out their hopes, wishes, angers, and despairs over relationships they have never released! Some as long as sixty years in the past.

7. Choose the crystal that feels right to use as an antenna to focus all the energies that are now present in your sanctuary.

You may want to choose a simple Quartz crystal to represent the other(s) on your altar. Before you use it, please deprogram it in one of the methods described in

"Crystal Profiles." After this has been done, speak the name(s) into the Quartz as lovingly as possible. Place it on the altar.

You need a separate crystal for yourself. It can be any one of the colored crystals that call to you emotionally, by visual liking or by energy transmitted through touch. There are many different ways to like a crystal. The colored crystals are already programed to transmit rays from various stars and planets, so they are focused energy and cannot be programed. The one you choose for yourself will be bringing to you the perfect program! Your superconscious mind will choose the crystal if you relax. Do not try to "figure it out" with your left brain —just follow your heart.

If you have no colored crystals available to you, use another Quartz crystal and go through the same cleansing and programing procedure that you did with the first one. Speak into the crystal what you want to accomplish with this active meditation exercise.

Your personal crystal will be kept with you throughout the duration of your meditation program. You need to keep it somewhere on your body between the throat (Power Center) and the solar plexus (Emotional Body). In the center between these two points is the heart (Spirit Body), which is a very comfortable place.

If you are using a loose stone, it will have a tendency to get lost! Make or buy a little pouch to put it in, or wrap it in a handkerchief or square of choice fabric. If possible, put it on a ribbon, string, or strip of leather around your neck and wear it under your clothing.

If you are using jewelry containing your stone, it needs to be worn in the same area, even if it is a ring, brooch, bracelet, or earring. Remember that gold, silver, and all the metals are crystals, too! Choose the metal as well by referring to the surprise crystals on pages 217–20 in the "Surprise Crystals" section. It is easy to tie this jewelry on a string or ribbon around your neck and wear it inside your clothing for a month. Take the crystal off at night and keep it under your pillow or beside your bed.

When you go to your special meditation place, lock the door, close off the noise from everything, sit on your meditation cloth, and light the candle on your altar, for this will be the most precious time in your life! Make sure that you choose a time when your resistance is low.

In my previous book, I had given instructions to do your active meditation exercises in the morning. I am now finding some clients are too eager to get started on their daily activities to *receive* at this time. Day people wake up "rarin' to go" and spend meditation time planning activities or making lists! This blocks the process. Night people are pretty "groggy" in the mornings, so this is a good time for their meditation. Day people need to monitor themselves to see when their energy is low, in order to be relaxed.

The most important part of your meditation time is the time when you focus on *your own* heart, mind, and emotions. In order to begin with this, take your personal crystal in your hand and gaze into it for a while. Allow yourself to see inside it, even if it is not transparent. A crystal such as Lapis Lazuli (Laz-U-lie), Turquoise, or Malachite can be studied in the same way. As you search for understanding of your stone, it will be affecting your energy, creeping into your electromagnetic aura field, and transmitting cosmic rays directly into your vibrating molecules!

At this point, the most successful body position would be lying on the floor, head pointing to magnetic *north*. Try to get as close to this as possible.

Place your crystal on your solar plexus (between the lower ribs and the waist), place both your hands over it, which completes an energy circuit, with Earth-Moon magnetic and Sun-planets energy coursing through your hands and the crystal. This will magnify and change the vibration of your Emotional Body, whose center is right there under your hands.

This area also is the home of the little child we were, at age three. The instinctual survival spirit animal we may have been eons ago continues to live there beside the inner child. Each of them needs to be treated.

For each of the crystals I have researched and studied with my clients, a strong sentence has been devised to repeat aloud on the solar plexus. This is important to say at least seven times or for two minutes (don't watch the clock!). Just let yourself repeat it as long as you need it.

This same procedure with a different sentence is practiced on the heart, which is the main generator and home of the Spirit Body. This is the part of us that never dies and can travel free in the Universe when not trapped in a physical plane such as Earth. When you are holding the crystal on your heart, feel your physical heart. Go inside it and ask it to talk to you. You will receive answers from your Spirit that are wise, true, and good for you.

Now move the crystal to your forehead, which is the place called the *third eye*. This accesses the pineal gland in the center of the brain, which remains or corresponds to the dorsal fin of a dolphin! The human brain is a fantastically powerful computer, broadcasting, receiving, sorting, and storing experiences and observations on many subjects, many levels of consciousness, and possibly close and distant invisible worlds. When we activate the pineal gland, we are turning on our *receiver*. We are

▲
▼

sending out to the Morphic Field and beyond to the Universal Conscious Mind a channel of light. This is like putting an electric cord in the electrical outlet and plugging in to *power*.

We have already asked questions of the inner child, the instinctual animal, and the true Spirit. Now it is time to wait for special instructions from the Designing Creative Force of All That Is.

Sitting or lying quietly waiting for inspiration may be the toughest or the easiest part of this active meditation exercise. Don't be discouraged if you receive worldly, mundane thoughts that seem nonspiritual or even selfish. Pay attention to every word or picture that comes. Let them pass until something strikes a chord within you, that excites you. Just wait calmly. It will happen. Be patient with your Self. Also be confident that underneath the level of your thinking, the changes in your brain waves are really happening. Do not demand anything of your Self because what you are doing is making your Self open to having a gift. Earlier, in the beginning of this chapter, I asked you a question: "Where are the sounds and the pictures when you have not turned on your radio or television?"

They are vibrating in the air all around us, invisible until we decide to turn the power on. When we go into our sanctuary, sit down, and surrender all resistance, it is like turning on the switch! All of the answers to all the questions that have ever been asked are available.

The secret is, love is the "stuff" that permeates the Universes, holds everything in place, keeps a balance, and produces the whole show. If we can tune in our receiver to that frequency, we can hear the broadcast.

The more consistently we go into our special place and wait patiently for the inflow of "stuff" we call love, the greater the changes that will occur in our outside world. Even though we may not experience conscious "mind-blowing enlightenment," we are receiving a peaceful and living vibration that strengthens us in a subtly powerful way. Others will even remark that we appear healthy and happy! Or they may just say, "You *look* different, what have you been doing?"

We are sending out to them different messages from our Emotional, Mental, and Spiritual bodies. This causes a reaction in them that follows the law of *reflecting effect*. We become givers because we are filled! All around us can be positively affected because we have taken a few moments to receive the free energy flowing everywhere, by simply sitting in silence.

> In realizing the groundless nature of ignorance, my former awareness, clouded and unstable, becomes transparent, clear and shining as crystal. Its light transforms all blindness.
>
> **—Milarepa**

Self-love

Driven by the forces of love, the fragments of the world seek each other—so that the world can come into being.

—(Pierre) Teilhard de Chardin
The Phenomenon of Man

In the religious atmosphere that has prevailed in all the lands conquered by the early Roman Empire, and spread to the new land of America by emigrants and conquerors from Spain, self-love has been a dirty word. In Catholicism and many Protestant religions, self-sacrifice, self-denial, unworthiness, and humility have been extolled as the most spiritual of all virtues.

The concept that we are born with evil or sin already inside our spirit, and must spend our complete and only lifetime pleading for forgiveness and begging for mercy from a vengeful creator, has held millions in bondage for hundreds of years.

The residue of this pre-Christian view has crept into the new religions even though the reformer Jesus, and his champion interpreter St. Paul, both stated without any doubt that we are totally loved and it is the Creator's great joy to give to us!

The biggest hurdle we face is expelling the thought that loving ourselves is an abominable act of sin and conceit.

My clients have sat in shocked amazement at my suggestion that self-love is the very first step toward learning love. Learning to love the Self is not easy. We have been brainwashed over centuries of conditioning that the basic self is a monster that must constantly be held in check.

"Why, I thought loving myself was the last thing a spiritual person would do," my clients say. "Aren't I supposed to love others, give to others, help others, be unselfish, and put myself last?"

My answer is, "If you are always growing a garden, harvesting the food, preparing it, and serving it to others, but you never feed yourself, how long will you last?" It is not only impractical, everyone you feed knows you're crazy! They don't think you're kind and wonderful, because they see your life going down the drain. They take what you offer; but there is no respect.

When we are constantly focusing on helping others without sufficient focus on our own growth, we distract ourselves. When we get continual signals of "no respect" from others, we become resentful: "Look what I have done for you and this is the thanks I get!"

The best reason in the world to give to and love the Self is to "make sure your own house is in order." Anyone practicing any of the healing arts as a daily profession is aware of how difficult it is to accomplish healing for a client if the healer is ill.

We meet a person now and then who seems to have a balanced respect for the Self. They are a joy and blessing to be near. The energy that emanates from them is nurturing without trying. How do they do it? These are some of the things I've discovered about people who love themselves:

1. They spend time daily (maybe only ten minutes) going within themselves to examine their thoughts and motives. They give their inner life attention. They contemplate their daily activities as positive action toward their goals.

2. They think healthy thoughts, visualize themselves as healthy, and do not dwell on little aches and pains. They do not create illness or accidents in order to rest.

3. They do not physically hurt themselves by eating, drinking, drugging, or smoking too much.

4. They don't need sickness to get attention or sympathy from others because they give these things to themselves.

5. They don't do good for others with a hidden agenda, designed to benefit themselves by receiving praise, social acceptance, or a tax deduction. They do not act out of duty.

6. They don't meddle in the affairs of others with advice or offers of intervention unless asked. They are generous and untiring during emergency needs but understand "tough love," which insists that others be responsible to help themselves whenever possible.

7. They know that "helping others" is the best way to avoid facing their own problems. They are usu-

ally involved in self-help, spiritually seeking knowledge of how to better care for themselves.

8. They are not selfish or self-conscious or self-centered. They are self-nourished so they are not "needy." What does "needy" mean to you? Do you say, "I have love, respect, and affection for my true spirit, and for the Designing Creative Force that is my total Self! I have love for others because they are a part of me." Or do you say, "I *need* love and friendship"?

9. There is a balance between working and playing. There is a balance between logic and intuition. (Not all mind, not all heart, or all feeling and no thinking.) There is a balance between acquiring worldly possessions and giving love, attention, and respect to others. They know that being poor is not necessarily a virtue, nor is having abundance automatically suspect.

10. Above all, they are willing to take responsibility for their own rescue, to continually focus on self-reliance, never blaming anyone or an outside force for circumstances in their lives. Simultaneously they are always willing to share and be intimate with significant others in their lives.

11. They have a good sense of humor and can even laugh at themselves.

These actions, practiced daily, add up to self-love, being a good caretaker, and a kind parent to the Self. It is very much like taking care of our car, or any machine we are dependent upon. Sure it is; think on this: The machine will run and run until there is no fuel. We must refuel. The machine will produce until the lubri-

cant is dry, then it begins to cause friction and deteri-
orate. Sometimes it will operate for a long time without
proper care, but eventually it breaks down. Taking
proper maintenance procedures with our precious Self
will insure our ability to share positive energy with everyone, without even trying!

The basic natural instinct, built into us by the Designing Creative Force, is self-love. It is called survival of the
species. This instinct is also involved in creativity and is
often designated desire.

The Emotional Body, being programed for love, is
constantly interacting with the cosmic love energy in the
invisible rays moving through the Universes. The solar
plexus is intertwined with ganglia of nerves receiving
these rays. The Self we are in the material world responds to the color vibration of these rays, without consciously realizing how colors vibrate and affect our lives.

The color of the ray that urges our survival is *red*. The
planets that emit red rays are Mars, Venus, Mercury,
and Pluto (Mercury, Venus, and Pluto also emit blue
rays). When the red ray combines with other rays attracted by colored crystals from Earth, it becomes a pink
ray, burgundy ray, or violet ray.

The gem-crystals that I use specifically for crystal therapy or healing that attract and transmit these rays of
survival at a basic level are all the red stones: Ruby,
Carnelian, Fire-Red Opal.

The more subtle energies, but not any less powerful,
are crystals that transmit other color rays with the red
ray, generally combining some degree of the white or
silver or blue rays. These stones are Amethyst, Sugilite,
Kunzite, Garnet, Rose Quartz, Pink Tourmaline, Rhodochrosite, and Coral (Pink or Red).

These red, violet, burgundy, and pink crystals are

vibrating to affect the Emotional Body. This invisible body is formed while we are becoming physical within our mother's womb. Science is showing us now with sonograms (sonic vibration photos of infants *in utero*) and sensors that the baby before birth is actually responding to outside words, actions, and emotions of others. The Emotional Body as the basic energy of all life is developing.

As we take on life in the physical form at birth, our Emotional Body makes decisions about the pain or comfort of the mother during delivery. Many of my clients enter Earth life with guilt, feeling responsible for their mothers' pain. Some, when hypnotically regressed, recall frustration or even anger at the person who assisted in delivery, because of the basic insensitivity often present in clinical birthing practices.

Thankfully new-old methods for human birthing are making a resurgence with sympathetic surroundings. There is less anesthesia being used on the mother due to prebirth trainings such as the Lamaze method that include the father's support and comfort. Hopefully, physicians are choosing not to use hard metal instruments to grasp the baby's head and pull, as was the custom several years ago.

Loving the Self that is our internal and recycling eternal spirit is the number one goal in the next step of evolution on Earth. This giant step for humankind begins with awareness of the Self in its true nature. So many of us are carrying genetic memory seeds from past lives in which we had strong opinions of *right* and *wrong*. In this present life we have taken the unconscious behavior of continuing to feel guilty or judgmental against ourselves and others.

Thanks to great pioneers in the study of the human

mind such as Sigmund Freud, Carl Jung, Abraham Maslow, Carl Rogers, Eric Berne, Rollo May, and countless other contemporary "avatars," we are breaking away from the old helplessness of inherited mind-set.

Within the United States, California has been an outer-limit pioneer. Things seem to develop from outrageous experiments into prescribed procedure, beginning on the West Coast and radiating outward.

The California legislature has established a task force to study ways of teaching self-esteem in the educational system at all levels. The belief that all crime begins with the personal lack of self-esteem is bringing a new attitude to education.

Jack Canfield, a counselor designated as a director for the California Board of Education, has a progressive approach in public schools.

He also conducts seminars and workshops for teachers, prisons, and corporations. His purpose is to make them aware of how important it is, for peace and less crime in our society, to encourage self-love and self-acceptance on all levels.

This approach seems so logical and practical for such a minimum investment, we wonder why it has taken so long for us to recognize a simple solution.

There are two opposing "slogans" that Canfield uses in his seminars to wake people up to their unconscious belief systems. The first one is the root of all arguments from mundane domestic disputes to world-level politics. His phrase rocks me back on my heels when I think of how many times I have unconsciously acted in this way: "I would rather be right than happy."

The opposite is a phrase that he teaches all levels and ages of people to affirm in all situations: "No matter what you do or say to me, I'm still a worthwhile person!"

In the language of psychology, there are two descriptions of personality types prevalent in society that are dysfunctional:

1. The inferiority complex
2. The superiority complex

Both of these types operate from an extreme end of the self-esteem possibilities.

People who talk and act as though they are superior to those around them often have a secret inner fear of not being good enough. They are not aware of their fears in their conscious everyday activities. Without thinking or acknowledging the fears, their personalities take on an acting role. They actually bury their feelings of inadequacy in exaggerated efforts to boost their own self-esteem. Both inferiority and superiority complexes are just as they say, *complex* within the individual but simple in diagnosis: not loving the Self! Each type is an unconscious victim of a harsh inner judge.

The "judge" is a combination of personalities that have influenced our "little child within" since birth (or before). There are several years when we are still sweet and innocent after we return to Earth as a baby human. During this time we can still remember the other levels of existence, where we have been while we were away from Earth. Many times we can see and hear things on these levels that adult humans cannot perceive. Did you ever have an invisible playmate? Were you able to talk to animals when you were little? Did you ever see elves or fairies or even scary apparitions in your bedroom at night? Who convinced you that you were wrong or even a coward to believe what you saw? Who told you that you mustn't tell lies or make up stories, that you were bad?

These statements made to you when your mind was very impressionable went into your brain like a handprint in wet cement. Psychologists call the age before five in the human child "the age of concrete thinking." Can you begin to see how the "judge-parent" within your own personality began to grow? These were the very first seeds of self-doubt, and the first step toward lower self-esteem. When we hear enough of this sort of criticism, and if it continues on into our preteen years, we lose all confidence in our own judgments and begin to listen to the negative "inner judge" we have created.

Religion has called this a *conscience*, which is a word derived from ancient English and French words. The word *con* means with, and *science* derives from the word *scire*—to know.

This is Webster's definition of conscience:

1. Knowledge or sense of right and wrong, with a compulsion to do right.
2. Moral judgment that opposes the violation of previously recognized principle.
3. Judgment that leads to feelings of guilt if one violates principles.

So how does a baby Earthling get a conscience? Certainly not if she is raised in the jungle by the apes or the wolves like Tarzan!

We can only be given a conscience—with science! Scientifically we must be methodically brainwashed by words and actions from big humans. Certainly, most of our caretakers loved us and wanted us to have a sense of right and/or wrong. They wanted us to "fit in" to society, to be accepted, to behave correctly. Most of our caretakers were very young themselves, inexperienced as parents or even as Earthlings. Their intentions toward us were good, most of the time.

There are as many ways of parenting as there are parents! There are as many ideas of right and wrong as there are humans. Sometimes when my children were small, I decided it was wrong for them to come into the house with muddy boots, especially after I had waxed the floors. They wanted to come in and out a lot, to talk to me or to get a drink of water. I was young and impatient about taking off the boots and putting them on. I am ashamed to admit that living in a wet climate, I eventually decided when they wanted to go outside, not to let them back in for a certain period of time! That seemed cruel to my neighbor. My children may have decided several things about themselves and about right and wrong because of my decision.

It was a selfish decision. I wanted my life to be easier. I may unconsciously have brainwashed those little minds, consistently telling them, "My waxed floors are more important than you" or "I won't love you if you are dirty." I didn't intend to give them that message.

There has been an obsession within our civilized societies for at least one hundred and fifty years to be more and more antiseptically clean. We had to discover and correct the effect of bacteria and germs on our health and longevity. We owe so much to the scientists who have done the work. But has the pendulum of evolution swung too far?

Self-esteem or self-acceptance in the Western world has almost become determined totally by a standard of physical characteristics:

1. I feel guilty if I haven't had a shower or a bath today.

2. I feel guilty if I haven't washed my hair.
3. I feel guilty if I haven't brushed my teeth.
4. I feel guilty if I detect any odor on myself.
5. I feel guilty if my clothes are wrinkled.
6. I feel guilty if I have dandruff on my shoulders.
7. I feel guilty if my whiskers show a little.
8. I feel guilty if I have too much fat on my body.
9. I feel guilty if I don't have enough fat on my body.
10. I feel guilty if I am too short/tall.
11. I feel guilty if my nose is too big/small.
12. I feel guilty if my hips, hands, feet, stomach, are too big.

Society and the commercial media have taken the religious and scientific reasoning to a ridiculous point of self-incrimination. "Cleanliness is next to godliness" has been the cry of the Puritans who settled America. We now lead the world in production of commercially marketable physical items that we can use on our bodies, clothing, cars, and homes—to keep ourselves squeaky clean, shiny, good smelling, attractive, desirable, on time, up the success ladder, and *totally out of touch* with our inner spirit.

For many years (even though I was naturally youthfully slim), I wore a tight rubber girdle to make sure that my body was acceptable by Hollywood standards! Lingerie manufacturers in all Western nations brainwashed women scientifically into having a social "conscience" about what was right and wrong with our own bodies!

The gentlemen did not escape. When razor designs changed and razor blades became a marketable product that must wear out and be replaced—off came beards!

It is only now, over a hundred years later, that males are allowed to decide whether or not to grow facial hair.

Isn't this silly? We have designed our own distractions, our own demons, and the "inner judge" who convinces us that we are not okay unless . . . ! The term for this attitude is *conditional love*. This is actually saying to the Self: I will only be able to love you if you produce on the outside of your shell, on your physical body, these certain conditions that the group consciousness (the herd) says are desirable and acceptable.

The innocent little child within our true Self says: This is too much, it seems so difficult, I would need to have plastic surgery, hair transplants, skin peels, bone grafting, jazzercise, weight lifting, jogging, cycling, rope jumping, scientific nutrition, and more willpower than I can even imagine. I can't do it, I'm a failure, I don't measure up, I'm not acceptable. I cannot love my Self.

I have small groups of people come to stay with me in a house that I have in Sedona, Arizona, for the purpose of remembering who they really are. Every month I have a different group. In the beginning people brought bags and bags of commercial products to use so they could be acceptable to the group! Hair dryers, hair sprays, shavers, lotions, soaps, deodorants, mouthwashes, eye, cheek, nose, lip cosmetics, shampoos, conditioners, and some skin things that only real "self-hate" would convince a person to buy! And of course they brought clocks: travel alarms and watches, so they could be acceptably "on time."

Since it is only a three-day retreat, it became very clear how far removed and insecure my intelligent, attractive, and spiritually searching guests had become from their true Selves.

Can you imagine their shock upon discovering that all of these products were to be put away in a closet and not touched for three days?

Being in an unfamiliar place is the greatest test of self-acceptance and self-love. Sedona has a special atmosphere, high, bright, clear, clean, and visually beautiful. Mother Earth is at her best in certain places, so it helps to reconnect with her in those places—unspoiled by human pollution. My guests have a chance to be naturally beautiful, naturally sensitive to their own heartbeats, their Emotional Body, and their inner perfection. They rediscover their inner knowings about time without a clock, direction without a map, and acceptance without "conditions."

These retreats are preliminary research toward the eventual large-scale rejuvenating, spiritual spa and healing center, code name Emerald City. This center is being envisioned by many people in many countries. I have received letters from around the world. How can we have peace on Earth without inner peace in the individual? How can we learn to love ourselves unless we love ourselves enough to build Emerald Cities to teach ourselves to love ourselves? We are all in this together.

Are you taking good care of your Self?

Are you nurturing your inner child?

Are you a harsh judge, are you living under a false sense of "conscience," with a demon that tells you, "You are not acceptable," because you have been brainwashed by the religion or commercial media of our time (and archaic times)? Do you need to shake off a lot of crazy baggage that you are carrying around in the form of *beliefs* that stop you from being real perfection and okay just as you are?

There are some helpers that Mother Earth continually

produces for us to use as receptors or antennas to attract cosmic energies to ourselves. Crystals are transmitters of light energy and vibrations for our physical, mental, emotional, and love health.

In order to help yourself to drop all the baggage you are carrying, and to become lighter and "enlightened," a gem-crystal can become a wonderful assistant.

The crystals that we will learn to use for self-love are varied and many, but this writing will deal with ones clients have found to be most effective. There will be some surprises, too, because several crystals are rather new discoveries! Others have never been recognized by the average person as crystals.

Prepare your Self to be open to an adventure! Tell your Self that these things cannot harm you, because they are beautiful expressions of love to us from God, Goddess, Designing, Creative, Mathematical Force in the Universe. They are like flowers and rainbows, they give us joy, hope, and comfort, because they are alive with light, color, and vibration. We can *be* with crystals as we can be in a garden or on the beach. They take on our vibrations and we take their vibration into our Self! It is "so simple, it confounds the wise."

How many more ways can I receive love?
How many more ways can I give love?
How many more ways can I be loved?

—**Lazarus, 1988,**
as channeled by Jack Purcell
Concept: Synergy

Passion

By annihilating the desires, you kill the mind. Every person without passions has no principle of action, no motive to act.

—Claude-Adrien Hervétius

I do not believe we can kill our passion and thereby become "spiritual." In fact I believe just the opposite. Religious doctrines that teach the active, creative Western mind that desire is evil and lack of desire is spiritual are out of balance with reality.

We are essentially spirit before we become physical. As such, we are small replicas of the Designing Creative Force in the Universe. We are bits of the Great Spirit. As such *we* have the passionate spirit to create.

The Earth is a spirit also. We are bits of her Great Spirit. Everything she produces has its own spirit: humans, animals, plants, and crystals. Each has its own passion to create itself, and to re-create its own kind.

Humans seem to have dominion over animals, plants, and crystals (Earth minerals) to care for and to use or misuse. We take what we wish for our aid, benefit, and comfort from each of these kingdoms.

Earth minerals are widely used as health-giving nutrients, vitamins, salves, ointments, skin treatments, and internal medicines. The use of a larger crystal as an antenna to collect, attract, and disperse useful cosmic rays to the solar plexus or Emotional Body to increase the will to life and will to love is not a phenomenon. It is as natural as ingesting a crystal such as iron or calcium.

The Spirit Body in the heart is moved and healed by the meditation exercises using specific crystals. Heart trouble is rooted in a troubled spirit that has lost the will to live, and the will to love the Self.

What I have observed in my clients over the years is not absolute clinical research, but when my records are checked, there are statistics. Using the right crystal can increase desire and a passion for life and love.

When a person is displaying very low energy, almost any other person (and possibly animals) can sense it. Mental depression causes the will-to-life energy to decrease. Hard work causing physically depleted energy is a different matter. It can be restored by food and rest. Depletion of energy through excessive stress can also be relieved by recreation or meditation, a change of focus.

When the will-to-life energy, which I believe is centered in the solar plexus, the Emotional Body, is low, there is an absence of desire. The person doesn't need sleep, can't sleep, doesn't need nourishment, can't eat, and does not want recreation, and has no desires, not even sexual.

This is Earth, not "Heaven"; we are on a physical plane of existence because we have chosen to learn to create!

In order to create, we must have a desire! Without the spark of Masculine Energy from the Sun to our solar plexus being stirred, nothing matters and nothing happens.

If you need physical proof in a simple way of the physical interaction between the Solar Planet and your solar plexus, expose your belly to the Sun! The next time you feel depleted of will-to-life energy, observe yourself refueling by being out in the open air. Even if there is snow, ice, or cloud cover, the solar energy penetrates. It also penetrates buildings; however, glass distorts the ultraviolet so necessary for optimum health. Spend as much time as possible outside!

The findings of the medical profession have been instinctual in many ways. Recuperating victims of battle fatigue, wounds, surgery, tuberculosis, and many other life-threatening diseases have been taken outside the hospital into the solar rays whenever possible for increased healing. We copy the instinctual self-healing activities of our animal friends.

The Sun's rays activate the desire, spark the engine of the solar plexus, and get things rolling again!

There is no spirituality without desire on this plane. The secret is to regulate and balance the passions. There is no true spirituality without passion, and no passion or desire can come into the Emotional Body that is truly creative without spiritual understanding on some level.

What is *passion?* It is a word, a sound; when spoken aloud it changes the vibrations in the ethers around the person who speaks and the listeners who hear the word. Something is stirred within.

Webster's dictionary says it derives from Middle English, Old French, and Latin. The first three definitions have to do with suffering or agony connected to martyrdom for one's religion: harm, destruction, and the emotions connected to this spiritual sacrifice are listed as joy, fear, love, grief.

The fourth definition is, extreme compelling emotion, intense emotional drive or excitement such as: (a) great anger, rage, fury; (b) enthusiasm, fondness; (c) strong love or affection; (d) sexual drive or desire, lust; (e) the object of any strong desire; (f) ardor, fervor.

The Crystal Love Secrets connected to "passion" are to be discovered in the energies of colored light sent to Earth by stars and planets in our solar system, attracted by specific crystals, and transmitted to our visible and invisible bodies when we use them. This is accomplished through vibrations changing within us from the center outward. Saying aloud the crystal meditations creates healing vibrations. In the study of vibration, the ancient scientists gave mathematical equations to sounds. Current sciences are showing by intricate measuring devices how sound waves create a geometric pattern in the air around us, made visible for us by computer! The sounds we make in chanting, singing, and positive statements have their effect magnified by the crystal we use.

To be passionate is to be at a high level of attunement on Earth. Naturally, as we remind ourselves over and over, there is a balance between the two polarities of passion: anger, hate, fury, and lust, and love, affection, ardor, and desire. We cannot separate in balance unless we are aware of the way in which we are feeling and using our passions.

> Passion is universal humanity. Without it religion, history, romance, and art would be useless.
>
> **—Honoré de Balzac**

The French have an expression, *la grande passion*—the grand passion for life! Not expressing sexual passion alone, but including it with every other facet of living. Living with emotion, excitement, desire for experiences, daring, courage, vulnerability, surrendering to weakness, enthusiasm, energy, curiosity, empathy, relatedness; interaction with all of humanity, animals, plants, clouds, fire, wind, water, stars, planets, and all things seen and unseen! The ultimate love connection realized somewhere between the mind, heart, and solar plexus is a passionate love feeling that equates with satisfaction of the soul!

Some of us have that feeling for our work, some for our play, and others focus that feeling toward another person, money, or objects in the physical realm.

In order to realize or actualize passion in our daily living, we focus on a balance of spiritual and physical. We cannot experience true passion without both, unless we prefer to experience the first three definitions in Webster, which have to do with religious martyrdom, pain, and suffering!

We must be *willing* however to endure all of the above if we are truly passionate.

Even in the holiest of all Western religious books is the quote attributed to Jesus Christ by his disciple John: "I know thy works, thou art neither cold nor hot: I wish you were cold or hot. So then because you are lukewarm, I will spew thee out of my mouth." (Revelation 3:15–16)

When I have a client in a state of depression, the vibration or energy that is sent out by their invisible Emotional, Spiritual, and Mental bodies is often so weak it can hardly be felt. Some fortunate persons can actually see these vibrations in the form of colors surrounding the physical body, called auras. The majority of us monitor our fellow humans unconsciously by a mechanism we call feeling, but not with our hands as in touching. We "feel" the energy or lack of it through different sensors, basically in our solar plexus.

Solar means "of the Sun." *Plexus* is a complexly interconnected arrangement of parts, a network. It comes from the Latin word that means to braid or intertwine. The solar plexus of the human is the physical area of the body that is intertwined with the Sun! The direct vibration of light to the solar plexus is as much a connection to the Universal Knowing as the connection we have from our Mental Body! The solar plexus is in the direct center of the human. This center is the most basic survival mechanism. Using this center is much more important than using any other method. This is called the Emotional Body, or the Desire Body.

There are cases recorded in history from earliest times of strong Spirits who overcame any or all of these terribly disabling deficiencies. A particular case in point in our times is Helen Keller, who was born both blind and deaf. Not being able to see or to hear, she still learned to *speak!* She spoke publicly on every continent. How did she do it? She had a passionate Spirit!

Recently, the most advanced book on astronomy and physics written for the public mind, *A Brief History of Time* (Bantam Books, 1988), was published by Stephen W. Hawking of Cambridge University, England. He has made numerous television and public appearances from his wheelchair, where he has been imprisoned for twenty years in a state of deteriorating physical pain and isolation. He educated himself, competing in a healthy normal world, by putting forth ten times the effort required from an average person. His writing was done in the most difficult way. His illness was diagnosed in 1964 as fatal amyotrophic lateral sclerosis, deterioration of motor neurons of spinal cord, medulla, and cortex. This disables skeletal muscles affecting speech, swallowing, limbs, and eventually the heart and chest. It does not affect the brain. He got married in 1965, which in his own words made him want to live. He received his Ph.D. in 1966. His physical body has deteriorated so much, at first sight his condition is shocking! He and his wife have two sons and a daughter. Why did he do this? How did he accomplish this? Because of his passionate Spirit!

The human activity is prompted by desire.

—**Bertrand Russell**

Our amount of satisfaction in the life we are leading is in direct proportion to our degree of passion! Passion is not a dirty word, but it is basically sexual. The original passionate desire is to survive and for the species to survive, to recreate ourselves through mating. The sexual urge is the creating urge. That instinct, when tamed, civilized, recognized, can be diverted toward other methods of survival for the species. The creativity of Homo sapiens, diverting the reproductive urge to an urge for the survival of the clan on a higher level of life enjoyment, is also an expression of passion.

The dedication of Mother Teresa, a religious devotee who has made it her passion in this life to feed the poor and care for the millions of abandoned, has contributed to all of our lives. She has exchanged her opportunity for sexual, romantic intimacy and reproducing herself in children for an Earth-changing crusade, more powerful than any war or invention. Hers is an expression of the *will to life* on the highest level.

All persons who devote themselves to redirecting that creative urge to creating for humanity's future are recognized as "saints." We cannot emulate or duplicate their actions, and so judge ourselves as "not spiritual enough." This is taught to us, but is not a fact.

Passion is a fact of life; it puts adrenaline into the center of our being and gives us an exciting shove. All the gurus, the Christs, the Buddhas, Muhammads, popes, Martin Luthers, maharishis, dalai lamas, Rajneeshes, Sai Babas, Mahatma Gandhis, and Mother Teresas are constantly surrounded by and drawing energy from the opposite sex! Whether or not they are celibate, they engage in a normal exchange of sexual energy.

When one reads the accounting of Siddhārtha (Guatama Buddha), one finds a normal married man. The accountings of Jesus show that several women were more intimately close to him than any of his male friends. One of his closest female followers was actually believed to have been a prostitute. It is common knowledge that many children have been sired between priests and nuns. Mahatma Gandhi was married and had children. When he declared his intention never to indulge in sex with his wife after he committed to a spiritual mission for India, he was continually surrounded by "special" young maidens and slept among them at night.

There is a basic instinctual need, and understanding of that need by humans, to feed or exchange the energy of our chosen gender body with a body of the opposite gender. The exchange can take place through proximity or touching. It is not necessary to have physical intercourse in a sexual union. The positive energy charge carried by a male body is exchanged with the negative magnetic charge of a female.

The effect of physical touch between opposite sexes (or even same sexes) has been studied now for a number of years. There are several levels of study, beginning with the Christian theory of the "laying on of hands" in order to miraculously heal physical disorders. I'm sure there are earlier precedents; however, two thousand years of history is sufficient for me.

Modern anthropological studies have shown how the Victorian age of strict morality concerning appropriate (mostly inappropriate) sexual behavior for society has affected the actual health of humans. There are national programs advertising and advocating more human exchange through touch.

In America there is an organization called HUGS. Their contention is that we must embrace another human at least four times a day to exchange a healthy amount of life-force energy.

One of the best examples of the successes in healing some ailments through touch has been the rise in recognition and acceptability of the chiropractic profession. These pioneers have gone up against a huge worldwide group of demigods called doctors. They have proven comparable abilities in healing through touch and physical hands-on manipulation of muscles, bones, and nerves.

Many persons, responding to their natural instincts and desiring more human contact, have gone into the profession of massage therapy. Massage is now becoming a prescription given for the reduction of stress.

This is not a new profession and is probably in direct evolution descending from Mary Magdalene, or the other women who followed groups of men from battle-field to battlefield. The women kept them strong, fit, and balanced through the exchange of their physical energy.

It is my personal opinion that this type of therapy, if legalized, would eliminate the cruelty of male pimps upon women. The drugs that are associated with illegal sex would also be unnecessary. Violent crime in pros-titution and rape would disappear, as regulated, clean sexual energy could be exchanged without fear or shame. It's going to happen anyway in its worst form as long as it is handled as a moral, religious issue, rather than a logical scientific realization for health. As Dr. Eric Berne said, "Good sex means better health."

Passion's first definition in Webster's is associated with religion, death, and suffering for a spiritual cause. We humans have used religion to attempt to control sex.

Our sexual epidemic now is the plague we call ac-quired immunodeficiency syndrome (AIDS). This is a result of passion gone awry. This passion is the negative description in action; great anger, rage or fury, sexual drive, lust. These eventually affect all of us.

Anything is a part of everything else, and there is always the positive and the negative included. When passion for life, passion to create, will to life, reaches its lowest level, it is humanity degraded to the animal in-stinct. Sex without affection or love becomes lust, and lust eventually deteriorates into violence. When sexual union becomes physically violent enough to tear the skin, the virus that lies waiting to bring us back into balance moves into our bloodstream. When one of us is affected, we are all affected. When thousands of us are affected, we wake up and change our ways. This sexually transmitted virus killing thousands is waking us to control our personal sexual habits. Meditating with the crystal that directs the rays from planet Pluto can help us to transform our motives and attitudes in sexual encounters.

The great plagues of the Middle Ages spurred humanity to "clean up its act" on a physical hygiene level. At this moment in our evolution it goes beyond the physical to the Emotional, Mental, and Spiritual bodies. We have to clean up our attitudes toward passion. Too many of us have been expressing our passion in negative ways.

In America alone the crimes of violent passion, rape and murder, are beyond belief in a so-called civilized, religiously structured society.

Our grass-roots, homegrown, internationally known "religious leaders" have publicly been exposed as secretly cheating, stealing, lying, and partaking of abnormal sexual practices. These men have made personal fortunes from the donations of their huge television audiences. Their messages to their people were so unreal, they could not be followed. The emphasis on negative acts called sin, the attempt to kill desire, only gave negative energy more power in their lives. They became what they despised!

Passionately preaching against passion is a dichotomy to the human mind. We cannot go against our own nature without harming ourselves.

Human sexual activity, practiced on a safe, sane, affectionate, mutually respecting level, may not sound as exciting as passionate, abandoned, instinctual sex, but the results are satisfying to all of the invisible bodies. The energy exchange benefits both.

Returning to the days in the cave in wild abandon can be fun now and then between a couple practicing affectionate, mutual respect. This is my prescription some-times when things begin to get too routine! Excite the passions!

On the reverse side of stories of wild, unregulated sexual passion are the stories I hear of total disgust. Self-criticism, lack of satisfaction, and a depletion of personal energy are brought about by sexual interaction without spiritual connection. These results of attempting to sat-isfy only the body lead to eventual dis-ease and infection.

To have sex without some form of love being in the consciousness is depleting to the Spirit at this point in our evolution.

Many humans on Earth are here in this lifetime to become instructed by their own choices and experiences in the facts of love and sex. They choose dramas and write scripts with characters played by Spirits who love them, but who may play an opposite role in this lifetime. The actual events described to me every day by men and women fit definite patterns. It is my greatest chal-lenge to disclose these patterns and find adequate means or formulas to retrain the reactions and beliefs that per-petuate pain.

I am passionate about my belief that conscious passion is perfect! Observe yourself. What is your greatest pas-sion? Circle the right word or fill in the blanks below with your response.

1. I have   no   some   many   passions.

2. My greatest passion is _____.

3. My passionate feelings concerning this make me feel   happy   angry   hopeful   fearful.

4. I   do   do not   usually act on my passionate feelings.

5. By not acting on my passionate feelings I believe

_____

_____

6. By acting on my passionate feelings I believe

_____

_____

Resolve now to be a more consciously passionate human, displaying a healthy will to life, and willingness to enjoy your portion of the Love Stuff!

In every chapter of "Crystal Profiles" you will find an active meditation exercise to increase or properly use your passion.

> Every human mind is a great slumbering power until awakened by a keen desire and a definite resolution to do!
>
> **—Edgar F. Roberts**

If you want further encouragement, I suggest you go to your local music store and buy a cassette made by a rock star named Rod Stewart. His long version of a song called "Passion" might wake up your solar plexus.

Music is another method humans have discovered to

use vibration as an invisible addition to stirring the Emotional Body. There are as many separate types of music as there are different human beings on Earth. From the intellectual and spiritual composers we have classical compositions that were rejected by their first audiences! Remember that humans have a tendency to want to continue what is well-known and comfortable. The contemporary compositions of the closing of this century are bewildering to many, because the vibrations of the sounds are in a different tempo. The mathematical equations of modern music are not soothing to those who have been scripted from birth on other vibrations. Your crystals will absorb and magnify your music.

Why does our music change? The history of Earth music and Earth art show that humans express their environment and unconscious understandings by their compositions. Each new generation of Earthlings create a new record of evolution by their music and art.

The "heavy metal" and "hard rock" of the presently maturing generation is passionate and aggressive music. The parents, grandparents, and great-grandparents do not feel attuned to these vibrations. It is widely criticized and rejected by generations who respond to a set of musical vibrations that reflect and trigger different emotions, and a different history.

My speculation is that the present generation is reflecting a world of chaos in their music. They are coming into incarnation during a period of drastic change, a time in which everything appears to be out of order, out of control, unpredictable. The analogy would be this: Imagine a scientist mixing two chemical solutions together in a test tube. When one chemical is poured into the other, there is instant chaos! Bubbling, boiling, vaporizing, violent reactions, crystallizing, reformings of molecules—and after the combustions subside, voilà! A new formula is developed!

The present music coming from the new generation is possibly a conditioning vibration. They may have a preknowing of their future in space. Many of the recordings made by our space explorers have been filled with the sounds that are similar to the sounds in the passionate new music. It is not at all suprising that the electronic instruments and amplifiers contain crystal frequency mechanisms.

The classical composers have also been visionaries presenting outrageous, nonmelodic symphonies years before the chaos of our evolutionary change was felt by the new masses. Many of us in frustration could only bear the sounds by listening with our eyes closed and imagining it was the sound track of a flying-saucer movie! It was disturbing our Emotional Body.

Music and art are emotional creations. The products of the emotional field made into physical expression have a definite purpose in our lives. Passion must be constantly stimulated to keep the life on Earth in the state of fresh new becoming.

The personal passionate life of any human can be enhanced by the vibrations of music, combining the vibration of crystals.

Desire is the essense of a man.

—Benedict Spinoza

A great majority of the passionate poetry, art, and music preserved by humans can be attributed to the male gender! They have all admitted in either their private writings or public conversations that the female gender inspires this romantic, spiritual approach to passion. Most always it is somehow connected with a woman's physical beauty. Now we have all seen the woman, un-beautiful to our eyes, who is the beauty to his. It must be more than the physical.

It seems that the love of beauty civilizes the world. Somehow the beauty carries an invisible meaning that cannot be seen, can only be felt. The beauty of a tree, rock, flower, mountain stream, moonrise, sunset, new car, piece of jewelry, sky-scraping architecture, old barns, clouds, woven fabric, painted canvas, antique chair, horse, gorilla, rhinoceros, desert, electrical storm, or another human does not depend upon eyesight alone. Can a blind person detect beauty? What portion of their instinctual nature do they use? Which part of our many terminals of perception is more reliable in detecting true beauty? Does it come from within, is it radiation, is it transferred by the builder to the building?

If something is consistently pleasing to generations upon generations, it is believed to contain some essence that came from desire and speaks directly to our desire. It was born out of *passion*. The passion is felt in the solar plexus because it is braided and intertwined with the life-giving, life-sustaining energy from a distant source we call the Sun!

The Sun may be the solar plexus or Emotional Body of the Designing Creative Force in our Universe! What-ever the explanation may be, passion is one basic and necessary element in the composition of the "stuff" we live and breathe that I believe makes up the whole Cos-mos, called love.

Passion, also known as desire, in its most positive form is the one element necessary to fulfill our destiny. We are meant to become Gods and Goddesses, creating in a physical, visible world, using only invisible ingredients. The vibrations of invisible emotions and thoughts are like magnets that attract particles of matter. A strong desire and a strong focus of mind cause molecules to form themselves into dense constructions that eventually become visible.

If you truly desire love, intimacy, passion, romance, friendship, family harmony, you can attract it. *Stir up your passion!*

When you purchase your musical cassettes, also purchase one containing the vocalist Tina Turner singing "Paradise Is Here!" Take some time to passionately invest in loving yourself. Learn the lyrics and sing along. Remember that you are singing to your Self!

We have determined that we cannot kill the creative desire within ourselves; it is a part of the Universe and the "stuff" that holds the Universe together. It is a major ingredient in that "stuff" we call love.

I hear your question: "I don't even have a small possibility of an intimate relationship. I'm not particularly in love with my Self. I don't know of any special talent I could get passionate about. How do I produce or get some passion in my life?"

You have the power to create your own passion!

You chose to come onto the Earth to experience life!

You are responsible for your own rescue!

You are not responsible for anyone else's rescue!

Unless you have a passionate desire to fulfill the first three definitions of passion, which deal with the suffering and agony connected to martyrdom for a religious belief. In that case you already have *passion!*

So what is your problem?

I was reading a newspaper in 1980 in which a letter

appeared from a psychiatrist, who said people always asked him this question: "Why do people see a psychiatrist?" He explained that the answer could be summed up in a particular behavior: Silently going through life screaming, For God's sake, *LOVE ME!* The client, he explained, goes through a million different manipulations to be acceptable—just to get someone to love them.

Healthy people are looking around for someone to love! If you see changes in the people who are screaming "love me, love me" it is when they realize if they give up screaming and go to the business of *loving* another human, they will get the love they've been screaming for all their lives. It's a hard lesson to learn, but life gets a lot easier once we learn it.

> It is the law of love that we have whatsoever we desire.
>
> **—Charles Filmore**
> Founder of Unity

This sweet and gentle man along with his wife, Myrtle, dedicated their lives to the teaching of the loving bounty of the Universe. Their focus was on a religious belief in the words of Jesus: "It is your Creator's great pleasure to give to you! Whatsoever things you desire, ask and it shall be given unto you, knock and it shall be opened. When you pray, pray believing."

The last sentence in the quote appears to be the stumbling block for most of us. We simply find it hard to believe that we can receive!

Charles Filmore also said, "You are not to sit back and wait for a miracle to bring you what you want: Having prepared your mind with positive, constructive thoughts, you should expect opportunities to be revealed, and be alert to their possibilities."

Are you listening? Did you get that formula?

In the chapters that follow in the "Crystal Profiles" section, you will be given many choices and formulas for creating passion in your life. The active meditation exercises that can be greatly enhanced by using a specific colored gem-crystal will be explained, along with the suggested music and fragrances!

The principle of pleasure will be reintroduced into your life, as all the senses you possess as a human can be awakened. The stimulation of the senses is called sensual. If you have had a fear of sensuality in the past, there are crystals, music, and fragrances designed by the All Knowing Love Energy in the Universes to overcome your hesitant heart!

Passion is what you used to get yourself created by your parents into an Earthling. Passion for life has kept you alive up to now. It is part of you and everything that lives. You alone can call it forth and direct your own creative, spiritual evolution.

Passion makes idiots of the cleverest . . . and makes the biggest idiot clever!

—François de la Rochefoucauld

Family, Friends, and Lovers

The moment we indulge in our affections the earth is metamorphosed. There is no winter, no night. . . . All tragedies vanish.

—**Ralph Waldo Emerson**

Male and Female energies have changed over centuries of evolution. The description *positive energy* is attributed to the active forces in the Universes, such as electricity, Sun energies, and also Masculine energies. These are interactive to produce movement, outgoing, assertive motion. This energy is neither good nor bad. The way it is directed can be helpful or destructive. The Sun can give us life-sustaining energy, or we can expect destruction if there is too much Sun. Self-assertiveness is a Masculine Energy that is admirable until it is overacted and becomes too aggressive. The word *positive* is a scientific term used to describe the Masculine Energy, not a judgmental or discriminating expression.

The negative energy in the Universes is attributed to the quiet forces that appear to be inactive, receiving or reflecting forces such as magnetism, Moon energies, or Feminine energies. These are interactive to produce subtle but equal forces to the Masculine Energy. This opposite energy we call negative feminine is an equal energy that must be present to balance the strong, uncontrolled, outgoing, active energy. The Feminine Energy is a grounding, receiving, nurturing, holding, creative, and blending force in the Universes. The word *negative* is a scientific term, as the Feminine Energy is neither good nor bad.

As the Sun nurtures our Earth, our Moon receives the rays from the Sun, reflects them back to Earth in a changed vibration, and nurtures the moisture in our bodies, plants, and oceans. The living planet and Universes operate on positive-negative, Masculine/Feminine energies.

This chapter describes how the Masculine/Feminine forces need to be recognized by men and women in personal relationships. All humans contain both energies within themselves. Our family, friends, and lovers are all acting and reacting to our Feminine/Masculine energies, and we need to identify these energies at work. We want to direct them to their most favorable use toward loving and receiving love.

The family is one of nature's masterpieces

—George Santayana

A definition from Webster's may be helpful to get us ready to explore this pervasive controlling influence we share.

> **Family:** (**1**) All those claiming descent from a common ancestor, tribe, clan, or lineage. (**2**) A group of people related by ancestry or marriage. (**3**) One husband, his wife, and their children.

I am choosing the second definition to begin a subject you may want to reject: "A group of people related by ancestry or marriage." Please overcome your resistance and stay with us, because your *love life* is so dependent on your open-minded willingness to realize your unworkable patterns of relating. *Relating* is the key word.

As an analyst, I have been listening to the stories (narrations; recountings) of my friends and clients for many years concerning their personal interactions with their families. They *relate* how they *related* to their *relations*. The stories include how they came to be related, how their parents related, how their siblings related (including parents, brothers, sisters, grandparents, etc., acquired through marriage, not blood), and how they are presently relating with the families they have created for their present drama!

A great majority actually believe they have *left* their original family behind! They believe they have overcome or "worked out" within themselves any disturbances or friction that may have influenced their early family relationships.

Whatever a current problem may seem to be, even if it is career, organization, personal performance, disease, chronic illness, temporary or chronic depression, emotional, criminal, violent rebellion or passive resistance, it can eventually be traced back to an incident or a way of *relating* within the original family. We learn every word and movement on how to be a human directly from our closest family associations.

As the planets Saturn, Uranus, and Neptune clustered together, many old government structures crumbled. The Communist-ruled countries broke free of restrictions that had been an important phase in the end of a very old system of monarchies. Almost on cue, two hundred years after the French and American revolutions, the new revolutions began in Russian, Chinese, and Middle Eastern family hearts! The quest for personal freedoms cannot be overridden for long by any type of rule!

The microcosm is always a replica of the macrocosm. The larger family of Earth is coming closer to the knowledge that each national family is related to every other national family. When there are hardships being suffered by other Earthlings, we can no longer close our eyes, ears, or hearts. The public media bring it directly into our consciousness. We are forced to acknowledge our responsibility to our Mother Earth and all her children.

Because of transportation and communication technologies, our families have separated and scattered to other states, countries, or continents. All human families continue to be affected psychologically by certain religious holidays (holy days). Many do not consider themselves religious, and yet the winter holiday calls to them on a deep subconscious level.

Why? Because those days have evolved into *family* traditional celebrations, a way to respond (and measure) family love and connection!

With the changes in family structure, brought about by evolutionary conditions, many live far away from any permanent central family. During these times the old belief systems are resurrected and there is a deep feeling of loss and grief.

Members within the family structures that are surviving continue to make pilgrimages back to the nest, never realizing what the real astronomical plan is. When the reunion takes place, it usually brings about family drama! Old patterns emerge, old angers and hurts are stirred up, and psychological pressures are put upon most families during the winter solstice, *whether they are together or not.*

There are new crystals recently being uncovered, as gifts from our Mother Earth, to help us with our family love relationships. They are described in "Crystal Profiles."

Try as we may, our ways of responding to each other are affected by the in-born Spirit in the emerging soul. Family relationships may be affected by past lives. The position among siblings (number one, two, three, etc.) has an effect on the experiences that will come to the individual. This could all be an accident of nature or just random chance, but I don't think so.

Talking to so many different clients over the years, hearing their stories of how sibling rivalries or closeness has left its indelible mark on their emotional outlook, I'm asking them this question: "What do you think your Spirit wanted to learn from this circumstance? If it is not an accident, if indeed you two agreed to play this role for each other, what could be the lessons you wanted to teach to each other?"

Taking responsibility for our own reactions begins to put a greatly different perspective on familial "love."

Remember, I'm only asking you to *consider* these possibilities. Allow yourself to go back in time as far as you can remember. If you now have a specific issue or just an undercurrent of unrest with a parent, brother, or sister, even grandparent, what is the initial memory? There lies the secret to your healing.

The Crystal Love Secrets that you will be learning concerning peace on Earth begin with you and your chosen family.

> Family life is too intimate to be preserved by law. It can only be sustained by love, which goes beyond justice.
>
> **—Reinhold Niebuhr**

FRIENDS

Webster's definition of *friendship*: mutual trust and a sharing of private thoughts. *Friend*: a person whom one knows well that is an ally, not an enemy, an intimate associate toward whom there is affection; one who is kindly and helping.

When we speak to each other of friendship between two humans of either sex that does not include the physical act of mating or sexual union, we often refer to it as a platonic relationship.

> The love existing between friends that are a man and a woman without sexual activity is purely spiritual or intellectual.
>
> **—Plato**
> 427–347 B.C., Greece

Who was Plato anyway, and why are we always quoting him? He's been dead and gone for centuries. Haven't we become much more evolved and intelligent in these modern times? Apparently not, as we have yet to find a way to improve on some of his observations. We have kept his description of this type of love in our educational literature for 2,500 years! It seems to live on because it strikes a chord of truth.

In some minds this refers to a relationship without passion! It may even imply that the relationship is not as consequential as a sexual relationship. Nothing could be further from the experience of anyone who has ever maintained a really good friendship over many years.

Biographies of famous persons throughout history have detailed some of the most gratifying, totally satisfying human love relationships ever recorded. The union between the friends was between their souls, but not their bodies.

Most of the famous references in history concern male-male friendships, such as Michelangelo Buonarroti (1475–1564) and his anonymous brother; Socrates and Plato; Jonathan and David. The most widely read account of friendship is between a daughter-in-law, Naomi, and her mother-in-law, Ruth, which is in the Hebrew Old Testament. This reference to friendship is in modern reference works, after five thousand years!

One of Thomas Jefferson's famous letters written to a female friend gives us marvelous insight into the human condition in general. It is a discourse in which he explains the dialogue between "his head and his heart." The lady was married to someone else, but they maintained a distant and passionate friendship for many years.

The only way to have a friend is to be one.

—Ralph Waldo Emerson

"Until one is committed there is hesitancy, the chance to draw back, always ineffectiveness. The moment one definitely commits oneself, then Providence moves, too." This belief is attributed to Goethe.

Think of the friendships that have been a contributing factor to your happiness. Realization that love is always available gives us such confidence in the future! Think back now over your lifetime, as far back as you can remember. Who was your first playmate? How long did that last? Were you willing to keep on trying even after a disagreement? Were you concerned about the things the friend could do for you? Did you forgive and forget? Well, these questions are all far beyond the thinking of a three-year-old. We just wanted to play, and even scuffling over a toy was considered part of the game. Our memory was short, because the next day, we began again with pleasant expectations.

As we grew in years, so did our expectations! We became more territorial, possessive, and less forgiving! For several years after we are born we are still fresh from the nonmaterial Spirit world. We can see and hear things adults cannot. We carry with us the "sweetness" of that other world, which includes the "stuff" we call trust, forgiveness, unconditional love. We must become fully human, to fit our Spirit into a changing Earth body, to walk, to talk, experience being tangible, and learn to create on this physical plane.

Learning to cooperate with everyone surrounding us becomes the first stumbling block to our innocence.

Imagine yourself lost in space, finding an unidentified planet on which to land your spaceship. Beings gather around and pull you out of the ship. They are giants, they have hair all over their bodies, they have teeth and claws, and peculiar glass and metal things over their eyes! The first thing they do is turn you upside down and hit your backside until you scream! That makes them very happy!

Then you meet the one who will be your keeper. This one will be replaced by several others who will keep you alive for a while. Eventually *she* will be your first enemy and your first friend, maybe.

Remember Plato's description of friendship? "Love existing between friends that are a man and a woman without sexual activity is purely spiritual or intellectual."

The mother and child sometimes have a sexual union if the baby is breast fed. This is healthy for the mother as it causes her uterus to contract and return to its normal size after childbirth. It feels sexual to her. It is healthy for the baby as her milk contains natural immunity compounds. Suckling is a sensual satisfaction for the infant. In reality our first caretaker becomes our first friend, and we begin this friendship with sexual overtones being built into our memory genes. Our relationship to this first caretaker determines our relationship to every other human we will encounter. She becomes our first sweetheart and lover also.

It is my belief that we spend the remainder of our time on Earth psychologically attempting to return or to rebel from that initial encounter! This will possibly affect all future friendships or love relationships.

In the "Crystal Profiles" section there are two specific crystals my clients have identified as being very helpful

▲
▼

in dealing with the areas of friendship and/or family love. The Azurite, Malachite, and Larimar crystals are activated now by the Saturn-Uranus conjunction.

The relationship established between mother and child may not be ideal. Sometimes the mother does not survive, or the child is placed with another caretaker. This may be planned in advance by the Spirits before Earth entry. I can hear your mind working madly, saying, "Why would anyone choose this?" There could be many subtle reasons why a Spirit would set this up for its learning. The most obvious would seem to be a knowing that a past life relationship between parent and child had been too dependent. There could be a possibility that the Spirit coming in as baby was the mother in a previous incarnation and may have abandoned the then baby! The changing places would be a lesson intricately interwoven with Spiritual learning.

I have had a number of clients over the years who have had extremely frustrating relationships with their mothers. In some cases, the feeling of being unwanted by the mother or father has damaged the self-esteem of the individual severely. This situation causes any kind of future friendships to be difficult and out of balance.

Unfortunately, when this information comes to me, I discover there has been little if any communication about this between parent and child! Adult children are afraid to confront their parents! On occasion the parent has left Earth or is not cognizant and so cannot be directly approached. In these cases the prescription is the same: communication! Talk to the Earth bound, talk to the Earth free. Get the feelings out of the body! Write everything down in letters, which you may never mail. It doesn't matter if the Spirit has left Earth. It can forever be contacted on some unseen level. The crystal of your choice can act as an amplifier and transmitter of your desires and feelings.

The friendships that we allow to nurture ourselves are all love affairs! We may experience "tough love" from some of our friendships.

I believe friendship is the ultimate goal to achieve in *any* human relationship. If we are interested in perfecting our friendships, or in learning the art of friendship, we must examine our relationships to our parents. This will help us to analyze how we really feel about women friends and men friends. Hopefully it will open our minds to allow fresh air to clean out dusty old ideas!

It is very exciting to know that Mother Earth is giving us friendship crystals! Did you know the constellation of stars called Aquarius sends the vibrations that rule friendship?

At this very important time in Earth history, the leaders of the nations (or clans) are beginning to visit each other, to offer friendship, affection, and help. There are two planets that give us energy toward this goal. Those planets will be traveling close together for a number of years. They are Saturn, sending a green ray of truth and stability, and Uranus, sending a blue ray of loyalty and peace. Saturn rules the crust of the earth and all structures. Uranus rules the electrical sky and all instant communication. This marriage of Earth and sky is symbolic of the Age of Aquarius, the *new age*, the age of friendships.

The four things most important to maintain in friendship are truth, loyalty, stability, and peace. The newly activated crystals we can use in meditation exercises to enhance our friendships are a combination of blue and green. The newest discovery is called Larimar, and the other is an Azurite/Malachite blend. These will be discussed in depth in the second half of this book.

> Friendship is always a sweet responsibility,
> never an opportunity.
>
> **—Kahlil Gibran**

Have you ever had a destructive or disappointing end to a friendship? Do you sometimes think back and wish you could have overcome the difference? Did it have to do with truth or loyalty? Did it have to do with possession? Did it have a connection in your own psyche with attempting to repeat a pattern with one of your parents?

Case History: A scenario that is often the reason that friendships are lost, and the amazing successful outcome.

Lisa is a massage therapist, Barbara is a counselor, and they are dynamic friends. They play tennis, go dancing, attend plays, cook for each other, exchange gifts; love is verbally expressed between them. They discuss their male relationships with each other, their problems with their work, money, children, or their parents. They have an intimate, kind, helping relationship, nonsexual, but with deep affection.

Barbara meets an exciting, romantic, intelligent man who has similar interests to hers in a private project she has been spearheading for several years. He travels internationally. He confides in her that he is rebounding from his marriage breakup, is searching for spiritual understanding. He wants to learn more from Barbara because he witnesses her leadership and teaching abilities in this area. He is up-front with her, explaining that he is on a quest and not looking for a permanent relationship.

Barbara is overwhelmed by his personality and becomes infatuated anyway. She brings him into her project and her bedroom. Barbara tells all of this to Lisa in telephone conversations over several weeks' time.

Eventually when he is visiting Barbara, she arranges to take him over to meet Lisa. She is so excited and elated now her two loves can meet each other! Sharing a friend with a friend is a pleasure. Have you ever said to your friend, "I can't wait to have you meet . . . ?"

The meeting seemed amiable. He mentioned that he had a slight headache. Lisa, being a helpful healer by instinct, offered to relieve the pain with special pressure-massage techniques. This was very pleasing to Barbara, because she wanted them to like each other. While Lisa was working on his neck, the conversation turned to a spa-resort in his home city. Lisa had a monthly contract to travel for a weekend of massage for the visitors there. What a coincidence! That very next weekend she would be there.

When Lisa returned from her monthly sojourn of massage therapy in the other city, she called Barbara. Before many minutes had passed, Lisa was telling how Barbara's friend had come to stay at the spa where she was working. Gently, she began to relate how he had requested a massage and asked the manager for her specifically. She went on to describe how they eventually had dinner together that night. You guessed it! Yes, they ended the evening in his room having sex.

Barbara was stunned! Several moments of silence that seemed like an eternity went by as emotions swept over her body. Her mind was racing, attempting to stabilize

▲
▼

her physical reaction. Adrenaline was pouring into her solar plexus as a combination of surprise, fear, betrayal, anger, self-pity, violation, and loss all rolled into one moment. . . . With every ounce of her civilized conscious self-control Barbara began to describe to Lisa how she was feeling! She paid strict attention to her physical body, monitoring everything that was expressing itself painfully. She said, "Oh, Lisa, I feel like my stomach is falling out of my body! My chest feels like it is full of fire and the flames are burning up my throat. My heart is pounding so hard it is causing my ears to ring, and I am just in terrible emotional pain!"

Lisa said, "I'm really sorry to have to be the one who causes you to react this way. I guess this will not seem possible that I love you and can be your friend."

Barbara replied, "Lisa, you knew how much I liked this man. How could you do this? I would *never* have done that to you!"

"You may not want to believe this," Lisa replied, "but when I saw how you were falling all over him, and giving away your power to him, I also saw that he was a roamer, open to any liaison. I wanted you to see the truth, because you were blinded by his personality!"

Barbara didn't like this explanation at all, but she remembered that he had warned her of his quest. She felt Lisa had acted selfishly and impulsively. She suspected Lisa wanted to experience him sexually because as friends they shared almost everything, but this was too much! She told Lisa she was temporarily "knocked out" and had to meditate on the situation further. She never made any verbal accusations or judgments aloud to Lisa. They ended the conversation by stating their original declarations of friendship.

Barbara had a long talk with herself about the situation. She spent time doing her active crystal meditation exercises. She weighed her long-standing friendship with Lisa against the short affair with him. She realized he was transient, but truthful. He had stated all along he wanted friendship only. She knew she had been hoping for more, convinced she could cultivate it. Now she saw she must decide to have two friends or lose both.

Barbara eventually allowed her mating instincts to subside as she used the friendship, unconditional-love crystals in daily ten-minute rituals. She maintained her friendship with both, through open conversations about her feelings to them. They know they have an eternal friendship.

Barbara was fortunate to have training that helped her to overcome the fearful response of loss that can attack anyone who becomes involved in sexual triangles. The average person has no instruction on how to handle this emotionally. Many valuable friendships are destroyed because of a widespread, archaic territorial or possessive emotional reaction to the sharing of love. The misunderstanding is subtly taught to us as children as we observe older models, adults, expressing jealousy or possessive tendencies toward another.

In Nancy Friday's monumental book *Jealousy*, the final analysis brings this historical affliction down to one crucial personal point: self-esteem. If we have not done our homework in the quest toward loving our Self, we suffer consistent hunger. This causes us to be in a habitual state of searching for food to feed our Emotional Body. We live in fear that we will not get enough. When we think that we have latched onto a source of emotional nourishment, we become wild creatures, protecting our "territory"! Anyone who encroaches on our "territory" becomes the enemy! We feel justified in expressing (or holding within) violent reactions we consider to be natural or fair against the intruder. To begin today to overcome these fears, choose one of the love crystals for opening your heart to love yourself. How do we teach that possessive passion is *not* love? How do we teach that love is in fact the opposite:

"If you love something, set it free; if it is yours, it will return to you! If it does not return, it never was yours."

FOR MEN ONLY

There has been some recent study on the psychological loss that we have all experienced because our fathers have been so distracted by their work. The Masculine Energy has slowly been fading from influence for several generations. It is becoming so painful to both sexes, it is surfacing in our interactions with our friends and lovers.

The direct result has been that Spirits born into male bodies now are suffering from a lack of male friendships. They have so little contact with their own fathers, grandfathers, or any other older males, they have no role models. The result is their inability to communicate with each other on a personal or intimate level. This leads them to attempt this type of contact with females, because females are practiced at mixing emotion with communication in many cases.

In intimate, sexual love relationships (either hetero or

homo) the Feminine Energy is the communicator on the *intimate* levels. Talking a lot does not mean communication is taking place. The subject of the message and the way in which the message is transmitted make the difference between mundane conversation and intimate communication.

A man may feel safe with a more intimate partner so he can attempt to express his deeper feelings. He can allow the Feminine Energy to comfort him. As a child he communicated with his mother, and he may also be able to express deep feelings with a platonic female friend. In this new age of friendship, the Male energies will be helped to communicate with each other from the heart.

What is the answer to this modern dilemma? Are there really some crystals that can unblock the inhibitions and fears of vulnerability for those with a belief that expressing true emotion signifies weakness? Yes, there are several crystals that change the vibrations of the Mental Body (beliefs) and the Emotional Body (fears).

Spirits that are in female bodies now have an obligation to look into their own Masculine Energy, to see if they, too, withhold their true emotions in order to appear more logical, more controlled, stronger. We do live in a left-brained society that has consistently rewarded mental acuity. Women have become more acceptable in the business world as they have displayed more of their Masculine Energy.

If we can be patient and empathetic with the men in our lives now, we must encourage them to open up to each other. The Spirits in male bodies are suffering from centuries of grief they have never been allowed to express. They have fought and killed and died and lost

▲
▼

what they have loved, but have never expressed their pain and sorrow. This buried emotion has handicapped their ability to feel or to describe what they feel.

The Feminine Energy must encourage men to spend more quality time together, breaking down the ridiculous walls of inhuman emotional control they have built around themselves. The time has passed for that role, or any role, to be taken by one or the other sex of the human race.

> Friendship without self-interest is one of the rare and beautiful things in life.
>
> **—James Francis Byrnes**

In our lives now, for the sake of peace on Earth, the platonic friendship is a most valuable prize we can achieve. A spiritual friend connection is a joy forever. Each one of us can cultivate a male-female friendship if we truly want it. Each one of us can create a male-male friendship or a female-female friendship. The actual moving back and forth between those energies *within* ourselves, and recognizing when we are, and loving ourselves for that ability, is the key to true friendship.

The crystals to help ourselves are all described in *Crystal Healing Secrets* and *Crystal Love Secrets*.

FRIENDSHIP WITH THE FAMILY

I have a client who for years has been totally frustrated with the inability of her husband to show affection or to communicate on an intimate level. When I listened to them together, he finally attempted to describe his confusion over what love was.

"The only time I have ever felt what I thought real honest love was all about," he said, "was on the battlefield! Another soldier, sometimes a man I didn't even know, would see me in danger and jump to protect me by fighting back-to-back with me. Then I felt pure, unadulterated love."

His wife, with deep understanding and compassion, said softly, "But honey, the children and I have been right there in the heat of your battle, protecting you from danger and fighting back-to-back with you for all these years!"

Yes, there is a crystal to use with meditation or to wear that will help bring friendship back into our intimate or familial relationships.

LONG-TERM FRIENDSHIPS

I have talked to many clients about their friendships because the ability to make friends is so interwoven with physical health! True friends often feel so uninhibited they hug each other whenever they are together. This human energy exchange is so powerful, certain metabolic rates in the body show a marked improvement. Recent studies have shown human need for positive human contact.

These connections of the heart have been described in every civilization:

Friendship is one mind in two bodies.

—Meng-Tzu
Chinese philosopher, 372–289 B.C.
(Called in Latin: Mencius)

The clients that have the highest quotient of self-healing appear to have long-term friendships. When I ask them how long they have maintained their longest single friendship, it usually equals more than half their lifetime! These clients have helped me to identify the friendship crystals.

Unfortunately many of us were raised in a time of history when friendship between the sexes was not even considered possible. The understanding seemed to be, "My friends are the same sex as myself. If I have anything to do with the opposite sex, it must eventually lead to sexual union. If I don't want that, I can't have friendship instead."

For many years there was a belief that the marriage vows automatically severed any ties of friendship between males or females outside the couple's home. Any interaction was suspect; ownership and jealousy reigned. This false conception never inhibited infidelity. It may have promoted extramarital affairs. It caused more excitement, more intrigue, more drama, to spice up the otherwise humdrum unromantic marriage.

Because of cultural and ethnocentric beliefs, many of us are just beginning to break those old barriers of thought. The more the physical passions cool, the easier it becomes; that is, aging helps! However, it is of utmost importance for *Peace on Earth* that younger, passionate men and women look at this question from a more universal or Aquarian position. Life can be just as exciting without making a "soap opera" or acting out a TV drama.

One of my clients is a primary-school teacher who is learning to balance his Feminine Energy in a male body. He has given me a Spanish word I believe we need to memorize: *granjear* (gran-hey-AR). It means to give, without expecting anything in return. This definition is the key to friendship, and the formula of the "stuff" of the Universes.

A very definite beginning to committing to true friendship is the surrender of any subversive, manipulative, unrecognized plans we may have to somehow benefit ourselves when we take on or offer friendship.

We can recollect in the past how this incorrect motive usually backfires. The Laws of the Universe are designed for balance. Unless the outcome is *win-win* on both sides, a relationship is out of balance.

If there are hard feelings between you and an exfriend or relationship, you can usually trace the problem to the *expectations* you were carrying into the original setup.

We all begin any new relationship with high hopes, expectations, and addictions!

The ability to be a friend or to have one is based on adaptability and the courage to be vulnerable. In both of the cases stated here (Barbara/Lisa and that of the male client), the focus was placed on needs or addictions unrecognized by the client. They were not focused on a balanced exchange of energy. The "playmate" friend can learn to mature emotionally by "adapting" to the schedules of others. The "strong and effective" man can learn to be vulnerable by telling the truth to his friends: "I don't feel strong and effective today."

In the later chapters we will discuss crystals that are

helpful in active meditation exercises to promote adaptability and vulnerability.

Questions to ask yourself about friendship:

1. Am I a good friend? _____ yes _____ no
2. Do I expect something in return for my friendship? _____ yes _____ no
3. Do I have enough friends? _____ yes _____ no
4. Do I approach new aquaintances for possible friendship? _____ yes _____ no
5. Do I have a good balance of male and female friends? _____ yes _____ no
6. Do I plan recreation with friends and invite them? _____ yes _____ no
7. Do I make an effort to notice what my friends like and offer it to them? _____ yes _____ no
8. Do I share what I like with my friends by doing things together, or introducing them to a new subject? _____ yes _____ no
9. Do I ever give my friends gifts for no reason? _____ yes _____ no
10. Do I communicate my true feelings to my friends? _____ yes _____ no
11. Do I trust my friends enough to be vulnerable? _____ yes _____ no
12. Do I trust my friends enough to let them know I'm human? _____ yes _____ no
13. Do I give them my moral and even financial support in their business or career by choosing their service? _____ yes _____ no

LOVERS

This particular subject is the one that is uppermost in the minds and hearts of humanity. In order to be prepared for the happiest, most successful use of the Crystal Love Secrets, you need to fully absorb the chapters before this one. If you have read them, I suggest you go back and read them again.

If you have not read them, please give yourself a chance to become more successful at loving. Tell the curious little child within you to slow down. Tell it you intend to really consider many different attitudes and opinions about love and loving. Tell the little child inside that reading the other chapters will make this one work for you so much better. Thanks for loving yourself. Start at the beginning.

Sex is the urge to create. It begins at the lowest energy center in the human. It is the primal instinct to continue its own species. Now we're talking about primitive *sex*. Sex without romance, sex without intimacy, sex without love, just raw drive to reproduce is still with us after all these years! It isn't abnormal, unnatural, or evil, and feeling this drive should not produce guilt. In the balance of the Universes it is imperatively necessary. Remember this half of positive-negative energies must be present for creation to take place. Sexual drive is good.

If this urge is out of balance, impaired, inflated, or missing, everything in the life of a human is awry. Our Mother Earth produces conductors of Cosmic Energy called gem-crystals that we can use to balance our sexual

▲
▼

drive. These will be detailed with explanations on how to use them in the "Crystal Profiles" section.

There was a natural evolving reason for each step of our progress toward civilized living and the structures that we have devised to control ourselves. We have been "on a roll" and not only survived, but overpopulated our planet!

In most of the civilized countries on Earth there began to be an unconscious "knowing" fifty centuries ago in our earliest written history about the need for more integration of the races. At this point humans had wandered around the globe, established separate languages, physical features, talents, and strengths peculiar to their special climates. Now it was time for the tribes to begin trading talents and strengths for the further evolvement of the total Earthling.

The few brave souls who set out to visit other lands led the way for establishing roads, and star maps for water travel. Many followed, camping on territory considered to belong to tribes already camping nearby. The Masculine Energy began a series of aggressive movements that have accomplished two very important things in our progress as a one-world race.

1. By moving into others' territory, the tribes intermingled sexually.

2. When there was a dispute over who owned whom or who owned the land, they either had a council meeting or fought a war.

This method and formula is still in effect. The results have been barely effective in controlling the Earth's population and evolution of the species known as Homo sapiens up to our time.

Now we can begin to talk about our great dream—

There is no instinct like that of the heart.

—**Lord Byron**

What is the greatest and most universal dream of Earthlings? When did we begin to dream this dream? How are we doing on making the dream come true? The question is really, now that we have almost perfected the physical Earthling, and the Mental Body is working rather well, can we now learn to direct the Emotional Body?

The dream is invisible and intangible. We *know* it exists, we desire it more than anything, we cry for it and search for it all our lives. We write about it again and again in books and articles. We create music and lyrics around the dream, we are drawn into violent action and even murder because we believe in the dream until it turns into a nightmare.

If we never accomplish the dream, we condemn ourselves as failures, trudging through our lives feeling incomplete. We overlook every other blessing and pleasure, while we pine in our addiction to the dream.

Emotion is not something shameful, subordinate, second-rate; it is a supremely valid phase of humanity at its noblest and most mature.

—**Joshua Loth Liebman**

The dream is *romance! Romantic involvement!* Again I turn to Webster's dictionary to help us with a definition: a Middle European word, Old French, coming from the word *Roman* (1) because the Romans wrote long verses about the adventures of knights and heroes; (2) a fictitious tale of wonderful and extraordinary events, characterized by much imagination with the emphasis on courting or wooing to gain the favor of a lover; (3) preoccupied with idealized lovemaking; (4) not practical, dominated by thoughts, feelings, and attitudes of a fanciful nature toward love.

When did we begin to change from merely mating into loving? Or thinking about an emotion connected with mating other than pure reproduction instinct? How have the Male and Female energies contributed to the dream?

From reading the many accounts of love stories in the ancient Hindu and Hebrew religious manuscripts, it appears the Emotional Body was awakened long before the earliest writing. Affection following attraction is a natural instinct. It is also observed among certain animal species in the wild. Lions, beavers, and wolves are some groups that mate for life.

> The sexes were made for each other and only in the wise and loving union of the two is the fullness of health and happiness expected.
>
> **—William Hall**

The moving planets, sending signals of light vibration to Earth, activate the crystalline structure of our mother. She produces a personal character and personality, like any mother. She guides and directs our actions at all times. When she wants our undivided attention, she either shifts her position or erupts. In these ways she sends crystals up to her surface. We have used these tools for talismans and communication with her since our early beginnings. We are now finding *new* crystals, never seen on Earth. These crystals are transmitting from the unseen new planets, bringing us new information.

The next level for our collective growth is our "dream" of perfecting our personal relationships. The dream we have of "peace on Earth" is gestating or quietly receiving energy as we pursue our dream of "romantic love."

The planets Uranus, Neptune, and Pluto (the newest, most distant, and powerful) moving through the constellations of stars called Sagittarius, Capricorn, and Aquarius, in the coming years, will send energies to persuade humanity to continue the quest toward personal growth and understanding. We now have *time* to learn these things through personal relationships for the first era in history. The planetary time is right. The collective dream of romantic love is gathering strength as more humans find time to dream. As we continue to search for love, moving from partner to partner, we continue to learn better ways of relating.

The crystals relaying energies to us from these planets are transmitting the colors blue from Uranus, green from Saturn, and burgundy (violet-red) from Pluto. The names of some of these crystals are Emerald, Larimar, Azurite-Malachite, Kunzite, Garnet, Rhodochrosite. These crystals and their uses are fully explained in "Crystal Profiles."

As the "Universal Transformation" is accomplished, the more we are aware of our personal role in the process, the easier it will be for us to move through the ensuing chaos. In order for the Universal Transformation to bring *peace* on Earth, each one of us must transform ourselves.

By starving emotions we become humorless and rigid. By repressing them we become "Holier-Than-Thou." Encouraged, they perfume life; discouraged, they poison it.

—**Joseph Collins**

The Living Essence

Remember when you were light, playing
in the amorphous mists of heaven, showing yourself
in luminous rainbow colors? I loved you then.

We all played together, building a sparkling star, remember?
We all agreed to do a great exploding act, not knowing
the outcome, but what an adventure in flying!

A swirling mass of red-hot lava we were, cooling
ever so slowly. We regrouped to form a mass called Earth
in this time. Do you remember I loved you?

You became water again and I was born from
your elements, a crystal between two huge rocks.
Earth shifted, stretched, strained, crushed us together
dying in each other's arms, remember?

You returned as a giant redwood tree, I as a
flower at your feet, still together after all these years!
A terrible storm, a fire, a flood, we died again,
me, bound in your roots.

Remember the animal times, the many millions of
times we loved and died? When we transform
this human thing at last, what shall we be next?

—Brett Bravo

Mating, Marriage, and Dissolution

Where there is marriage without love, there will be love without marriage.

—**Benjamin Franklin**

With the movement of the planet Uranus sending its blue ray to Earth magnified by the constellation Aquarius beginning soon, new ideas will explode. This energy is strong because the planet and the stars involved affect quick thought, insight, electronic inventions, unexpected instant change, and telepathic communication.

At this moment the planet Saturn, which rules form, structure, tradition, status quo (the old way), and the career or life status of each Earthling, is in its own group of stars. Saturn represents an immovable object. Uranus, traveling in the same area of the heavens, represents an irresistible force. To illustrate the results of these planets' sending simultaneous messages to Earth, imagine a huge, immovable mountain. Suddenly, without warning, it explodes from the inside and changes its shape and the surrounding terrain! Volcanoes are often like this, it's natural.

Worldwide the effects of these planetary influences are visible to all of us because we are linked together by electronic media (Uranus rules radio and television). We have been watching events that are changing history and the total status quo of Earth politics. These events were unexpected and unforeseen. The nations in psychological slavery and physical oppression suddenly without warning broke out of the old way. This has affected the careers and status in life of millions of humans.

When Uranus and Saturn travel through the constellation of Aquarius beginning in 1992, there will be great changes in other areas of life on Earth. New ideas will replace the old. New communications, new discoveries, new ways of thinking in the areas of friendship, our dreams, our hopes and wishes, will suddenly be revealed by Uranus energy.

The visionary person usually receives these messages from the stars long before the actual occurrences. It has been noted by philosophers that we are given previews of change from one to five hundred years before the deadline. We are not aware of our gradual growth. The visionaries who attempt to describe what they can see happening in the future are commonly shunned, ridiculed, and in the past, persecuted.

A good example of this is the Polish astronomer named Nicolaus Copernicus (1473–1543). He predicted accurately that the Earth is not the center of the Universe. He speculated that we were one of many heavenly bodies revolving around a central Sun. For that kind of unexpected information, he was put under arrest by the Pope, threatened with expulsion from his profession and the church, and generally harassed!

Synchronistically in another area, Leonardo da Vinci (1452–1519) was making sketches of flying machines. These two visionaries were extremely sensitive humans who felt and received the energies of great change four hundred years ago.

In those times (and up to the present) it was a sacred ritual in the church to perform an actual wedding ceremony for the women who chose to devote their lives to the church. The nuns received a wedding band and were declared married to the Spirit of Christ. This marriage was supposedly replacing sexuality with "spirituality." This created a separation in the mind of humans, leading us to believe that one cannot coexist with the other.

> The substance of our lives is woman. All other things are irrelevancies, hypocrisies, subterfuges. We sit talking of politics, and all the while our hearts are filled with the memories of women, and the capture of women.
>
> **—Sir Thomas More**

Yes, all of this history, all of this astronomy, astrology, politics, war, and suffering are intertwined with our Emotional Body, our solar plexus, our Desire.

So you want to know how the visionaries of our past are contributing to our future? And how the planetary movements are encouraging a new Renaissance? Remember, Aquarius rules friendship, hopes, dreams, new ways of thinking, new ideas.

In how many marriages have you observed and noted the participants to be "friends"? Isn't it a fact that often they appear to be enemies? What type of nonsense is this? Is it time for a renaissance in relationships? Is it time at last to remove the meddling of the political and religious from the human natural process of pairing up?

The church and state may not think it is time because those entities love power. One old saying is "Absolute power corrupts absolutely." After all, those big corporations continue to exist because humans pay money to be governed. It may seem small or unimportant, but by collecting fees for marriage licenses, recording marriages in public records, and performing marriage ceremonies, several financial chains are perpetuated. This includes the profession of *law*, which has to untangle the messes created from religious and/or legal ceremonies combining the assets of two "lovers."

The ceremony of divorce is not new, but the changing times have made it expensive. The lovers lose, and the corporations win.

Marriage, as we know it now, is the old way, the centuries-old way. Uranus traveling through Capricorn and into Aquarius will be the beginning of the final phase. A new way of relating is coming.

In ancient times religious writings such as the Bhagavata Purana (third century B.C.) alluded to the marriage of sexuality with spirituality.

In the traditional Christian and Hebrew Bible of today, there remain passages concerning the incident of the "Sons of God" mating with the daughters of men.

Pairing has not always been related to marriage. As we trace the evolution of "marriage," we note the interference of the political authorities and the religious grand pooh-bahs of the tribes. That was a necessary fabrication of laws to protect and insure survival of the species of humans. We have survived, we have over-populated, the complete cycle has been run.

So what is a marriage without friendship, love, or intimacy? How can we do this to ourselves? And why? Because we are cowards! We are afraid to trust for fear of being betrayed. We are afraid to disclose because we fear judgment. We are afraid to give our gifts of spirit because we are afraid our gifts will be rejected. We are afraid to uncover our naked bodies because they don't match famous figures. We are afraid to give any love away because we may not get it back from the person we give to (and it must be that person or we have failed somehow). We are convinced there isn't enough love to go around.

> A coward is incapable of exhibiting love; it is the prerogative of the brave.
>
> **—Mahatma Gandhi**

Our personal fear of failure is such a strong emotion. What we fear happens! Remember the Emotional Body has its center in the solar plexus, the Sun center of our being. From that center, energy pours out to track down, and bring together like a magnet, all the ingredients of our emotion. We can create any happening or object or result, depending on the intensity or focus of our emotion! Crystals magnify this energy.

Fear of failure. FEAR of FAILURE. *Fear of failure!* This unconscious, subconscious emotion is being sent out firmly from the center of our very being. In our close, love-starved relationships, what is being called and attracted? Fear of rejection is truly the coward's excuse.

I'm not talking about new encounters here. I'm discussing folks who've been married and living and sleeping in the same bed for thirty-five to fifty years. I'm talking delusion and cowardice! I'm talking lies and deception through omission and withholding! I'm talking about *creating* failure by fear.

How many times have I heard a female client say, "Oh, I couldn't do that, my husband would kill me!" A lie. She uses him as an excuse for her cowardice. The same result is inevitable when I listen to a man tell me, "Oh, I couldn't do that, she would be destroyed." Not only a delusion, but a false belief that the partner is weak (because *we* are), and our false sense that we are so responsible for "fixing" the partner. They couldn't get along without a personal "savior-mechanic" as we have imagined our role.

The use of subterfuge, evasion, sidestepping the issues, withholding of true feelings (good and bad), and judging the partner as "needing fixing" are all our own ways of avoiding our own cowardice. If I can just focus my conscious mind on what is wrong with you, I don't have to concentrate on my own insecurities—right? Wrong, because what I have judged as your weaknesses are my own weaknesses, blown out of proportion. If you want a visual picture of this, think of the funny mirrors at a carnival that make a person look very fat or very tall, or crooked. This is how your mate looks to you, a reflection of yourself, not recognizable.

There are two tragedies in life. One is to lose your heart's desire. The other is to gain it.

—**George Bernard Shaw**

If there truly is a correlation between the battle of the sexes and the warring between nations (which I believe), we should be encouraged. Consulting history, I discover thousands of years of daily *war*. Getting up in the morning and going out to chop off somebody's arm, leg, or head in a gory battle was just routine. All these acts are still taking place. The encouraging part is, we have millions more humans on Earth and only have a *big war* about every twenty years or so now.

The Male and Female energies continue to *wake up* to the dream of the collective unconscious for idealized romance in love relationships. Slowly we are beginning to realize our responsibility for our own rescue. We have dreamed of finding another human who will be just like our Self! We have said of our mate, why can't she/he be more like me?

> More tears are shed over answered prayers than over unanswered prayers.
>
> **—St. Teresa of Avila**

It is happening, whether we realize it or not. Our prayers are being answered. Women are becoming more like men, men are becoming more like women.

Since you have been a crystal, on some level you can communicate with a crystal. It is a slow vibration compared to your fragile human body, vibrating at a high frequency of light. The crystal cannot be observed as moving or growing because it is at such a different rate. However, when we allow ourselves to return to our primitive solar plexus way of perceiving (not with eyes, ears, nose, or fingers) we can feel a relationship. It is something akin to "love feeling" when we hold an Earth crystal. We are attracted to it as a thing of beauty (even if others think it ugly). We hold it to our heart and feel comfort or strengthening or some other emotion, usually indescribable. The fact is *we know* the crystal is stored energy, stored information, and a healing tool from Mother Earth.

In our "quest for vision" (the Native Americans call it vision quest) we need help in rerouting all those little neurons of electric thought and beliefs that have made the grooves and canals in our brain. We need a stored energy that can help our Self to redirect millions of years of brainwashing about marriage and relationships. There are formulas of light refraction in the crystals that can change our own vibrational thought patterns. We can synchronize with the crystal's knowledge and its million years of experience. It can help us to open our minds to new ways of relating and mating.

> Until the middle of the last century, a series of marriages, each terminated by the death of a partner, was a common pattern. Modern methods of medicine and hygiene altered that program. Society had to alter. The seventies established divorce as a part of life. Instead of marrying and waiting for death, we get married, divorced, and marry again. . . .
>
> **—A. Alvarez**
> As quoted in Mary Singleton's
> *Life After Marriage*

If you have already been married, or have lived with a sexual partner in a monogamous relationship for six months or more, you are carrying some emotional baggage! Your brain computer is carrying some old pro-graming on an obsolete disc.

If you have never married, mated, or paired up for at least six months, you are also afflicted with some very old and outworn ideas that need trashing!

Feeling *guilty*, feeling *failure*, feeling *fear*, is such a killer! This tendency runs rampant in our Western society. It is the underlying anxiety reported to me by every client I see.

As a way of helping those New Age partners bring extra energy into their verbal commitments, I have created a "crystal wedding ceremony." In the past it has been customary for partners to exchange rings as a sign of mutual agreement (or mutual ownership). The jewelers have made this custom into a multibillion-dollar industry.

Many a wife has been valued by herself or her peers by the value (or size) of the Diamonds she wore in her engagement and wedding rings. The Diamond is a crystal with a high frequency vibration. It was chosen as the "love crystal" on a superconscious level by humans only a short time ago. Underneath the materialistic, obviously capitalistic business-profit motive lies the metaphysical meaning of the Diamond. It is the hardest natural substance known to exist on Earth. It is durable. When it is faceted and polished, it refracts every cosmic light ray in our Universe. It was chosen for the symbol of promises to faithfulness, steadfastness, and honor. It is such a high-frequency crystal it does not need to be large because it is strong. The symbol of the Diamond is for a durable, strong bond between the partners. Its symbology is lost in our materialism.

The Diamond has lost favor with many New Age partners because they feel attracted to other gem-crystal vibrations. A few of the more awake individuals are sensing the need to choose a different place on the electrical nerve system to wear the wedding gem-crystal. Bracelets or pendants on chains to touch the throat, heart, or solar plexus are being chosen. I even made earcuffs for one couple! Each partner chooses the gem-crystal he or she feels most attracted to. Each partner chooses the place to wear the crystal on his or her body, where he or she feels the most need. This is an intuitive process. The choices are made by desire and feeling, not by a left-brained analysis of which crystal would be the best prescription for what you believe to be your problem!

Do not look at one of my lists of crystal descriptions to decide which crystal would be the best prescription for what you believe to be your problem! Let your heart do the choosing. It will choose perfectly.

There are two other crystals involved in making the wedding talisman. They are Gold and Silver. (All Earth metals are crystalline in structure and refract cosmic light rays.) The Gold reflects the Masculine Energy of the Sun. The Silver reflects the Feminine Energy of the Moon. Please refer to the chapter "Surprise Crystals."

When the gem-crystal and the type of talisman have been chosen by each partner, the Gold and Silver will become a part also. Each person is attracted to either the Gold or the Silver. This choice must also be from the heart and must not be determined by the value of the metal. There are many preconceived ideas concerning what "appears" to be fashionable, glamorous, or successful. These are psychological aids to build a false sense of self-esteem. When each has chosen the Gold or Silver, it will be the major metal used for their talisman. There will be a smaller portion of the opposite metal crystal included. Each piece will include both Gold and Silver with the gem-crystal.

One partner may choose a pendant, the other may choose a bracelet or ring. Each choice is significant because it is the subconscious or superconscious (God-Goddess connected) mind making a statement of fact. Each area of the body is a symbol of the male or female energy and also points to a psychological issue. The partners can begin their relationship with knowledge of how they can be of assistance in the spiritual growth of the lover.

I always suggest the wedding talismans be worn on the physical body, every day. Attempting to carry them in a pocket or purse is adding another misplaceable, losable item. Talismans do not need to be expensive. There are many craftpersons in every area who can help design and construct jewelry costing under five hundred dollars.

It would be advisable to have just a small chip of Diamond crystal placed somewhere on your talisman because it magnifies the vibrations of all other crystals. It is a long, strong bond between you and your Universe, a symbol from your Mother Earth. It signifies the everlasting "stuff" of the Universe that we call *love*. It attracts every possible ray and vibration to treat our invisible bodies.

When the talismans are completed, each partner will make a gift of the talisman to the other. There will be a written metaphysical description for each crystal included in the talisman (metal, gem, and Diamond), which will be kept by the partner who gives the gift. This written description can be referred to at all times for clues as to how the lover can be encouraged and helped to achieve their highest spiritual understanding.

In the Crystal Love Ceremony for pairing, each partner describes the meanings of the gem-crystals, metals, and other symbols in the design of the talisman and the place on the body where the talisman is to be worn by their lover, to their lover, witnessed by friends or family.

The Crystal Love Ceremony cannot take place until each partner has full knowledge of what the other needs and desires from the pairing, based on the ingredients of the talisman.

In the center between the couple a single natural crystal is placed during the ceremony. This crystal can be any size or color, but must be chosen by both partners as a symbol for the third entity that is always created by pairing.

This entity is the relationship. The crystal that represents the partnership contains "the holy spirit" of Mother Earth and Father Sky. The relationship is like a baby or a business and is some of both. It must be nourished, fed, watched over, cared for, worked for, and sometimes sacrificed for. Our personal childish whims, fears, and issues of control must be placed aside, gratifications postponed, and absolute freedom curtailed for our responsibility to the relationship.

Theodore Roosevelt said, "It is better to be faithful than famous." Joseph Barth claimed, "Marriage is our last, best chance to grow up!" The most practical description was given by Antoine de Saint-Exupery recently when he stated, "Love does not consist of gazing at each other, but of looking outward together in the same direction."

These are the things that I choose for a positive *primary* relationship or partnership or both. The definitions for *partnership* according to Webster's are:

1. company
2. association
3. companionship
4. fellowship
5. participation
6. coworking
7. teamwork
8. joint effort
9. mutual assistance
10. union in action
11. cooperation
12. shareholder
13. comrade
14. associate
15. colleague
16. teammate

I have a perfect soul mate
I adore him/her.

I am a perfect mate for him/her
He/she adores me.

Love comes
Love chooses us.

Because we have persevered
I am a perfect mate.

I adore that man/woman within me.
I have my primary relationship.

The physical man/woman
is my mirror.

There are two fast-moving evolutionary forces at work in all levels of society bringing changes in marriage. Easy access to information and convenient transportation have given even undeveloped countries more personal freedom. Television is close by in even the poorest neighborhoods, and schooling is fast becoming universal. The farm-grown food and families are easily transported to the cities. Exposure to new ideas is a part of the overall decline in lifelong marriages.

In the poorest country on Earth, Bangladesh, Muslim women are learning to write and bank their own money. Their husbands are angry, and now divorce is an immanent new way of life.

This working Universe has a plan. When we see the overall picture, divorce no longer carries the painful stigma of failure. It becomes one of the major initiations in the never-ending spiritual growth of humans.

> It is better to have loved and lost
> than never to have loved at all.
>
> **—Alfred, Lord Tennyson**

Divorce as initiation . . . what does that mean? When I experienced that traumatic event, my lawyer called it dissolution. I was a little bit relieved when he used that word. I thought often, "What is a solution?" It can mean to solve something, as in finding the solution. Or, a solution can be a combination of things that make something else. A chemist makes a solution.

If you add the prefix *dis* in front of *solution*, it means you are unmixing or dissolving something. When two people have mixed their molecules in a close sexual and emotional relationship, they have made a solution of themselves. For a while they think they have found the solution to loneliness.

When these two people decide to dissolve their solution (the mixture of their molecules), society gives it the harsh-sounding word *divorce*. It was a relief to me to realize there was another word for us that could make the whole thing a little softer.

Put sugar or salt into water and they dissolve, but neither will disappear. Sugar and salt are both crystals.

They dissolve into the water and the water is never the same. Two people who have mixed their physical molecules also mix the molecules of their invisible Emotional, Spiritual, and Mental bodies every time they hug, kiss, make love, and come close. Their molecules are mixed into a solution.

This solution doesn't make anybody disappear. Out of these two sets of energies a third energy is created. When that is dissolved, they don't disappear, but the solution changes them. When two people have done this, they've made an agreement to change, to turn into another element they've never been before.

The same things happens in the dissolution. When the water evaporates, the salt or sugar become crystals again. But they're in a little different form because they were once mixed in water. They reform in a different way. When the water dissolves, it doesn't disappear, it simply evaporates and changes form.

I define divorce or dissolution as a transformation. Two people have come together to make a solution; now one of them is leaving. But neither of them will ever be the same because they have touched each other and they have affected each other.

In most of the cases I have known, it's never easy. There is a lot of temptation on the part of the one who is leaving to have extreme guilt, which stays with them for a long time. They must go through intense soul-searching to mobilize their courage to make this break. Anyone who leaves understands the pain it will cause. All of us have been left at some time in our lives.

A child is left by its mother when it's young. Even if she's just going to the post office or the grocery store, the child experiences dissolution of the bond it has with the mother. Everybody on Earth knows exactly how it feels to be left.

Therefore, the person leaving is having just as difficult a time, knowing on a subconscious or superconscious level they are going to cause extreme pain to the other person. There is a tendency to amass all kinds of reasons from the logical mind. A long list of gripes or complaints may be made. Two underlying causes for dissolution are: (1) a blockage in the learning of a lesson; (2) the lesson has already been learned and it's time to move on.

The soul knows the lessons it is here to learn; the spirit remembers the contract made before they were born. They would play the role for each other . . . whatever they wanted and needed to learn. One would play the good guy, one would play the bad guy; one would stay and one would leave.

These two people made an agreement to teach each other whatever lesson they needed to learn, and they would remember when it came time to leave. But being on the Earth plane, we find it's tempting to forget about it from the spiritual standpoint. That's why we rake up all kinds of earthly reasons that really have nothing to do with the big picture.

One experiences the agony of having been left. That person is faced with the temptation of dredging up all kinds of reasons why they have been "done in." They have logical explanations why they don't deserve this kind of treatment. They will attempt for months, sometimes lifetimes, to get sympathy. They would like nothing more than to have everyone feel sorry for them and become an ally.

These are our earthly temptations and we fall prey to

them. Divorce, or dissolution, becomes tragic in our mind and in our hearts. The Spiritual Body is wounded. The Emotional Body is scarred. When we choose this way of doing it, scar tissue forms. This makes it even more difficult to have another love or to form another solution.

We also set up barriers so that no one else can get into our Emotional Body. The mind can carry this on indefinitely. I have clients who have been divorced for forty-five years and they're *still* angry at the one who left them. They've wasted their entire lives telling everyone their sad story and not getting on with it.

Let's talk about divorce as initiation. We experience systematic initiations all our lives. When we go to school, we leave our mother, we experience initiation in that first dissolution. It is often traumatic, but we don't remember it. At about fourteen, we experience separation again when we reach puberty and change from children to young adults. This represents initiation as we are separated from innocence, the freedom of the childish mind. We become dissolved as children. We never feel the same again. We reach the point when reproduction is possible. The Spirit Body in the heart knows love outside the family. This is felt as sexual attraction to another human. We seek to form the close chemistry we have with our family even if we don't consider our ties as good or loving. From this time on, we never again feel the freedom of childhood. The instinct for forming a bond with a mate becomes a constant quest.

At the age of twenty-one we go through another passage as we become legally responsible for ourselves and our actions. There will be no more excuses, no real protection from the family. We are no longer even a "half child."

The next initiation usually occurs when the time comes for people to dissolve their marriage. It's interesting how frequently that happens between the ages of twenty-eight and thirty-one when people marry young, or between the ages of forty-two and forty-five if they marry a little later. If they really hung in there and had a lot to learn from each other, divorce as initiation might occur between forty-nine and fifty-one years old.

The initiation of divorce appears to be one of the strongest any human being can experience. Now the law and religion are both involved when the time comes to dissolve the wedded solution. Physical things, possessions acquired by the couple, even children, become pawns in the game. Couples separating focus their Mental Body on dividing the goods: "Well, I'm going to keep the stereo" or "You can't have the car because I need it to go to work." This part of the drama is our mechanism of self-distraction. We are focusing on trivia because we are attempting to protect the Emotional Body. At this point we do not want to *see* how we must transform. We do not want to look at what this initiation *really* is.

How we handle this initiation means all the difference if we are ever going to find a solution again. The first tendency is to lose all kinds of self-esteem. We immediately begin to feel like a total failure.

I experienced one of the most difficult initiations in my life over a marriage that was neither religiously nor legally sanctioned. I had made the decision to leave, but I was so bonded to that person I went through a two-year initiation that was the most important in my entire life. I went so deeply inside myself I could barely leave my house.

The pain of separating the molecules can be tremendous. I'm practically positive initiations like that occur when people have been together in other lifetimes and the molecules have been mixed century after century. We meet again in this lifetime without realizing it on the conscious level. This type of bonding may be an agreement. There will be a solution for a certain length of time, after which we need to experience separation. This kind of dissolution is the greatest initiation because the lesson is life transforming! Both people are absolutely born again.

The initiation of the divorce experience takes us through our greatest soul-searching, possibly into a greater state of perfection. If we are able to change our beliefs about marriage, mating, pairing up, we can experience dissolution in a more conscious state.

This does not mean we will be relieved of all pain. There seems to be a requirement on the Earth plane that we must "go through the fire" to achieve the worthwhile understandings.

What is the rebuilding required after dissolution? Think about the different crystals we can use on our body and the simple exercises outlined in this book. During tough periods of dissolving a marriage, many of my clients have used the crystal therapy. They have reported back to me their feelings and results.

This invisible energy that is coming from the planets is there for us. We just need to know how to harness it . . . just like electricity. It was always there but we didn't know it. Then somebody discovered it and figured out a way to trap it. That's exactly what the crystals do with some of these invisible energies.

> Talk not of wasted affection!
> Affection never was wasted.

—Henry Wadsworth Longfellow

PART II

CRYSTAL PROFILES

Crystal Profiles

I love to think of nature as an unlimited broad-casting station, through which God speaks to us every hour, if we only tune in.

—George Washington Carver

In the first half of this exploration of the Earth crystals to use for the promotion of love in our lives, we explored scientific, psychological, and emotional areas. A good deal of the information was my attempt to convince you with logic, research, and experience.

In this portion the strategy will be using both my right and left brain (Male and Female Energy).

Here is a short example of how "star energy" has brought me to this approach. Try not to be confused as I make an example of my own horoscope:

For those of you who study astrology, the Sun was in the sixth house in Virgo, with Aries rising, the Moon in Aquarius, and Uranus in the first house when I was born. To those of you who have no knowledge of astrology, I believe I came to Earth in this lifetime to teach my Spirit how to use both Male and Female Energy in proper balance. Virgo (female), ascending Aries (male), the Moon (female) in Aquarius (male).

Since I did choose to reincarnate into a female body, I also chose to be born at the moment when my Female Energy coming from the planet Venus would be located in the group of stars called Leo, which is a Masculine Energy constellation. Believe me it has not been easy.

I must encourage you to study your own astrological star map to help yourself become more familiar with your own plan to teach your Spirit Earth lessons. I want to testify how important I believe astrology has been to my self-understanding and self-acceptance. I also want to encourage you to read the writings of my beloved guide and avatar, Dr. Carl Gustav Jung (1875–1961), Swiss psychologist and psychiatrist. His writings introduced me to astrology as a viable science in counseling others and my Self.

As I mentioned, my Spirit is in a female body, therefore I believe that in this life I pursue the perfected use of my Female Energies. For this reason I allowed myself to leave the world of clinical, traditional psychology to become a "psychic" counselor.

> Women reason with the heart and are much less often wrong than men who reason with the head.
>
> **—De Lescure**

> A woman's guess is much more accurate than a man's certainty.
>
> **—Rudyard Kipling**

Woman's advice has little value, but he who won't take it is a fool.

—Miguel de Cervantes
Don Quixote

You will notice most of the historical quotes in this book have been recorded by men, from men. I believe the Earth has been dominated for the past five thousand years by the Masculine Energy, in divine order. We are in the closing stages of this era, but the majority of Earth government continues to be predominantly left-brained, Masculine Energy.

We are in a state of transformation that many are experiencing as chaos while the Feminine Energy gradually emerges. Therefore I take this opportunity to express my Feminine Energy as feelings, knowing that I have "covered my tracks" by preceding this with quotes from respected men!

HOW I "FEEL" ABOUT CRYSTALS

There are many folks I've met who have the special tactile ability to physically detect crystal energy. They can hold the crystal or simply pass their hand above a table or tray of crystals and receive vibrations. They describe these as "hot" or "cold" or "tingling" or "stinging" or as a "motion"! I am envious of their sensitivity, because touch does not affect me in this way. Possibly if I took more time or concentrated more, I could do it.

▲
▼

I am a visual person. I would rather *look* at the crystal. When I look at crystals, I get pictures like movies in my mind. I also feel the crystal is speaking to me telepathically. I meet a crystal as I would a new aquaintance. In fact, they introduce themselves with descriptions of their abilities, like giving me a résumé! (For astrologers, I have Saturn in Capricorn, in the tenth house—all rule Earth crust, rocks, minerals, and crystals.) Yes, I talk to rocks!

Nature creates ability: God provides opportunity.

—**Francois de la Rochefoucauld**

Years ago, when I "came out of the closet," abandoning traditional left-brained approaches to healing, I took a moral stand. At that time I received national publicity overnight. A newspaper article with my photo was picked up by a national news service and distributed to every major radio station in the United States and Canada. For six months I received at least two interviews over national radio each week, and often many more. Mail began to come in with requests for personal "prescriptions" on healing with crystals. I soon realized I had to find a way to answer mail quickly. I printed literature on how to use crystals and mailed it back with no charge. The telephone rang and I gave free advice on the psychic "hits" I received from the callers' voice vibrations. After the first six months it became clear I had to begin to ask for a fee. The Universe had supported my "moral stand" on alternative therapy methods, but it was up to me to support my expenses.

Since that time I have had over five thousand clients. Most of them have been referred to me by other clients. I have not advertised either the healing crystal amulets I design, or the psychic counseling I give. Recently I have begun monthly seminars that have been advertised in the journals that print my syndicated crystal columns. Otherwise the crystals themselves have been the carriers of my messages!

I have cleansed thousands of clear Quartz and colored crystals. I have washed them, loved looking at them, and marveled at their faceted, orderly, sparkling symmetry. I have placed them in trays under the Sun all day and in the moonlight at night. I have given them away and sold them with a tiny instruction booklet. I have stood, bent over, searching for all types of colored gemstone crystals at mine sites, in riverbeds, or at gem and mineral shows for years. I love the crystals! I am addicted to their beauty! They speak to me on a level I cannot describe.

Faceted gemstones are wonderful, too. They have the same healing vibrations; they remain crystals even after being cut and polished. The difference for me is this:

A beautiful zebra is better than a zebra rug.

A beautiful rosebush is better than a dozen cut roses.

I do wear faceted crystals such as Opals that really must be polished to reflect light, or Diamonds for the same reason. I marvel over their natural beauty also; before they are improved they are wonderful. Polishing and cutting crystals is similar to a woman's using hair color and makeup (I do both) because it is usually more glamorous. Maybe letting in more light, which makes them sparkle, might even enhance their effect. However, it does not change their identifying vibration on a meter.

I am convinced humans will once again discover a source of power by focusing a special type of light through a polished crystal. We have done this with a Ruby crystal in a laser, but have not adapted it to larger uses yet. I am predicting huge energy sources will be discovered.

Within the past three years, some enormous Quartz crystals have been found in South Africa. They were uncovered on a site being mined for the new gem-crystal, purple Sugilite. The largest Quartz crystal I have seen was eight feet long and three feet thick.

The "new energy" crystal may not be a clear Quartz. I *have* felt for years that it would be the Amethyst. Recently, larger Amethyst crystals have been mined in Brazil. The Amethyst is a form of Quartz that contains a mineral (or minerals) that are in dispute among crystallographers and gemologists. The violet color is caused by light's passing through the Amethyst except for the ray of violet, which is reflected back to our eyes by the mineral inside. Some scientists say it is Iron, others say it is Manganese. Whatever it is, "I feel" it is a power source waiting to be tapped by humans. "I feel" it may have been used by earlier advanced civilizations on Earth (such as Atlantis) for such purposes. "I feel" I may have been active in the field of science in that time, or on some other planet at some time, using crystals.

"I feel" a special affinity and communication takes place between a crystal (or gemstone) chosen by a human and the Spirit of the human.

I have experimented with other meditation mandalas or "objects of focus" for my clients to use in self-healing. Nothing has been more effective as a "promoter" than the crystal. No one has ever responded to a rabbit's foot, lucky coin, or symbol made of metal or wood or any other type of fetish made by a healer to the degree of healing I have seen with a crystal. In my previous book, a chapter is devoted to the influences observed when using crystals with premature babies and animals. They cannot be explained as "mind over matter."

I have observed mature men and women, adolescents, and small children all respond to the vibrations of the crystals on a personal, intimate level. I have seen grown men cry simply from touching or holding a crystal that was attuned to their personal vibration.

"I feel" the crystals are "thinking" entities. I know the plant and animal kingdoms respond to music, language, and human touch. These things are obvious to some, and to the skeptic, proven in laboratory tests! As they were the original and first Kingdom of Earth, *I know* the crystals are wise. They have recorded millions of years of Earth information. "I feel" the crystals are workers for Earthlings' benefit. They have groups, categories, families, and races. They have each their own gift to us. Some are doctors, teachers, scientists, dictionaries, protectors, spiritual priests and priestesses, comforters, strengtheners, pacifiers, warriors, and some are actually flowers! They just bring beauty and joy. Some are young, some are old. Some are wise, some are dull. For example, Diamonds and Sapphires are used as beautiful faceted gemstones when they are clear and colorful, but when not, they're used as sharp dust on a grinding wheel, as workers.

Gold crystals are fused into wonderful jewelry or are used as actual medicine in the treatment of human diseases such as arthritis. Rubies, mentioned earlier, are working in lasers, and Quartz work in many electronic information modalities.

Nature does not complete things. She is chaotic. Man must finish, and he does so by making a garden and building a wall [or cutting a gem].

—**Robert Frost**

The crystals seem to have been written into my life script. Many people have asked me, "How did you get started in this work?" It began when I was very young, but I wasn't consciously aware that my life had chapters leading to this occupation. Many different choices seemingly unconnected at the time came together like a jigsaw puzzle.

The stars, Sun, Moon, and planets cannot be separated from the crystals. The knowledge of planetary cosmic rays is crucial to understanding the use of crystals. Our Universe is now described by all physicists and scientists as vibrations of light at different speeds.

"I feel" the personal, physical vibrations of plants, animals, and people; that is, "I sense" them through my solar plexus, right brain, and left brain. It is a process I cannot explain because it is so subtle. In this same way "I sense" the crystal communication.

There must be at least fifty books in print now on the healing use of crystals, written since 1980. I have most of them in my personal library. Many of them are self-published and/or "channeled" information, not based on crystallography, gemology, or research. The authors have "tuned in" to the "morphic field" of knowledge that some scientists believe circles Earth. This "field" is a level of vibration where all thoughts are stored. This is like a giant computer, and like any brain, it takes in *everything* without discrimination. In computerese there is an expression: *garbage in—garbage out*. Many authors of the New Age are not proficient at (voluntary) clair-voyance. They accept and allow all and any information to come through. Sometimes they receive garbage. You as the reader must be discriminating as to what you can accept as viable information.

> The practical effect of a belief is the real test of its soundness.
>
> **—James A. Froude**

CLEANSING OR PROGRAMING YOUR CRYSTAL

There are full and complete explanations and descriptions of how many of my colleagues in science and my mainstream clients have experienced crystal energy in *Crystal Healing Secrets*. Descriptions of various ways to "cleanse" or deprogram a crystal as practiced by various cultures are covered there also. I will give a brief explanation here:

Clear Quartz crystals have a regular, reliable, and stable vibration of molecules that allows other vibrations to be held in layers inside it. That is the process they perform in electronic equipment such as radio, TV, computer, telephone, and Quartz timekeepers. They can hold a frequency.

When the crystal has been handled or used by many others on its way to you, it has stored unnecessary vibrations. They may all be neutral or not. When you

▲
▼

begin processing with a newly acquired crystal, cleanse or deprogram it. This is my favorite method (there are many others):

Wash the crystal in cold water. I use a little dishwashing soap. Place the crystal where sunlight and moonlight can vibrate it, unobstructed by glass, for twenty-four hours. Ultraviolet is a cleanser and leveler.

Colored crystals are already full of a vibrational program due to the element inside the structure that reflects a colored ray of information. They cannot be deprogramed or reprogramed from their messages. They can be cleansed however from surface vibrations they have acquired in their travels. I always use the identical ritual with colored stones, just to be sure, and to make them personally my friend.

The clear Quartz crystal, after deprograming, can be given a verbal or brain-wave program by the owner. It will hold this until cleansed again.

The difference in colored crystals is their specific strength of a one-pointed, very clear program. They are stronger medicine, specialized, to help you accomplish your goal, without distraction.

> Nothing is so firmly believed as that which we least know.
>
> —**Michel de Montaigne**

CRYSTALS AS ART

This part of the introduction to "Crystal Profiles" is concerned with the crystals that have been written about as healing crystals without practical research or discrimination.

These specific groups will be included in the general reference list as art. We all agree art is healing in the form of color, form, music, and poetry. Nature's art is the most healing in the form of sunsets, cloud formations, oceans, flowers, trees, mountains, musical babbling brooks, and birdsong.

There are many crystals too fragile, too gentle, too soft for "working" instruments; however, they give us healing. When they are forced to "work" for us, by being cut and polished into tools, carried around in our pockets, or made into jewelry, they break. Some of them are fragile, like flowers, have the same healing effect as flowers, and must be treated as we would a tender plant.

These are a few of the crystals I have found listed in other books as "working" crystals that I believe are only to be used as *art* or *beauty* in our lives: Calcite, Celestite, Selenite, Fluorite, Apatite, Wulfenite, and Dioptase. These crystals are all beautiful, and most (excluding Wulfenite and Dioptase) are inexpensive. The colors are varied and often transparent. The growth patterns are exciting to our eyes. They "heal" us by their very presence! They are the "flowers" of the gem world. Used as a sculpture on an office desk, possibly as a paperweight, or as a larger specimen dominating a room, the vibrations affect us positively.

Collectors keep faceted gemstones or carvings of these fragile crystals locked in glass cases. I do not advocate that extreme. Please use discretion in finding a balance. I have a great fondness for Fluorite. In its natural uncut, unpolished double-pyramid (octehedral) crystal growth formation, it is astounding! The range of colors from green, yellow, blue, to purple is such a joy to behold. I even have a green sphere polished to perfection (I see an underwater city inside) on my coffee table. These various forms of Fluorite are similar to the prize-winning different species of roses I have grown. I can hold the Fluorite, gaze into it, lose myself in its natural beauty, receive its loving, soothing vibrations, and put it back in its place of honor. "I feel" this way concerning all crystals that break easily. They are *art*.

There are various other materials, listed by "channeling" authors as healing crystals, that are certainly *not* crystals. Some of them are:

Obsidian and Tektites (Moldevite), which are glass caused by Earth heat or Earth-entry heat fusing sand, are not crystalline in structure. When Mount Saint Helens, an old volcano, erupted in Washington State in 1980, pale-green glass modules were found later. The Moldevite Tektites now being marketed as healing are found in Czechoslovakia in a meteorite crater. The "channeled" information calls them extraterrestrial or UFO stones. They are glass, exciting glass, formed in the meteorite as it entered Earth.

Amber is a wonderful material, so golden, so smooth, so transparent, especially interesting when a tiny insect can be seen trapped inside. Amber is petrified tree resin. It has no crystalline molecular structure. It is ancient, it may have some memory, but even light does not cause it to vibrate like a crystal. It may be healing in some other fashion, but at this time, Golden Topaz is the highest form of the golden ray, followed by Citrine. Amber is untested.

You may wish to see and handle a specimen of each of these types of "art by Mother Earth." You may disagree with my findings. You may heal yourself or attract more love into your life using any of these "flowers." Please write or call me, I want your information.

In the following chapters of "Crystal Profiles," several crystals will be introduced as a result of my considerable research with clients. One of the new crystals is a recently uncovered type of Pectolite, found in the Dominican Republic in 1974. It is rare because it is a mixture of sky blue, white, and green. Occasionally it will contain streaks of red Hematite. When it is polished into ca-bochons (domed gemstones for jewelry) it often resembles turquoise. This new, blue variety is commercially called Larimar. The Uranus-Saturn influence on Earth has now brought this crystal from hiding.

Rhodochrosite, a pink, red, and white crystal combination will also be discussed. More deposits of this beautiful mineral are coming to light now at the time when love is the only answer we have left to maintain Mother Earth.

Rhodonite is another pink, amorphous crystal with black inclusions, coming out of hiding to help us integrate our "shadow self" for more self-love.

The "dark crystals," Black Tourmaline (Schorl) and Smokey Quartz, have been described by my clients as mirrors into the "dark side" of their nature. We will discuss how these crystals can help us in using that "other" energy to create more love.

The "surprise crystals" will help in understanding the total focus of light rays through metal crystals such as Gold, Silver, Copper, etc. We have used these crystals longer than any others. From our earliest history in creating crystal amulets for healing, the metal crystals have played the most integral part.

Come and explore now the new formulas and ancient

prescriptions for attracting more love, romance, friend-ship, and spiritually satisfying sex in your life!

> There can be no theory of any account unless it is corroborated with the theory of the earth.

> —**Walt Whitman**

MEDITATION

This is a reminder of the step-by-step procedure to follow with the active meditation exercise for each crystal in this book. Lie down on the floor on your back. Hold the crystal in your palm and gaze at it for one full minute. Place the crystal against the:

Solar Plexus (near waist): Cover with palm, repeat seven times . . . use the sentence for your chosen crystal.

Heart: Cover with palm, repeat seven times . . . use the sentence for your chosen crystal.

Forehead (third eye): Cover with palm, repeat seven times . . . use the sentence for your chosen crystal.

Sweet Surrender

Crystallizing in pink and blue rainbow
Tourmaline, lying in the bosom arms of
Mother Earth, I was in the Middle East
when Muhammad was born.

Deep in the bloodstream of Gaia I became
her bloodred Ruby gem of India, before Krishna.
I am Gold and Silver, all metals.
Confucius loved me in the polished stone of jade.

In Persia, Tibet, and the New Land
Turquoise was my name, before Christ Consciousness
or the native shaman spirits came.
The Swahili witch doctor carried me, an octahedral
sparkle in his pouch, until the Dutch moved in.

In every part of my Mother I crystallized for
future generations to discover my miracles
disguised as beauty for the rings of Popes
and crowns of Queens.

I now lie down on your sacrificial altars.
I smile, "Slice me into minute slivers, enlighten me!
I empower you, in lasers, computers, and magnificent futures!"

—Brett Bravo

Reference List of Love Crystals

Crystal	Planet and Color Ray	Love Quotient	Page
AMETHYST	Mercury–Violet	Forgiveness	287
AZURITE/MALACHITE/CHRYSOCOLLA	Saturn–Green, Uranus–Blue	Friendship	243
EMERALD	Saturn–Green	Truth	151
GARNET, RED	Pluto–Burgundy	Sexual Arousal	243
GOLD	Sun & Jupiter–Gold	Masculine Energy	221
HEMATITE	Space–Black	Strength	209
KUNZITE	Mercury–Violet, Pluto–Burgundy	Unconditional Love	296
LARIMAR	Saturn–Green, Uranus–Blue,		
MEXICAN FIRE OPAL	Mars–Red	Family Connections	236
ONYX, BLACK	Mars–Red	Erotic Love	276
QUARTZ, SMOKEY	Space–Black	Surrender to Unseen Help	203
ROSE QUARTZ, STAR	Space–Black	Shadow Self–Love	197
RHODOCHROSITE	Mars, Moon, Sun–Pink	Self–Love, Gentleness	165
RHODONITE	Mars–Red, Total Ray–White	Personal Charisma	176
RUBY, STAR	Mars–Red, Space–Black	Sweet Dark, Balance	183
SILVER	Mars–Red, Moon–Silver	Six Points of Passion	259
SUGILITE	Moon–Silver	Feminine Energy	226
TOURMALINE, BLACK	Pluto–Burgundy, Mercury–Violet	Fear Changed to Love	291
	Space–Black	Shadow-Self, Discovery	190

The crystals produced by Mother Earth act as receiver—transmitter for directing Cosmic rays.

NATIONAL AERONAUTICS AND SPACE ADMINISTRATION

The planet Earth, as our Mother, is a living breathing entity. Along with her Moon, she is one of the major magnetic (Feminine) energies in our Solar System.

We on Earth receive electric (Masculine) energy from the Sun and half of the other planets to help in balancing our Earth-Moon rays. These same magnetic rays are projected to the electric planets from Earth. Our Solar System and our Physical, Emotional, Mental, and Spiritual Bodies are interdependent on these gifts of Love.

Emerald—
The Truth Crystal

Love is the pain of being truly alive.

—Joseph Campbell
Interview with Bill Moyers
on public television, 1987

The Emerald has a significant impact on truth; giving out of love, stability, and reliability.

When I came to the perfect time and place to begin the actual pen-on-paper writing of *Crystal Love Secrets*, I made a list. The first crystal that presented itself was the Emerald. Somehow it seemed prominent in my own psyche. My Higher Self whispered, "This is where to begin."

I replied, "Shouldn't we start with the easier crystals and work up?"

My Higher Self said, "First you eat your vegetables, *then* you get your dessert." "Gee," I managed, "this sounds just like home. Is that why I chose my Virgo Mother?"

Higher Self replied, "You know the answer to that. Whatever you believe is true for you."

"Okay, so I choose this Earth-sign Mother who would make sure that I did everything in the correct order, right?"

"Right."

"I also chose her to always tell me the truth, right?"

"Wrong. You chose her to tell you the truth as she understood it, and consequently to give you double messages so that you could learn to discern."

"Learn to discern." I think I'll use this as the Emerald slogan from now on. "So you are saying that truth can be hidden in double messages from the ones we trust most in the world?" I questioned.

Higher Self replied, "Sure, and the truth is, it's your choice to discern what is true for others might not be true for you."

So I refocused on the subject of the truth. Truth as my mother knew it and truth as I have known it is constantly evolving into a broader spectrum of possibilities.

TRUTH

The truth for my mother was, "Until death do us part, but I'm not going first." So my dad went first. Her truth became my truth. Being a little bit aware, not wanting death involved, I managed to get my children's father to leave first, and he left with someone who could make him happier. Now that is the truth for me.

Do you think I believed the truth when I experienced it? No way. I played the victim role for quite a while. So who witnessed me playing the victim role and decided to make it their truth? My children. They are susceptible to carrying my pain, right? Am I going to beat myself over the head and defeat my Higher Self because my children suffered? No, because I believe my children chose their father and me, as well as all the subsequent psychological circumstances for their own personal growth. What they do with my pain and my truth is their choice.

Does this mean I have everything figured out and that I never feel guilty? No. It means I've been meditating with an Emerald crystal, my truth is beginning to change, and I'm starting to come clean.

When I begin to come clean with the truth, I begin to take responsibility for every circumstance of this lifetime and all previous lifetimes. I stop playing the victim role, which includes, "There is only one way to do it right, and he/she did it wrong!" I stopped believing my mother messed up because she gave me double messages. I now realize that I'm a little shifty myself and I give off double messages, especially about love.

"Higher Self, we talked of truth, and now of all things, I'm going to tackle the biggest question in the whole world: love. Am I crazy? Come on, Higher Self, shouldn't this be the very last chapter, the grand finale, the American flag with fireworks?"

"No, kid," replied Higher Self, "the reason we're starting here is because you need to know right up front that you don't have any answers that will work for everybody. This book is just your way of giving out love, as you understand it, and that's all you can ever do."

> The meaning of the "I-thou" relationship is that I treat you as if you are myself.
>
> **—Martin Buber**

EMERALD

CHEMICAL COMPOSITION: $Be_3Al_2Si_6O_{18}$ (cyclosilicate)
CRYSTAL SYSTEM: Hexagonal
COLOR: Clear medium to dark green
HARDNESS: 7½–8 on Mohs' scale
PLANET AND COLOR RAY: Saturn, Green Ray
LOVE QUOTIENT: To come clean with the truth. To give out love.

WHAT IS AN EMERALD?

Most of us are familiar with the clear-green Emerald as a faceted gemstone in expensive jewelry. Before it was cut into a shiny jewel, it was taken out of the ground in the form of a six-sided (hexagonal) crystal, growing in some form of mother (matrix) rock or even metal veins. The chances are it was found somewhere in Columbia or Brazil in South America. There are deposits in other countries, but they have been mined for thousands of years and are almost depleted.

Because the Emerald crystal is no longer plentiful on Mother Earth, its price is higher than Diamonds when found in a bright, clear-green color. There are, however, very inexpensive Emeralds available that are not clear and/or have flaws that would cause them to crack. The vibration on a spectrograph, a scientific instrument, would still measure "Emerald." The effect the crystal has on any life form will be the same whether it is a gem or rough, clear or murky, expensive or inexpensive.

WHAT IS THE EFFECT OF THE EMERALD ON LIFE-FORMS?

The vibration works on the mind (Mental Body) as well as the physical body. The crystal sends out its own electromagnetic energy, which is triggered by the cosmic rays that are invisible and by visible rays of light. The Emerald then acts as a transmitter of Cosmic Energy. This energy commingles with the electromagnetic energy of the life-forms (animal as well as human and plant) and balances or changes the field. This field is sometimes called the aura by those who can see it.

The mind (Mental Body) has a specific vibration in each person. The Emerald commingles with this vibration, allowing the mind to change. The cosmic ray that is transmitted by the Emerald is green and can only be seen when there is a rainbow or a green crystal gem to trap it. That ray originates with the planet Saturn in our solar system. Saturn's rays affect the understanding or foundation or structure of everything on Earth. The planet Saturn also affects the crust of the Earth and all rocks, minerals, and crystals. Saturn helps us to build proper form. It even rules the calcium skeleton that supports our bodies. The rays of Saturn cause things to crystallize, including thought. When thought is crystal clear, it is pure and good. When our thoughts have become too encrusted, they are like the barnacles on a boat, which not only cause friction but weigh and slow down progress.

When we use a crystal such as Emerald to heal any of our bodies (Mental, Emotional, Spiritual, Physical), it actually rebuilds the form. To describe the process, imagine the green ray entering the aura around your body, penetrating your body, going into your brain (the home of your mind), and changing the little canals through which your thoughts travel. Imagine it rebuilding the canals and making new roadways.

THE EMERALD CRYSTAL VIBRATIONS MESSAGES

It seems such a simple formula to insure love, respect, affection, and emotional support from our significant relationships by following one pattern, that is, to first give to them what we desire! "Oh, my, how deceiving," I've heard people cry as they try in vain to follow that golden rule. The spiritual avatar Jesus told us, "It is so simple it confounds the wise."

One of the greatest mistakes in learning love techniques is buying gifts (I've noticed that my clients do it, too). You know what I mean: You choose a gift that you like or something "you" want and attempt to satisfy yourself by giving it to someone else in the form of a gift. The end result is that both of you are disappointed. Often, the gift creates serious emotional disruption when the receiver is not overjoyed; this is a common consequence of the "not honest" approach to showing affection.

The approach is the purely physical manifestation of an underlying misunderstanding of how to build or support love in relationships. When this same misuse takes psychological form, you might find yourself angry, disappointed, or judgmental. This happens when your "other" doesn't use the loving techniques you prefer in conversation, such as supportive encouragement, verbal compliments, validation of your work, etc. Of course, you may feel disturbed because you want the other person to express love *your way*. This might even flow over into other areas when you subliminally demand proof of your specialness to the "other" by complaining or accusing them of not loving you, when it is your own self-love that is inadequate.

Wanting your "other" to fill your emotional needs, your ego needs, and your consolation needs is not honest of you, nor is there any *truth* in those expectations.

The Emerald crystal has a double light refraction. It causes a twofold vibrational action that helps us to:

1. Come clean with the truth
2. Give out love

When you're perturbed, disturbed, and diseased, it is usually when you haven't "come clean" with the *truth*. I've played those roles where I'm a victim attempting to shift responsibility to the "other" or even less significant others, haven't you?

The meditation with an Emerald crystal brings us back to the *truth* of the situation. We can then proceed to correct it by direct action or confrontation, or we can decide to say, "Well, I should have been awake or conscious at the time of occurrence," then forgive ourselves. Forgive ourselves for being asleep during waking/working hours and know that the "other" or "others" have acted according to their understanding. Even if we suspect that the "other" is not in integrity, we must continue to accept the *truth* that we had choices at every moment, to "wake up" and act in our own best interest.

In some cases, it helps to embed this lesson in the mind of our inner child (our subconscious) by honest communication to the "other" in a discussion of the situation so admission of unconscious inaction can be dealt with by both.

This reassessment of our own actions is a daily review that is encouraged by meditating with the Emerald crystal. Coming clean with the truth is our own responsibility in every interaction, with every kind of relationship.

Looking into our deep-seated belief systems is another way of coming clean. Things we decided as children with impressionable minds, including truth about relationships, may not now be truths. Those childish truths as seen through the eyes of an adult may very well be distorted. Decisions that we make at the age of three can remain with us into maturity. We have received many negative subliminal emotions from our parents.

Many grow up with parents who have an inability to discuss their opinions and differences openly. How many undercurrents in your personal belief system did you receive?

Were you one of those who received these deceptive signals? As a little one did you falsely decide:

Women/Men were to be feared.
Women/Men were not affectionate.

Women/Men were uncommunicative, inarticulate,
  and shouldn't be disturbed.
Women/Men wasted money.
Women/Men were workaholics.
Men were not really interested in the home or
  family.
Men/Women were "in service" or dominated by
  men.
Men/Women were afraid of confrontation.
Men/Women were thriftier, smarter.
Men/Women cared more about children.
Men/Women were cleaner and neater at home.
Men/Women were more creative, affectionate,
  understanding.
Men/Women were morally or spiritually stronger.

All of these *untruths* have affected personal relationships at school, work, play, and later in romantic, sexual
love. Some men and women continue through life without even consciously being aware they've made those
erroneous, concrete decisions. These childish beliefs are
hiding in the dark recesses of the mind. They can still
affect relationships in every area, unless we consciously
bring them out into the light. Meditating with an Emerald crystal will expose untruths of this type and eventually help us to replace the mind-set that causes friction.

The truth is, we all have masculine and feminine abilities, strengths, and weaknesses. The spirit is androgynous. We come back to Earth each lifetime to experience
the development of the positive aspects of both energies.

GIVING OUT LOVE

The second vibration caused by the double light refraction in the Emerald is "to give out love." Searching for love seems to be the great human pastime. It took many years before I discovered that I was free to love anyone I wished. Are you ready to experience this freedom?

Many of us hesitate to give love out unless there is a guarantee that it won't be rejected or casually accepted. We believe our love must be equally returned.

The Emerald teaches us to give out love. Sure you say, "Hey, I give out my love all the time! I love my dog, kids, car, my country. I leave big tips. I wash and clean and cook for my family. I go out on the job every day for my family. I love my secretary. I love the trees, flowers, oceans, mountains, nature, and God, but nobody loves me. At least not the way I want to be loved."

Carl Rogers, one of the great humanistic psychologists of this century, had a definition of love that has helped many clients:

> Love exists when the health, welfare, and happiness of any other is as important to me as my own.

Being able to say "I love you," to give out the love whether it comes back to us from the same person or not, is the greatest first step in improving relationships. It seems to take a lot of courage for most of us to risk that first step. The Victorian age of proper rigidity and suppression of emotions has left its mark on all of us. We are fearful of telling the truth of our feelings because others may judge us as foolish or weak. The secret is, the "other" is fearful, too. How long has it been since someone said "I love you"? How many days since you've said it?

I'm thoroughly convinced that health on all levels of body, mind, and spirit would be significantly improved by the spoken word vibration in any language if most of us said "I love you" more often every day.

Okay, I can hear your mind working now. "Oh, gosh, how can I do that? I just can't go around saying that to people!" The Emerald meditations will help you to overcome your fears.

Case Study: I'll call her Janelle.

When Janelle chose the Emerald crystal to hold during our consultation, I had a psychic feeling that the conscious problem she had come to solve was *not* the real problem. I asked her to do a meditation for ten minutes a day using the Emerald because I felt an estrangement in her family. I did not hear from her for about three weeks.

She returned to report that after about ten days of the meditation, she suddenly felt she needed to contact her father. They had been in a stubborn disagreement and had not spoken in over three years. She telephoned Brazil only to find he was seriously ill. Janelle immediately flew to see him. They had a week of loving reconciliation, and he died in her arms . . . peacefully. She was grieved, of course, but free from guilt because she had been willing to *give out love*.

A synopsis of the green ray from Saturn and how it vibrates the Emerald to affect our way of giving out love to our family and friends is contained in these key phrases. The vibration of your words changes the vibration of the energy that surrounds your body. It will eventually radiate out to reach the ones you love.

Emerald Meditation Exercise for Family and Friends

Lie down on the floor or ground, head pointing north. Place the Emerald against the . . .

Solar Plexus (between waist and ribs in the center where you feel surprise or fright): Hold your hands over the crystal and say aloud at least seven times or more, "This Emerald is vibrating to help me discern why I chose my family (or friend)."

Heart: Cover with both hands, repeat seven times aloud, "This Emerald is vibrating to crack the wall I have built around my heart."

Forehead: Cover with hands, repeat seven times aloud, "This Emerald is vibrating to jar my mind about my past lives with my family (or friend)."

If it is a specific member of your family, or a specific friend, use his or her name. This will enable you to realize his or her "inner spirit" and will help you to focus upon his or her positive personality.

Emerald Meditation for Romantic Love

Follow the ceremony for all meditations in this book: Be in complete privacy. Lie on the floor or ground, head pointing north. Do this when the mind is at low ebb or the body is at low energy. Place the Emerald crystal on:

Solar Plexus: Repeat aloud at least seven times, "This Emerald is vibrating to calm my erotic emotions until I can discern my *true* motives in relationships."

Heart: "This Emerald is vibrating to shake my *true* heart into feeling!"

Forehead: "This Emerald is vibrating to bring my mind into balanced, structured assessment of my desires."

If there is a specific person involved, use his or her personal name in this meditation exercise.

Emerald Meditation for Self-love

Follow the ceremony for all meditations in this book found on page 144. Hold the Emerald on the following parts of the body, repeating aloud at least seven times:

Solar Plexus: "This Emerald is vibrating to settle the emotional fears I took on as a child."

Heart: "This Emerald is vibrating to uncover my innocent heart's desire."

Forehead: "This Emerald is vibrating to help me be a kinder parent to myself."

Emerald Meditation for Unconditional Love

Follow the ceremony for all meditation exercises in this book. Hold the Emerald on the following parts of the body, repeating the mantra at least seven times.

Solar Plexus: "This Emerald is vibrating to awaken my Emotional Body to receive from all good sources."

Heart: "This Emerald is vibrating to open my heart to trust the Universe as a safe place to be."

Forehead: "This Emerald is vibrating to allow all negative habitual judgments to crumble in my mind."

The Emerald is one of the most versatile crystals for all types of love energy. Each following chapter has only one special meditation exercise.

PART III

SELF-LOVE—
GIVE YOUR "SELF"
A BREAK!

Star Rose Quartz for Self-love, Gentle Love

I suddenly knew that I was alone forever, that I would lose the people I love at any time . . . the only thing I had in this life was myself.

—**Judy Chicago**
Through the Flower:
My Struggle as a Woman Artist, 1975

CHEMICAL COMPOSITION: SiO_2 (Rose Quartz)
   Inclusion of rutile crystals: TiO_2
CRYSTAL SYSTEM: Hexagonal (trigonal) Rose Quartz
   Inclusion of rutile crystals: tetragonal
COLOR: Clear pink to rose with white star
HARDNESS: 7 on Mohs' scale
PLANET AND COLOR RAY: Mars, Sun, Moon—Red,
   White, Silver Ray
LOVE QUOTIENT: Self-Love—Gentle Love

In Custer, South Dakota, there is a spectacular cliff of pink stone over one hundred feet long. The earliest

American inhabitants that we know of, the Dakota Indians, used the pink stone for personal healing. Used by the medicine woman or man to treat other members of the tribe, it was a medicine stone. Mothers taught their children of the vibrations or "Spirit" in pink crystals. Tiny deerskin pouches were sewn and hung around their necks to hold pieces of the rosy rock. The early intruders from Europe realized they were witnessing a special kind of healing and called them medicine bags.

Approximately 30 percent of the Earth's surface is Quartz crystal, a common clear element, found in beach sand and growing in underground veins everywhere. When conditions are perfect, the mineral elements of iron particles enter into the liquid solution of silicon dioxide. These eventually crystallize into Rose Quartz with thousands of years of Earth's inner heat and pressure.

When a second element, called rutile (titanium), mixes with the two original elements in the liquid and simultaneously crystallizes, they produce a miraculous natural phenomenon called asterism. This is from the Greek word meaning star.

Recently, Mother Earth has given us a new bed of Star Rose Quartz. Deep in the jungles of Brazil a new discovery of gem-quality clear and rosy-glowing veins have been uncovered. When the huge veins are shifted by Earth's underground movement, she pushes them up to the surface for our use. As we have learned how to cut and polish these chunks into crystal balls and domed gemstones, we have discovered her message to us in the form of a six-rayed star practically bursting out of the crystal! The only way to see the star is to change the surface of the Rose Quartz into a spherical shape.

The Rose Quartz is refracting two rays of our light

spectrum. One is the silver ray of the Moon, a soft feminine vibration, and the other is the red ray of the planet Mars, an assertive masculine ray. They are blending into the pink ray. This blending causes a soft and gentle way of loving. When the rutile crystal is present within, it adds a third ray refraction, the white ray or total color prism of the Sun. The white ray contains all colors—the star in the Rose Quartz is white. The Sun contains all rays, making it a white star in the Rose Quartz.

The six-rayed star that is produced creates a subliminal message in the form of wavelengths through our eye to our brain. In a typical cloudy-pink Rose Quartz, the vibrational pink ray (combined Mars and Moon) brings a message of refining the primitive, red, aggressive love energy with the gentle, receptive, nurturing mother-love energy. This translates to us as a more gentle way of treating ourselves and others. First we must be accepting and nurturing to ourselves. We must return to a state of innocence and perfection that we experienced as toddlers, cradled by loving arms. The Rose Quartz has this effect on the majority of clients who have used it as a meditative focus. It has also been claimed by special intensive-care-unit nurses to aid premature babies in survival.

When the star appears in clear Rose Quartz, a third dimensional vibration occurs, entering the mind subliminally. The all-encompassing white ray from the Sun brings a special *power* into the understanding of gentle love. It promises a new invisible and encouraging energy in the everyday transactions of our workaday lives. Mother Earth has moved into a new and different section or division of the cosmic rays that effect change in consciousness. The "Star of Bethlehem" was probably a conjunction of two great planets, heralding a new age for humankind on Earth. The star seen in the rosy crystal ball sings to us of the possibility of more love in our lives as we become the "star" of our personal drama. We write the script.

As two great planets (Saturn and Uranus) again come together in line with the Sun shining through a group of stars called Capricorn, we have another choice to make in favor of self-acceptance and Universal love. Love thyself and it is easy to love thy neighbor.

To use a Star Rose Quartz crystal ball, egg shape, or a domed, polished gemstone in meditation, sit under a spotlight or sunlight or use a flashlight. This will bring the star reflection to the surface. Gaze intently at the star and follow each of the six rays from the center of the star to the tip of the ray. Give each ray a name or a word that relates to love. Say these words aloud several times around the star. Hold it next to your heart, your waist, and your forehead. Repeat the words at each location.

Meditating with a Star Rose Quartz, carrying it or wearing it on the body, gazing into it, or simply appreciating the natural wondrous beauty of Earth's treasures will make you feel better and could possibly change your life.

In my previous book, *Crystal Healing Secrets*, you will find the scientific, historical, and physically healing properties of Rose Quartz.

For *Crystal Love Secrets* we are dealing with the Emotional Body and how we can actually use crystals to attract love.

The best way for me to explain the vibration of Star Rose Quartz is to describe the mixing of two energies. The red ray from the planet Mars is fiery, energetic, assertive, passionate. The silver ray from our Moon is peaceful, tranquil, dreamy, and soft. When these rays are mixed and trapped inside a Star Rose Quartz, it is like coffee with cream! There is a dilution of the high energy red ray. The result is a soft pink ray, and a white, six-pointed star on the rose crystal.

Each human child begins to learn discipline and specific boundaries within the family structure and society at around age three (if not sooner). At this point, parents or day-care centers must teach socially acceptable behavior and Self-control to the tiny one. In this stage of development we little Earthlings have a Mental Body that is classified by psychology as "concrete mind." The meaning is, what we hear, see, and experience is what we believe to be concrete fact. We ask no questions. We do not analyze, interpret, or allow for adjustments.

When the adults tell us, "You're a bad boy, Johnny!" or "Let Mama do it, honey, you can't do it" or "Your mother is just a crazy woman, son" or "Your father is a drunken idiot" or "You're acting stubborn just like your aunt Judy!" or "Isn't she just like Joe's sister" or "God, sometimes that kid is a monster!" we automatically believe the negative (or sometimes positive) statement is true. We accept the accusation or description, put it into our mental computer, program the outcome, and frequently believe this about ourselves for a lifetime.

True, it sinks into the dark recesses of our mental library and sits on a back shelf. We forget many of those statements or work ourselves away from them by proving to others and ourselves that we are not like that at all.

The key word is *work*. The Spirit knows the words coming to our childish Self are false. The energy to prove our "Self-worth" becomes focused on *effort* in living. We are challenged to grow and accomplish, to strive for perfection. This energy we focus is good for us; it forces us to conform to the rules of the clan and to be socially acceptable. Unfortunately, we never forget those concrete ideas we formed at age three. We continue to *work* to dislodge those negative hidden descriptions we have formed of ourselves.

Our conscience is built around "bad boy, good boy" and "bad girl, good girl" concepts.

The older civilizations such as China, Japan, and some of the Middle Eastern countries have been so bogged down in "rules of conduct" and protocol, they have gone downhill by their efforts to control individual personality. The overcivilized culture squelches the spirit of inspiration by inhibiting free thought.

In the Western civilizations, our religions have attempted in vain to subdue the Spirit, and yet their strict influence lingers in our memory. We have been taught by osmosis or by direct religious training that we must be "good" to get to "heaven." The decisions we made at the age of three were very simple: "I'm a bad girl/boy, I have to change."

We are our own tough parent! When we do anything we feel we shouldn't, we punish ourselves mentally. We psychologically cause our dreams to collapse, our business to fail, or our relationship to dissolve, never realizing it happens by our own feelings of guilt! Overeating, drugs, and alcohol addictions are self-punishments.

Self-punishment, self-control, self-denial, can be much more extreme than self-indulgence. We are products of a Protestant, Puritan, hard-core work ethic. Somewhere deep down inside each of us there is the feeling of guilt over pleasure. We really do not deserve love because we are not "good" enough.

The Star Rose Quartz is transmitting the cosmic pink

ray of gentle, soft, sweet love. When we were three years old, we were precious! We were innocent, we had no calculating thoughts. We wanted to help with any task. We never thought anything was work. We were open to affection. We would hug or kiss anyone if our parents taught us to do it. We felt good about ourselves. We weren't concerned about our Earth body or how it appeared to others. We liked ourselves, we were okay and never compared ourselves to another person. We were totally Self accepting.

The love we felt for our toys or our parents or our pets wasn't erotic or passionate (red ray). Our Emotional Body at three was operating on the pink-ray energy of gentle love.

When my clients choose a Rose Quartz to hold during consultation, it is a clue to their inner knowings. I know they know that they are being too hard on themselves. Their "little child within" is crying out to say, "Give the Self a break!" I can then encourage them to do an active meditation exercise for ten minutes a day with the Rose Quartz. I can give them the phrases to use with the crystal as they use it to attract the pink cosmic ray into their solar plexus, heart, and Mental Body.

This is a case history concerning a very good man who couldn't give himself a break:

Jim was married to Joan, an intelligent, happy, personally successful woman. They had intelligent, healthy, normal children without major problems. The children were growing up and out of adolescence.

Jim was successful at his independent career, and respected by his peers. Although Joan had a career, she ran their lovely home and managed all of the upkeep and family affairs so Jim could pursue his hobby, which was playing the stock market. She felt he needed to have the freedom even though she personally did not believe in gambling.

Joan entertained his business clients and took an active part in social functions with his associates.

Jim worked hard. When he wasn't working, he was pursuing his hobby, attempting to make more money. He read all the journals daily and hardly ever had time to talk to his family.

Every year Joan wanted to take a vacation, and Jim would say, "I can't afford to take the time off," even though he was his own boss. His frequent statement to guests or friends was, "I haven't had a vacation since 1955!" In a manner, this was bragging, saying, "Look how hard I have worked!"

He traveled and had good relationships with every one of his business associates. He could relate well as long as he was *working*. When he and Joan entertained or attended social functions, he frequently became politically argumentative, or antisocial, retiring to a corner. Sometimes he even went to sleep. Naturally Joan was perturbed and embarrassed. She had difficulty understanding the mood swings. He was such a good man. He never quarreled or raised his voice around the house, and when they were alone, they enjoyed many diverse activities.

After quite a few counseling visits with Jim, he finally remembered a day when he was six years old. Walking to school, he looked down at his baggy overalls. His schoolmates had made a joke of them. He remembered his father saying to his mother that she was making a crybaby and sissy of him because she was being overprotective. He took in all of the past negative discussions between his parents, the taunting of his schoolmates, added it all together, and made a decision concerning himself:

"I decided that day that I was ugly. I didn't like anything about me, and I was going to make myself rich, and that would fix it."

These periods of ferment in early childhood actually begin at age three, and final decisions are triggered when we go to school to compare or be compared by our peers. At these times our "Spirit" is fragile. The negative thought forms of history on Earth are floating around in the atmosphere and can form an entity if given a chance. Taking a term from Socrates, I call this entity a *daemon*, or demon in our language. These entities can creep into our psyche when we are at a weak point, especially defenseless, in those younger years.

We actually performed an exorcism with Jim. We had a ceremony and demanded the demon come out and take leave of Jim's body! His addiction to work, to prove that he was okay, was as strong as any addiction I had ever experienced. He had had the addiction for over fifty years and a drastic measure seemed in order.

The Rose Quartz active meditation exercises were set in motion. He agreed to do it at least fifteen minutes every day for twenty-eight days, and to wear a polished piece on a chain around his neck. The Rose Quartz necklace was to be Silver for the soft ray of the feminine Moon vibrations. The chain was long enough to place the Rose Quartz over his heart. Remember, the heart is the home of our Spirit.

As an added emphasis on keeping the entity we call the demon at bay, I gave him a cassette recording of a song he could play in his car. I asked him to sing along and memorize the words:

I love myself—the way I am—there's nothing
I need to change.

—**Jai Josefs**

The Star Rose Quartz is for unconditional love of the
Self, and to balance Eros in our love for others.

Star Rose Quartz Meditation for Gentle Love of Others

Follow directions given for all crystal meditations.

Solar Plexus (Emotional Body): "This Rose Quartz is vibrating to soften my passionate feelings into a gentle love for others."

Heart (Spirit Body): "This Rose Quartz is vibrating to connect my Self at the Spirit level with all those I love."

Forehead (Mental Body): "This Rose Quartz is vibrating to keep my thoughts focused on sweet, childlike love."

Star Rose Quartz Meditation for Self-love

Follow directions given for all crystal meditations.

Solar Plexus (Emotional Body): "This Rose Quartz is vibrating to reassure my little child within that I love her/him."

Heart (Spirit Body): "This Rose Quartz is vibrating to connect my Self to my wonderful perfect Spirit."

Forehead (Mental Body): "This Rose Quartz is vibrating to erase all bad thoughts I have had of my beautiful Self."

Rhodochrosite for Personal Magnetism and Charisma

I decided long ago, never to walk in anyone's
  shadow
If I fail, if I succeed
At least I would live as I believe
No matter what they take from me
They can't take away my dignity!

—**Linda Creed and Michael Masser**
"The Greatest Love of All"
Arista Records © 1985

CHEMICAL COMPOSITION: $MnCO_3$ (manganese carbonate)
CRYSTAL SYSTEM: Hexagonal (trigonal)
COLOR: Rose red to white striped, opaque to transparent
HARDNESS: 4 on Mohs' scale
PLANET AND COLOR RAY: Mars, Sun—Red, Multiray
LOVE QUOTIENT: Sex appeal, personal charisma

The name *Rhodochrosite* refers to the Greek words for rose red. Raspberry red is the most common color. The most important deposits are in Argentina, near San Luis, 144 miles east of Mendoza. This crystal has formed as stalagmites and stalactites in the Silver mines abandoned by the Incas in the thirteenth century. Because of this location it is sometimes called Inca Rose.

The crystals, beautiful and rarely seen except by collectors, are rhombohedral. Usually marketed in large lumps of amorphous crystalline tubular shapes, it shows concentric circles similar to Malachite (green) and Larimar (blue/white) when sliced.

Deposits are found in the U.S. in the state of Colorado, and new discoveries have been made on the African continent.

Gem cutters and lapidary specialists are making beautiful jewelry and meditation stones available to the worldwide public for the first time in history. The most common shape available in a polished stone is a cabochon (an oval or round-topped ring or pendant stone). Spheres and egg shapes are also being cut as well as six-sided crystal shapes. Because of the structural shape of the hardness factor, thin shapes will break easily. Egg and spheric shapes are more durable.

Slices of a polished stalagmite show beautiful radiating patterns of alternating raspberry pink and white. These are very desirable for jewelry or meditation.

The Love Quotient in Inca Rose

After using the Rose Quartz as a transmitter for cosmic rays to the "little child within," our solar plexus, we progress to the Rhodochrosite (Inca Rose). This crystal is brighter, vibrant, and has more visual "movement" because of the alternating currents of white-ray energy.

Remember the solar plexus is also the home of our "instinctual animal Self." This energy, radiated out from the center of our being, has been recognized and actually described as *animal magnetism* by scientists in the field of emotion. Serious papers have been written by physicians and researchers as to the actual results of this human energy when focused purposefully.

Julia Lorusso and Joel Glick in their 1983 book, *Healing Stoned*, said, "This will be one of several gems holding the key to force fields and what can be expanded and clarified. Its great value lies in the ability to work in the lower physical realms."

Scott Cunningham's *Encyclopedia of Crystal, Gem and Metal Magic* was published synchronistically with my previous book, *Crystal Healing Secrets*, in 1988. At that time my research on Rhodochrosite was not complete, and it was not in my book. Cunningham's last statement on this gem was, "Rhodochrosite is also carried to draw love."

The "love secrets" that we already know have to do with our consciousness of our own magnetic power! Some would just get right down to Earth and call this energy *sex appeal*! Charisma is the power to vibrate our Emotional Body, our Spirit Body, and our Mental Body simultaneously until they hum! All of this is invisible to most human eyes, but it can be *felt*, even by lower animals. It is common knowledge that horses and dogs take advantage of humans that have low self-esteem or put out signals of fright!

I have many clients who desire more companionship,

and especially an intimate love life. Their main obstacle is overcoming their fear of their own sexuality.

Let me mention a short case history of a lonely, love-starved woman:

I felt Dina had everything going for her. Her children were grown, she owned a lovely apartment, she was professional in her career. She was tall, slim, tan, blond, firm, and attractive. She had a good sense of humor, a pleasant personality, and was eager to travel or try new things. She liked to swim and hike, go to plays, do almost everything for fun and entertainment. Did she *do* any of these things? No. Why not? She buried herself in her work and ran home every night to tend to her cats. She said many times, "I want a man in my life!"

In the career and work area she felt confident. She had mastered the left-brained Masculine Energy in herself, but her "power animal" was sound asleep. She had inhibitions about what was the proper way to dress. She had a wall around herself in any male-female encounter to stop any of her animal magnetism from leaking out. She was programed on a strict religious regimen in her early life. She wasn't particularly proud of her role model, her mother, who had been an alcoholic. Her complete sense of her own Feminine Energy was blocked.

Even though she had had cosmetic surgery to ensure a youthful face, dieted and exercised to keep a youthful figure, all her engines were off. Nobody home.

Charisma does not originate in the outer shell of the physical body. The ability to attract a significant other human into a relationship begins in the solar plexus. The Desire Body, in the center of our being where our animal magnetism originates, is the sensual sexuality we attempt to cover, hide, destroy, and squelch. We have been taught through religion and Victorian-age proper behavior that to let the power animal show itself would bring criticism or shame.

In order for Dina to become a real candidate for an intimate relationship, she needed to relax her own restrictions and stop "acting" proper, whatever that was.

The twenty-eight-day meditation with the hot-pink Rhodochrosite (Inca Rose) being used as an antenna to attract the red ray from Mars and the universal white ray would certainly stir the slumbering animal!

When gazing at an Inca Rose polished stone, remember the white ray contains all colored rays. This strong vibration represents the blessing of our Creator. We were created with charisma and sex appeal, and these energies insure our survival as a race. They are gifts to us, not meant to be condemned or misused in any way.

Everyone has the power inside to attract! I also have male clients who use the exact same self-defeating subterfuges to refrain from allowing their sensuality to surface. The usual excuses are shyness, lack of confidence, or lack of a proper technique to make verbal contact with a woman. I have often contemplated holding workshops on "how to" meet your possible companion, and "how to" allow yourself to be honest and real using a technique.

No one has to be a supersalesman or a smoothie to make a good impression. The technique is really simple. Tell the truth. Just say, "I've always felt insecure about how to act when I feel attracted to someone." This is an admission of a feeling of yours and a compliment to the other person. It states that you have a feeling of attraction. It doesn't force the other person into a yes-or-no situation. The next statement is also usefully true: "My fear of being rejected has caused me to miss out on past friendships, but now I want more fun in my life. I'm looking for more friends."

These statements of desires, intentions, and admissions are true, therefore there is no acting, no anxiety, and no pressure on the other person. This simple approach is strengthened and encouraged by doing active meditation exercises with Rhodochrosite. The open Spirit within you becomes uncomplicated, without any hidden agenda or manipulative intentions. This comes across to the other person as genuine, *real*. The real person is irresistible like a baby or a puppy, because we feel safe. Do not misunderstand this: .

Disarming a potential conquest is *not* the purpose. This only works when the things said are the truth. The power animal inside each human can "sense" the false vibration of anyone just acting a role. The Inca Rose is a vibration for unconditional love of our own Spirit.

Rhodochrosite, the hot-pink, almost edible raspberry vibration combined with the white ray of Divine Order, is a perfect blend of physical sensuality and spiritually satisfying vibrations. To encourage your Self to allow its own perfect nature to express itself in a balanced way, to attract others into your loving life, try these exercises with your crystal:

Use one of the three names of the crystal. Follow the procedures for all active crystal meditations.

Solar Plexus: "This (Rhodochrosite) (Inca Rose) (Hot Pink Crystal) is vibrating to free the power animal within my Spirit."

Heart: "This crystal is vibrating to nurture and recognize my magnetic Spirit."

Forehead: "This crystal is vibrating to clear my mind of restrictions to my *God-given* sensual charisma."

Rhodonite—
Sweet and Shadow

I do not ask for any crown, but that which all may win; nor try to conquer any world, except the one within.

—**Louisa May Alcott**
(1832–1888)

CHEMICAL COMPOSITION: $MnSiO_3$ (manganese metasilicate)
CRYSTAL SYSTEM: Triclinic
COLOR: Red pink with black veins or inclusions
HARDNESS: 5½—6½ on Mohs' scale
PLANET AND COLOR RAYS: Mars, Sun, Space—Red, White, Black
LOVE QUOTIENT: Sweet Dark, Balance

This unusual gemstone is rarely seen in its platelike crystal form, but is usually seen as compact, grainy aggregates. It has a double light refraction. The hot-pink ray is a Mars vibration and the black ray is, like the white ray, a combination of all colored rays coming from the Universal Energy.

There are deposits of this gem in Australia, India, Malagasy Republic, Mexico, U.S., Vancouver Island (Canada), and South Africa. It is most often cut and polished as cabochons (oval or round or free-formed domed ringstones, or pendant pieces) and is also made into beads, boxes, sculptures.

The word comes from the Greek, meaning rose. This could get confusing because there are three different gemstones that begin with *Rhodo*:

1. Rhodo*lite* describes pink Garnets and Tourmalines.
2. Rhodo*chrosite* is a hexagonal hot pink with white inclusions.
3. Rhodo*nite* is pink with black, different geometry.

There is another one called Rhodo*zite*, but it's very uncommon, so let's not complicate things.

I'm sure you can guess by now, if you've read *Crystal Healing Secrets* and the other chapters on the crystals transmitting the pink ray, how the Rhodonite transmits similar rays to the other pink or hot-pink stones. Here is a great formula to help you remember this important new crystal:

The black ray is visible at *night* (rhodo*nite*) and represents the dark side of Earth, when it turns its face to the Moon. The dark veins or spots in the bright-pink crystal are reminders of our Shadow Self. The bright-pink rays remind us of our vibrant, innocent, fresh, creative, animal spirit of life.

This crystal makes a wonderful amulet or meditation

stone for us to have and use anytime. It is especially helpful when we purposefully set out to attract a meaningful relationship.

In the chapters on Rose Quartz and Rhodochrosite we first learn gentle love, Self-love, charisma or animal magnetism.

In "The Dark Crystals" we begin to accept and explore the necessity for *total* acceptance of our Shadow Self. The power of our dark side is necessary in the universal formula of creation.

These two energies are mixed by Mother Earth in the Rhodonite. It is a constant reminder, or what I would call a "maintenance" stone, that each part of our invisible Emotional Body must act in tandem.

The candy-pink color is sweet Self and the black is Shadow Self. During the day we are a personality; when we are asleep at night, we become another entity altogether. We cannot remain awake or in light indefinitely. Eventually we must leave our bright world and retire to the dark world. We recuperate, rejuvenate, incubate, and hatch, subconsciously, the eggs our conscious mind has laid. No human has ever been able to change this pattern. This is the way we are, split personalities. Half Male Energy, half Female Energy, half Sun, half Moon, half candy pink, half black, swinging back and forth then blending into one, is our goal.

If you have a gem and mineral club in your area, or a natural-history museum or just a plain rock shop, call and ask if they have a specimen of Rhodonite for you to see. Try it, you'll like it! This crystal is for unconditional love of our balanced Self.

Rhodonite Active Meditation Exercise

Follow directions for all crystal exercise procedures. Hold crystal on:

Solar Plexus: "This Rhodonite crystal is vibrating to help my inner child and power animal coexist."

Heart: "This candy-pink and black crystal is vibrating to balance my innocent and erotic spirit."

Forehead: "This crystal is vibrating to bridge my right- and left-brain work."

PART IV

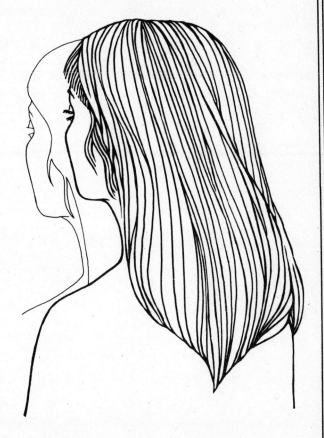

THE DARK CRYSTALS—
OUR SHADOW SELF

The Dark Crystals

There are four black or dark-gray crystals that I have researched and found helpful in therapy.

1. Black Tourmaline, called also Schorl
2. Smokey or Black Quartz, caused by irradiation
3. Hematite, which is iron-metal crystals
4. Black Onyx, which is Agate Quartz

Black Tourmaline is listed first because I have found it to be the most effective of all dark crystals in balancing the shadow side of our personality or Spirit.

When I was growing up in Texas, there wasn't much to do, but my town had two "picture shows." I began to go alone to the movies at about age seven. My favorite shows were the Frankenstein (Boris Karloff) and the Wolf Man (Lon Chaney, Jr.) series. Each portrayed scary monsters with a heart of gold, sweet and kind, especially to children. The original novel *Frankenstein* was written by Mary Shelley, the wife of poet Percy Bysshe Shelley. These stories, like "Beauty and the Beast," are myths we write about ourselves in an attempt to understand our *dark side*.

Black Tourmaline
for Discovery

You are what you are. It is my opinion the trouble in the world comes from people who do not know what they are and pretend to be something they are not.

—Lillian Hellman

CHEMICAL COMPOSITION: $Na(Mg,Fe)_3A_6(OH)_4(BO_3)_3$ (Si_6O_{18}) (aluminum borosilicate)
CRYSTAL SYSTEM: Hexagonal (however, three-sided crystals are common)
COLOR: Black (common in five other colors)
HARDNESS: 7½ on Mohs' scale
COLOR RAY: Black, all sources of space
LOVE QUOTIENT: Getting friendly with the inner child

The Tourmaline crystal family is highly complex in its ability to reflect and vibrate with many different elements in a consistent geometric shape. Each color is produced by a different element. In the Black Tourmaline, the element emphasized is iron. This variety is called Schorl, which is an old mining term.

The most abundant sources of Schorl have been found in the U.S. in the New England states, South Dakota, New York, and San Diego County, California.

Schorl with a termination (point of ending) at each end of the crystal is found in lengths up to two inches long in Kragero, Norway. This is a rare phenomenon of nature, suggesting the crystallizing in liquid, rather than growing from a base, as a plant and many other crystals do.

The largest deposits now being mined of all colors of Tourmaline are found in Brazil, with others found in Madagascar and Mexico.

Schorl has never been in great demand for jewelry because the more colorful and transparent gems are so spectacular. The Black Tourmaline has been somewhat of a castoff.

In the 1980s more and more deposits of Schorl came to light in almost every site where Mother Earth provides these healing crystals.

As I have stated earlier, my teacher and respected guide, Dr. Carl Jung, first introduced me to the field of mind study, the theory of "The Shadow." This invisible entity is the other side of our projected personality. It has been my clients' responses to the use of the crystals in healing that have led me to believe the dark crystals relate to our recognizing our own Shadow Self. Please do not be alarmed at the thought of a darker side of yourself. Let's light a candle and have a gentle look, okay?

This is a simple illustration: Imagine a coin. In America we often toss a coin into the air for a game of chance, or to make a decision, "heads or tails." The coin has a face or profile of a person on one side; on the opposite side is another type of emblem. When the coin falls flat after the toss, one side is not visible, but it remains a part of the coin. It is hidden from us, but we know it is there. One side of the coin is the part we show to the world (how they see us acting), the hidden part of the coin is what is suppressed or unseen or dark in our feelings and thoughts. This part is often referred to as our subconscious. *Sub* means underneath. A submarine goes underwater; we can't see it, but it is very real. If the submarine is directed to be destructive, it is dangerous. Because we cannot *see* it, the Shadow Self can sneak up on us.

These are two illustrations of how we can interpret our own Shadow Self: as a coin or as a submarine.

This is important: *There is nothing intrinsically evil* about a coin or a submarine. The coin can be used in many ways, as money or as a tool. It is a symbol of energy exchange. The submarine can be used for marine research or as a weapon of war. It has a lot going on inside itself, as does the coin.

When we think of ourselves as Spirits who decide to come to Earth and be a human in physical form, we know our Spirit is part of All That Is. We also know, now in this twentieth century of space travel, that once we leave the Earth's atmosphere, outer space is dark. All That Is includes "darkness." All ancient religions, philosophies, and myths have included the light and dark symbols and have pictured them as inseparable. In the Christian religion God does not destroy his dark side, who is personified as Lucifer and is every bit as powerful.

Humans have been experiencing light and dark periods on Earth exactly as a seed experiences being planted: covered in dark, then breaking free, transforming into a plant in the light. We know this on some level because our historians have used words such as Dark Ages or Renaissance or Enlightenment.

Without the time spent in the dark or hibernation or gestation, nothing can transform or be born. The land must rest, trees must rest, humans must rest, during the dark days of winter. The Earth turns away from the Sun; our mother says, "Now, plants, animals, and human children, take your refreshing nap!" We go inside. We do not die, but we stop giving and begin receiving for a short period. We are provided this time to take in nutrients, to refuel. If you don't recognize this and pull your energy in toward your center, you will have colds, flu, and sickness all winter. You are going against the cycles of light and dark. It is possible that your body in its infinite wisdom decides to break down, be sick, and force you to get in cycle.

These are physical expressions and illustrations of the inner and outer life we all have. The inner life is also an emotional, mental world of thoughts and feelings we never disclose. The object of exploring the Shadow Self is to see its proper function and to communicate with the underside of the coin. We cannot separate the underside of ourselves, so we must ask for its cooperation. We must also give it recognition, and praise, because it is basically responsible for our successes. If we do not engage, cooperate with, praise, and recognize it, it can become a destructive submarine and responsible for all our failures.

Our Shadow Self is a combination of our little child within and our power animal. These two live side by side in the solar plexus, the Emotional Body.

Most of us are so deathly afraid of these two remaining

sides of ourselves, we despise and ignore our Shadow Self. Therefore we receive no help, random help, or destructive energy, which causes our outside world to observe us as inconsistent, unfocused, or neurotic.

LOVE QUOTIENT

The Schorl branch of the Tourmaline clan are acting as undercover agents for us. The black crystal is strong in iron. When most of us picture iron, we see symbols such as weights, chains, large anchors, structural beams in large buildings, heavy machinery, etc. Iron is a basic metal, and a basic ingredient in the soil necessary to grow food or healthy plants, and a basic element in the blood of a healthy person. Iron equals strong.

The Shadow Self is equally as strong as the visible side of the coin, but it is undercover. In order to find out what's going on in the underworld, the undercover agent moves into the neighborhood and gets friendly.

The Schorl helps us to move into our own underworld neighborhood and get friendly. Frequently an undercover agent becomes truly a friend of someone being observed; they become partners helping each other. The Schorl seems to help my clients move into that strange and unfamiliar neighborhood. They often make friends with both their little child and their power animal.

This is a case history of a mature physician whom I met in Detroit and for whom I did a psychic reading through the mail using the outline drawing of his hand as a connection. I asked him to use the Schorl as an experiment to help with my research. I did not tell him anything about the crystal, only to hold it on the three places I consider to be the most powerful, every day, then write feelings and thoughts, or pictures received in his mind.

After a month he reported he got frequent flashbacks into his babyhood, nursing at his mother's large breasts. He had married and always been attracted to women like his mother. His mother had had to work and left him alone often. He was angry at his mother. She was harsh and tough on him. He continually searches out women like his mother but never reconciles this conflict. This is his angry, lonely "little child within."

When he does make a female contact, he wants marriage, commitment, guarantees of affection and total presence. He hangs on like a bulldog. His power animal is a bulldog!

These invisible forces have been bringing him financial success, far from happiness. This ignorance of the existence of these two entities meant that he never talked with them or asked them for help.

The Schorl disclosed their presence. The crystal can act as an antenna to draw in the black ray of the Universe, which is a positive force. When he realized his inner child needed mothering, attention, and affection, it was too late to get it from his mother, who had left Earth. He did not have a wife at the time and had never been able to get enough nurturing from any wife. His only alternative was to become his own nurturing mother!

His power animal, a bulldog, had been of great help in his career and now was being asked to help in the Self-understanding, Self-nurturing process. The bulldog perseveres, it "hangs in there," it is courageous. He had to divert that energy away from his female companions or career and focus it upon his own rescue. As he continued to become friends with these two in his underworld, they became allies and helpers. He used the Schorl crystal in an amulet hanging near his heart for almost two years, until he knew his Shadow Self intimately.

He writes to me on occasion when he discovers something new about his Shadow and its power to hurt or help him. He is still using the Black Tourmaline and gaining strength (like iron) to focus on integration and cooperation with his dark side. He's married again—he will never give up on love! (That's his power animal!)

Schorl (Black Tourmaline) Meditation

Follow the procedure for all crystal meditations. Say aloud seven times, placing the crystal on:

Solar Plexus: "This Schorl is vibrating to help me make contact with my inner child and power animal."

Heart: "This crystal is transmitting the other powerful black ray of the Universe to my Spirit."

Forehead: "This Black Tourmaline is directing my mental energy to work with my other side."

If you have better ways of saying these ideas, please create your own phrases.

Smokey Quartz
for Childpower

What I consider my weaknesses are feminine traits: incapacity to destroy, ineffectualness in battle.

—**Anaïs Nin**

CHEMICAL COMPOSITION: SiO_2 (silicon dioxide)
CRYSTAL SYSTEM: Hexagonal
COLOR: Dark brown to black
HARDNESS: 7½ on Mohs' scale
COLOR RAY: Black, all sources of space
LOVE QUOTIENT: Uncovering our destructive inner child or power animal

This crystal is one of many Quartz (seven cousins) found everywhere on Earth. Quartz is the most common crystal on our crust. Most of the beach sand in the coastal areas is Quartz. This chapter is only concerned with the Smokey Quartz as it applies to invisible energies transmitted by the black ray of the Universe.

When Quartz crystals are growing in the same areas underground where radioactive materials are deposited, there is a natural irradiation process. This proximity causes the clear crystal to take on a dark brown to gray color.

Many faceted gemstones of Smokey Quartz have been sold to unschooled customers as "Smokey Topaz." Occasionally colorless Topaz is exposed to natural radiation and turns a root-beer or golden-brown color—not gray. Clear, flawless Topaz is rare and expensive; Quartz is not.

Naturally irradiated Smokey Quartz is not as common as the clear natural Quartz, but there are deposits in every area. Some of the most beautiful Smokies found anywhere are from Switzerland. They are beautifully shaped and very transparent. Darker Smokies are found in many areas in California and Nevada in the United States.

I felt lucky when one of my clients brought a six-inch-long Smokey Quartz Scepter to me from his brother in northern California, who is what is commonly called a rock hound. The Scepter is a special growth pattern, an anomaly peculiar to Quartz. The crystal grows straight and long, then suddenly becomes larger, like an onion at the top. It looks like a king or queen's scepter or a magic wand. I am holding this crystal now as I write.

Radiation can be positive or negative. We can radiate love or hate. Radiation from Mother Earth creates beautiful gemstones by the power she holds down inside herself. Why does she use radiation on some crystals and not on others? Many scientists (who are not crystallographers) would claim the process is simply chaos or random chance, how the Earth just "happened" to go together. I don't believe that. I believe if we could go up to Saturn and turn a giant Xray onto Earth, we could see her whole skeleton, muscle structure, veins and capillaries of crystal, and the ingredients of her internal organs including heart and brain! I believe radiation is the energy that comes from her solar plexus, her Emotional Body.

LOVE QUOTIENT

The Smokey Quartz crystal can help us to discover our most destructive little-child or power-animal energy. The Smokey can "smoke it out" of hiding!

Radiation is caused when uranium and thorium are close to each other and decay. This causes gamma rays to be born (similar to X rays) that can penetrate several feet of rock.

Two elements die so a gamma ray can be born. The Smokey Quartz works in helping us to let our frightened or angry child be born again into a helpful toddler. The Smokey is a symbol for the power buried beneath our feet, and beneath our solar plexus.

Have you ever noticed how many TV commercials are done by children? Why? Because a child has much power over our emotions. The innocence, cuteness, and sweetness of our inner child can come back into our lives by meditating with the Smokey. Our inner child does not have to remain unnurtured and angry/lonely.

The power animal needs "smoking out" of its cave also. Animals often retreat into the darkest, smallest corner they can find when they are ill. When our power animal is sick, it needs nourishment and caring.

"How would my power animal get sick?" you ask me. Any animal gets discouraged if it is continually whipped and beaten. Soon its tail and head are drooping, it has no appetite, there is no sparkle in the eyes, the coat is dull. Many of us in this traditional religious culture are taught to mistreat our power animal and it is called ego or desire with a nasty, disgusting tone of voice.

The Shadow Self needs supervision and guidance, acceptance and praise, plus an invitation to be involved helpfully. The Smokey Quartz can be a gentle master. The dark crystals are direct transmitters of "tough love."

We are all suffering from the results of inexperience. Our own parents were inexperienced when they were teaching us to have a social conscience. They had been taught by their own inexperienced parents. The governing rulebook we all use is a cassette that plays within our brain, recorded from before birth. It has a lot of do's and don'ts. Hopefully we grow up to become more discriminating and self-governing, but unless we are awake, the old tape keeps playing. This causes us to feel guilty or wrong even when we are free to act *without* guilt. This is when we punish or suppress both our inner child and power animal.

I have had clients so depressed because of guilt over something perfectly appropriate they had done, out of anger, the result was self-punishment through illness. When I asked them to do a Smokey Quartz meditation exercise, the sickness left.

Our culture teaches us to judge and punish ourselves! The subconscious knowings are ignored (the little child), and our power is denied (the power animal). As a result our Shadow Self receives too much of our energy in attempting to suppress it. When this occurs, the Shadow Self becomes belligerent and violent. We have created an unprecedentedly violent society because we have not taught ourselves to use the Shadow Self constructively.

It is up to each individual to go inside themselves to the very beginning of this lifetime and remember, yes, *remember*, the earliest days of their perfection and innocence as a baby-child. It is also necessary for each of us to find the rage and courage of our animal instincts for self-protection and survival. We must acknowledge the Shadow Self and say, "Yes, I have all this potential energy inside, it is necessary, I like it, I can use it, I won't misuse it, and even if I ignore it, *it is there*."

I think self-awareness is the most important thing toward being a champion.

—**Billie Jean King**
The Sportswoman, 1973

Smokey Quartz Meditation Exercise

Follow the procedure for all crystal meditations. Say aloud seven times, placing the crystal on:

Solar Plexus: "This Smokey Quartz is vibrating to help me discover and love my inner child."

Heart: "This dark crystal is transmitting to stir awake the 'power animal' of courage and rage."

Forehead: "The Smokey crystal is vibrating the black ray of the Universe to strengthen my Shadow Self."

Black Onyx
for Surrender

It's ironic, but until you can free those final monsters within the jungle of yourself, your life, your soul, is up for grabs.

—Rona Barrett
Miss Rona, A Biography

CHEMICAL COMPOSITION: SiO_2 (silicon dioxide)
CRYSTAL SYSTEM: Hexagonal (microcrystalline aggregates)
COLOR: Various or banded grays/blacks
HARDNESS: 6½–7 on Mohs' scale
PLANET AND COLOR RAY: Space—Black
LOVE QUOTIENT: Surrender to the Feminine Energy—Receiving

Black Onyx is a name for a Quartz cousin of the Agate family. It is never found growing in separate crystals, as they merge into amorphous masses or nodules of roundish fist- to head-size boulders. *Agate* and *Chalcedony* are synonyms for murky masses of cloudy Quartz growing intertwined in clumps in cavities.

At the beginning of the nineteenth century, most of the mining for Agate was done in Germany. A complete town was dependent on and developed the Agate industry. These deposits seem to be depleted. The emigrant Germans with the mining experience uncovered new deposits in Brazil in 1827.

The German Agates were found in natural colors in circular or horizontal layers of pinks, browns, reds, yellows, and pale blues. These could not be dyed. The red color is Carnelian, the pink-browns are Onyx, and the black/whites are Onyx.

The Brazilian Agate is basically gray in color. The Germans learned to color Agate from the Romans and perfected their processes in Idar-Oberstein in the 1820s. The uninteresting Brazilian Agates became beautifully colored imitations by their techniques.

To create Black Onyx, the solution is concentrated sugar with carbon or cobalt soaking, followed by heat treating in sulfuric acid. Few natural Black Onyx are being mined, but many exist from centuries past. If you find a Black Onyx that has not been dyed, you have a treasure. The natural black is from Earth radiation like a Smokey Quartz.

The black ray of space is the combination of all colored rays. Out of this blackness is born all energy. The black of an Onyx is not translucent or transparent; it is thick, solid, opaque black. Black on black! The blackness of space is the hibernating, holding, waiting, gestating, total energy that all civilizations have described as the negative force, Female Energy. The receptive womb, the night, when we surrender to the dying of the light, go to sleep, leave the physical awareness, enter the other worlds we call dreams, unconsciously living in our original state, is our *re*-creation. We surrender to the "little death," we die to our conscious Self, and we become out of our own physical control, surrendered and safe. We look forward to sleep; if we can't sleep, we feel frustrated, out of balance, wrong!

The other Self we are is active in the darkness behind our closed eyelids in sleep. Many humans must sleep during daylight hours, so they voluntarily block out the light, close the curtains, wear a black eye-cover, or cover their heads completely. The human being is designed to have a split personality and lead a double life. If we are deprived of this routine, we become irritable, depressed, nervous, inefficient, and eventually insensibly confused until we *cannot* remain conscious.

LOVE QUOTIENT

The black ray of the Universe calls us back into a state of surrender: "Give in, children, you are not in control, you do not have to work, strain, and worry twenty-four hours a day. Surrender your mission, surrender your control (your imagined control), come back home to the comfort of nothingness for eight hours. Be born again all fresh in the morning after dissolving yourself overnight. Re-create, live free, out of your body, flying in the astral planes, live your dreams. Surrender to all that you already know. Your dark Self will work with your light Self to help you remember the answers, surrender."

Doing an active meditation exercise with the Black Onyx can help anyone realize that the other Self is a resting place as well as an active place of ideas. The Black Onyx while transmitting the black ray of space to our invisible and physical bodies is allowing us to surrender to unseen help, relief, renewal.

Self-realization, Self-discovery, Self-awareness, Self-respect, Self-trust, are all the positive antidotes to Self-*denial* that lead to Self-reliance. Self-reliance proves Self-love (taking care of the Self like a loving parent), which affords us the luxury of giving good amounts of our love to others.

The Black Onyx meditation allows us to have a rest from our worrisome conscious responsibility to know all the physical-world answers and to just turn it over to the shadow! When I was a little girl, we had no television, so I sat next to the big floor-standing radio with my ear close to the speaker and listened to stories. One of my favorites, because it was so mysterious and supernatural, was called "The Shadow." The masculine voice was deep and powerful. Every program began and ended with the phrase "The Shadow knows!" *Your* Shadow Self knows; surrender and allow it to share with you.

In many native myths and stories, the bird most praised and revered is the raven or crow. This bird lives in many places worldwide. The shiny black color and size of the raven make it different and instantly recognizable by everyone. It is interesting how supposedly primitive peoples gave superhuman powers to this black-ray bird. Science has echoed their beliefs in giving the crow high marks in intelligence. The myths of civilization give us clues to the *symbols* we most need to recognize: *Black is beautiful* and most wise. It is the combination of all color into *one*. *White is light* and most enlightened. It is the combination of all color into *one*.

The answers we all seek, the object we all follow after, the ultimate desire deep within the darkness of our inner space, is love, to be loved. To have our inner dark center be acceptable and okay is our dearest dream. We are the only ones who can fulfill our own dream. Self-acceptance through surrender to how perfect we are with our so-called imperfections can be accelerated with Black Onyx.

This crystal is a visual reminder of night, of sleep, of rest, of freedom from the physical body, of the other personality who is our partner in the dark world of hidden secrets and invisible equations. We can dissolve ourselves, our cares and worries, and just turn the whole mess over to the Shadow!

Recently, at the end of a monthly workshop I call Crystal Encounters, a young man approached me and asked me to tell him what the meaning was of the tiny crystal in his newly acquired earring. After examining it, and deducing that it was a faceted Black Onyx, cut to the hexagonal shape of a Quartz crystal, I told him, "The Black Onyx has a vibration to help you get to know your Shadow Self better. Did you choose this for yourself?" He said yes, he had looked at hundreds of different ones and this was his most favorite of all.

A few weeks later I heard from him and he said, "I was just speechless the night I asked you about my black crystal. I was blown away because I have had a new loving relationship with a woman who has caused me to look at my 'dark side.' The very first time we met, she used those words with me and I didn't understand them then.

"I have been in the Marines for four years. I have been overseas in bad conditions. I have smoked a lot of pot; in fact, I was into heavy-duty marijuana all the time. I didn't like my life or myself. I joined a hard, heavy-metal band and became a spike-haired punk rocker. I only wore black—the message was chaos!

"I just recently began to look at my life and get happier, stop being addicted, and got a different job. I am getting to know, accept, and acknowledge my partner, my own dark side."

Now he can surrender and allow the Feminine Energy, the little child, and the power animal inside his Self guide and help him.

Black Onyx Meditation

Follow the procedures for all crystal meditations. Place the crystal on:

Solar Plexus: "This Black Onyx is vibrating to help me surrender to my Shadow Self, my partner and constant companion."

Heart: "This crystal is transmitting the energy of space to comfort and rest my Spirit."

Forehead: "This dark crystal is vibrating to help me communicate and remember my conversations with my negative power."

Hematite
for Iron Strength

The first problem for all of us, men and women, is not to learn, but to unlearn.

—**Gloria Steinem**
New York Times, 1971

CHEMICAL COMPOSITION: Fe_2O_3 (iron oxide)
CRYSTAL SYSTEM: Hexagonal (trigonal)
COLOR: Metallic, dark gray-black
HARDNESS: 5½–6½ on Mohs' scale
PLANET AND COLOR RAY: Mars—Black (all sources in space—especially red)
LOVE QUOTIENT: To use strength and Masculine Energy (from the inner child or power animal)

The most significant feature of this metal, iron crystal is the dual color of red and black. The name *Hematite* derives from the Greek word meaning bloodlike. The crystal looks black or dark gray, but when it is cut into thin slices, they are transparent and red. The dust that is left in the liquid that cools the cutting wheel turns the liquid bloodred. We know that iron can rust and become red when exposed to moisture. Often when the tiniest Hematite crystals are trapped inside Quartz crystals, the Quartz takes a peachy-red tone.

In ancient times large pieces of Hematite were polished and used for mirrors. The Latin word sometimes used was *specularite* (speculum—mirror).

Another healing use of Hematite prescribed by the ancients was to wear it as an amulet against bleeding.

Over the years, I have discovered that when a client chooses Hematite over all other crystals, it often indicates a lack of iron in the blood (anemia). This can be corrected by improved diet. Eating habits are often indicators of Self-love or the lack of Self-love.

Few Hematite crystals find their way to the marketplace. However, tumbled polished stones are readily available and inexpensive. When the crystals are collected as specimens, the most beautiful are thin plates, six-sided with many natural facets along the edges.

The cutting, polishing quality of Hematite is found in England, Germany, Norway, Sweden, Spain, Brazil, New Zealand, and the U.S.

When it was fashionable to wear mourning dress after a death in the family, Hematite was jewelry for the grieving. It is a good stone for beads and rings.

When using Hematite to treat the Shadow Self, we need to focus on our Mars energy, because the predominant red ray is active *within* the black ray. Mars energy is masculine and fire, assertive and intuitive.

When Hematite is chosen by a client, their super-conscious mind knows there is a lack of strength, either in the blood or in their Spirit. Homeopathic medicine and holistic healing both teach us how the body responds to the mind, or the mind responds to the body messages. When we refuse to be a loving, nurturing parent to our Self, often the first symptom is bad eating habits. When we do not properly fuel our machine, it breaks down. The body says, "Hey, wake up, you're not loving your Self!" If sickness comes, it is the body talking. Mars rules iron and directs the energy of iron in our blood. When our body doesn't receive enough iron through food, because we have not focused on nurturing our Self, it gets weakened until the machine stops.

LOVE QUOTIENT

Hematite will transmit the red ray of Mars within the universal black rays to strengthen our "little child" and the "power animal." We need to call forth the strength of our Shadow Self, and especially the assertive Masculine Energy. Hematite helps us to "take control" when we have been acting weak.

Recently during a workshop I was doing at a metaphysical bookstore, an attractive gray-haired woman "fell in love" with a powerful Hematite pendant that I had made for "someone." I always create these power pieces knowing that I have made contact somewhere in the psychic plane with the person who needs it. They will find their healing amulet. That is why I travel to other cities and countries to teach crystal therapy and Self-empowerment. Maybe I am already creating a powerful healing crystal amulet for you!

When the pretty woman put the Hematite neckpiece around her throat, she felt a change in her body. I had a psychic sense that she was feeling emotionally weak. She was dressed in a fashionable, contemporary denim sports ensemble with shiny metal studs on the collar and jacket front. She looked great on the outside, but some spark was missing.

I asked if she wanted any psychic information (it isn't good to do unsolicited work; it is an invasion of personal privacy). She said she would be grateful for any insights. I said, "I feel a great deal of weakness in your body; you look good, but your energy is low and has been for at least six months. Have you been eating well? I think you are anemic, and it is because you are feeling emotionally weak over your personal life."

At that point she broke into tears and said her husband had died six months ago. She had been going to exercise classes, jogging, doing everything she could to stay healthy and entertain herself, but she just couldn't cook for only one person. Her weakness was a psychological feeling of no personal strength to live alone and make her own decisions. This emotional weakness moved into her personal physical habits. She also said she had just had a physical checkup and did have low blood hemoglobin (anemia—lack of iron).

She took her Hematite neckpiece and followed the twenty-eight-day active meditation exercise program. She reported a complete reversal, both in attitude and physical strength. She also mentioned how others had responded to her new "power piece." Strangers had commented on its unique beauty; friends were struck with how it complimented her appearance. She was attracting new friends just by the conversations invited by the crystals and the symbol built into the piece.

The truth is metaphysical; on a subliminal level every-one "felt" her new magnetic power, enhanced by the sweet medicine of Universal Energy flowing through her. Her life *is* different now. She has called forth her strong happy child and her courageous power animal!

Hematite Meditation

Follow directions for all the meditations in this book found on page 144. Place the crystal upon:

Solar Plexus: Repeat seven times aloud—"This Hematite crystal is vibrating to strengthen my little child and power animal."

Heart: "This crystal is vibrating to strengthen my heart and blood."

Forehead: "This dark crystal is using the black ray to strengthen my Self-reliant mind."

PART V

SURPRISE CRYSTALS

Surprise Crystals

The pattern or organization of any biological system is in part determined by its atomic physio-chemical components. Energy fields surround, power and maintain every living system.

—**Dr. Harold Saxton Burr**
Professor of anatomy, Yale
Electrodynamic Theory of Life, 1935

Whether you have experimented consciously with crystal energies or not, you have been affected by them all your life. The evidence is growing in scientific research that the human body may soon become defined in physics as "a crystal." It is known now that there are crystals observed in certain areas of the bone and brain of humans. Crystals found on and in Earth have been used by humans instinctively in all recorded history.

Somewhere in our distant past around 3500 to 1000

B.C., humans used the first crystals to make useful things. This period was called the Bronze Age. Somehow after the Stone Age, humans uncovered copper and tin crystals and learned how to melt them together producing bronze. They also learned to mold this alloy into bowls, tools, and weapons. This era comprises 2,500 years of our history.

Metal crystals have been so very important in human evolution that another complete section of time has been named after a crystal metal, Hematite, iron. Europeans introduced iron tools and weapons in 1000 B.C. This phase of culture lasted until A.D. 100 and is called the Iron Age.

The fact is now being accepted by our foremost physicists (mathematical scientists) that our solar system, galaxy (the Milky Way), and Universe are an integrated *whole being*. Everything we know of operates in relationship with and depends on everything else.

Each planet in our solar system has a chemical content that gives it a mathematical formula and a molecular structure that causes it to vibrate. This chemistry causes a sound or signal to be sent out into the Universe, which can be measured in waves by instruments on Earth. Each planet sings its own individual song. Since Earth is part of this *whole being*, it stands to reason that Earth also sings to all the planets. These vibrations or signals represent energy—or some kind of "stuff"—that holds the universe together, in perfect timing and balance.

Before you were born, your mother was being influenced by this "stuff" that permeates and affects everything on Earth. Let's call it cosmic rays. You know of many: ultraviolet, infrared, radio wave, microwave, alpha, beta, gamma, etc.

Your mother was using many common crystals every

day while you were building your body inside hers. One of the most surprising crystals to almost everyone is the one she probably wore on the third finger of her left hand. The crystal is *Gold*! It has a crystal atomic structure with a high light refraction. It transmits energy from the Sun. It is a strong positive energy (known in metaphysics as masculine) that helps with assertive action and logic. In the 1960s when women the world over began to emerge as leaders, asking for equal rights, Gold became a fashion rage. Especially in the U.S., almost every female had at least one Gold chain around her throat chakra or power center. Some women wore ten or twelve together—now that's powerful energy! The superconscious mind was telling women that they needed more left-brain activity and assertive action.

Another crystal surprise your mother may have had around her (and so do you) was the *Silver* crystal! Knives, forks, spoons, candle holders, as wedding presents or family inheritances, are in constant contact with us in everyday life. Your mother may have worn Silver jewelry and likely had some Silver tooth repair also!

The Silver crystal has a high light refraction also, which we believe is attracting the invisible rays emanating from our Moon. In every ancient mystery school, religious order, philosophy, cultural ceremony, and/or natural pre-science, humans have written of the Moon as a feminine force. The Moon rules the body cycles of the females on Earth. The Silver crystal transmits those cosmic rays to the electrical systems of Earth beings to help bring the opposite negative energy (called feminine) to balance our actions. The Silver crystal evokes the right-brain activity of intuition, creativity, and reception. Silver became a popular fashion accessory for men several years ago. Today, many men worldwide find themselves bachelors or fathers in charge of their children, learning the feminine role of self-nurturing, creativity, and intuition.

When I design a crystal healing amulet for my clients, I usually combine both Gold and Silver metals in proportion, using a smaller amount of Gold. As in everything, there must be a balance. This affects our electromagnetic balance in the body mind and spirit.

Your ancestors, your parents, and you have been using crystals for centuries. Every metal on Earth is a crystal—all your money coins are some form of crystal, your car, bicycle, and tools, even your thermometer is filled with mercury, a metal crystal.

We are all interrelated and interacting in a crystalline Universe. Treasure your *surprise crystals* for their special energies transmitted to you daily.

There are several newly discovered metal crystals in use now such as uranium, plutonium, titanium, etc., but here I will help you to focus energy through Gold and Silver.

These two crystals are our constant companions, and we must know them to appreciate their abilities.

Gold Crystals
for Masculine Energy

Throughout all of history, books were written
with male sperm, not menstrual blood.

—**Erica Jong**
Fear of Flying

CHEMICAL COMPOSITION: Gold, Au, ordinarily contains
10–15% pure gold; Silver up to 30%
CRYSTAL SYSTEM: Isometric—rarely in distinct crystals.
Octahedrons most common and cubes. Sometimes
thin plates with equilateral triangles.
COLOR: Rich yellow, opaque, luster metallic
HARDNESS: 2½–3 on Mohs' scale
PLANET AND COLOR RAY: Jupiter, Sun—Multiray, White,
Yellow
LOVE QUOTIENT: Logic, action, Masculine Energy, du-
rability

The Gold crystal is malleable and can be hammered flat without breaking. The molecules remain together when pounded even into the thinnest sheet of Gold-leaf paper. Gold cannot be made soluble by acid, but rather low heat causes it to form a perfect spherical shining bead that does not tarnish.

Gold is usually found as a companion to veins of Quartz. When Gold nuggets are found in river or stream beds due to erosion from host rocks above, they often have small pieces of Quartz attached.

There are several counties in California where splendid crystal specimens are found: El Dorado, Placer, Siskiyou, Tuolumne, and Nevada. Colorado and Idaho are also good sources of fine crystal specimens. Other countries where beautiful crystal specimens are found are Mexico, Romania, and Australia.

The Gold crystal is reflecting, attracting, and transmitting the rays from the Sun and Jupiter. It is a Masculine-Energy vibration. Like the Moon, Earth, and planets, the Sun is round to our visual perception. In all known civilizations the circle is used to describe in symbols the most spiritual essence. The Sun is so immense it is nurturing the complete galaxy. To our sensual nature, the Sun is life.

The Sun as a symbol for *The God* was used from the beginning of history. In most native cultures the Sun is given the character of Father and the Earth is called Mother.

The ruler of our space, Sun is electric. The giver of our life, Earth, is magnetic. These two energies are necessary to intermingle for our survival.

Jupiter is also a Masculine-Energy planet; the color of his ray is golden. The yellow-gold ray from Jupiter is attracted and transmitted by the Gold crystal. In metaphysics that ray influences our abundance in life. It has a joyous effect on humanity. If the financial situation becomes strained or uncomfortable, there is usually another planet (or more) blocking or redirecting Jupiter's influence. When this happens to nations, there is often a recession, depression, or war. When it occurs in a private life, there are lessons to be learned. There is always a scarcity of Gold crystal when these times come.

It is surprising to find large amounts of heavy Gold jewelry worn by women of some Middle Eastern and African countries who own nothing else! Our mother Earth provides Gold for everyone and anyone.

Gold is used in the process of making red glass, and also as a medicine in the treatment of cancer and other diseases. Recently a process has been discovered to fuse Gold dust to Quartz crystals with electricity, which turns them a beautiful blue similar to Aquamarine or Blue Topaz. Dental work with Gold is the most durable. The use of Gold for personal adornment leads all others.

There are many religious stories and ancient myths concerning Gold, such as the Golden Age of Greece and Rome. It is known as a time of great progress, prosperity, and cultural achievement. Some of the myths by Ovid relate it as an imaginary early age in which mankind was ideally happy, prosperous, and innocent. In the Bible stories of the ancient Hebrews, there was worship of a Golden Calf, which is the symbol of greedy pursuit of riches in opposition to spiritual understanding.

There is also a golden wedding celebration after a couple has been married fifty years. They are given golden objects as gifts. The increasing life span is making that pleasure more likely for happy couples, but the changing of partners makes it highly improbable for many others.

The practice of exchanging rings when a couple marries is still popular, and the majority of wedding rings are Gold. I believe the man needs to wear Silver, to help bring out his Female Energy, and the woman needs to wear Gold in order to balance her Masculine Energy. I also know cases when this could be reversed with great success, when a man needs more Masculine Energy or a woman needs more Feminine Energy. I sometimes suggest to couples that they exchange their wedding jewelry with each other during trying times. It has been very effective.

The Gold crystal appears in fewer places on Earth, yet there seems to be enough to go around. It is almost indestructible, and therefore all the Gold that has ever been mined in one and a half million years is still in use or storage, somewhere. It would be an interesting research project to search for a pattern of Gold veins that run through the body of Earth from reported deposits. I feel that Gold and Silver crystals are major arteries and other crystals are capillaries, etc., in her giant system.

LOVE QUOTIENT

Gold as a Masculine Energy certainly gets things done! Money talks. In refracting the rays of the Sun and Jupiter, it helps anyone to take action. Gold crystals give anyone a sense of power. Many wars have been fought for Gold, and many crimes committed, using the negative aggression of the Masculine Energy in the Gold crystal.

The durability and the malleability of Gold as a Masculine Energy has not been given enough significance. In the Crystal Love Secrets that are revealed here, please take note of the positive Masculine Energy in Gold. Many Spirits inhabiting masculine bodies have suffered untold misery and horror while bravely protecting their families. Their courage and ability to continue with an adaptability (malleability) although they have been beaten and stretched into a thin sheet is much like Gold.

If you wish to take on the marvelously durable qualities and endurance of the Masculine Energy, in order to balance your Self and your role in your loving relationships, meditate with and wear Gold on your left side.

> Psychic bisexuality as a deconditioning process can eventually eliminate sexist limitations for both men and women.
>
> **—Charlotte Painter**
> *Confessions from the*
> *Malaga Madhouse*, 1971

Gold Meditation

Follow the procedure for all other meditation exercises. Place the crystal upon:

Solar Plexus: "This Gold is attracting rays of strength and durability to my inner child and power animal."

Heart: "This Gold is reminding my Spirit of other lifetimes as a Masculine Energy."

Forehead: "This Gold is bringing the prosperous, joyful, logical, assertive Masculine Energy into balance in me again."

◆

Silver Crystals
for Feminine Energy

Woman magic and Earth magic are the same.
The whole Universe is the body of the Goddess.
The gods are her children. The female is the
giver of forms.

—Joseph Campbell, "Myth of the Goddess"
Interviews with Bill Moyers, PBS, 1987

CHEMICAL COMPOSITION: Silver—Ag
CRYSTAL SYSTEM: Isometric, mostly crude cubes but also
  octahedrons, wires, and sheets
COLOR: Silver—while tarnished, gray to black
HARDNESS: 2½–3 on Mohs' scale
PLANET AND COLOR RAY: Moon—Silver
LOVE QUOTIENT: Intuition, creativity, Female Energy

Silver is found in many different areas on Earth. However, there are noteworthy deposits of crystals in the
Northwest Territories of Canada, Michigan, Arizona,

Colorado, Mexico, Norway, Germany, Australia, and South-West Africa. We know the word *silver* is Anglo-Saxon, but the origin is lost.

Silver is extremely ductile and malleable, capable of high polish, and refracts light in a beautiful way for jewelry and artistic objects.

Silver is a precious metal crystal in many ways other than for adornment or art. In chemistry and industry it is the best metal conductor of heat and electricity. Silver salts are used in photography, and our mirrors are coated with Silver. Mirrors are used in many industrial products, telescopes, and energy reflector-collectors. Silver is a vital crystal in many areas of our taken-for-granted civilization. Every time you use the rearview mirror in your car, Silver is serving you. Silver nitrate is a medicinal antiseptic. Silver protein was formerly used as a medicine to treat inflammation of mucous membranes.

The word *silver* is constantly used as a complimentary adjective to mean beautiful or engaging, such as silver-haired, silver-tongued, silver-toned voice, silver screen (motion pictures), silver thaw or silver frost, silver fox, silver birch (tree). There was also a Silver Age in Roman mythology. A marriage celebration called the silver wedding anniversary of twenty-five years is marked by gifts of Silver to the couple.

> By the light of the silvery moon, I want to spoon with my honey, I'll croon love's tune.
>
> —**Song of romance**
> American, 1910

The silvery Moon has been so romantically linked to the loving, sexual side of the human experience, it could be considered a natural instinct awakened by Moon vibrations. The coyote howls at the distant mate; the wolf, owl, bat, and cat prowl in search of sexual satisfaction; when the "silvery beams increase loves dreams, we'll be cuddling soon, 'neath the silvery Moon."

The Silver crystal is attracting, collecting, and transmitting to us the ultraviolet light rays, reflecting from Sun to Moon to Earth. The Moon is visible in the daytime sky also. On some dark nights the circle of the Moon places it in the blue sky of another area on Earth. No matter if we see it or not, it is affecting the movement of the water on Earth, and inside each living thing.

LOVE QUOTIENT

The Moon directly affects the Feminine Energy or is a *physical* part of it. The Moon and its cycles create for us a pattern recorded in the menstrual flow of human females. Fecundity, the abundant ability to have children or reproduce the same kind, is attributed to the silver ray from the Moon. When the female has not mated during the cycle, the Moon vibration sets off fluid and hormonal balances to eliminate the nest her body prepared for the possible sperm to meet with her egg. She then begins another twenty-eight-day buildup of the nest.

The Feminine Energy is the receptive energy in the universal scheme. The Silver crystal awakens this energy in both male and female humans. The male gender has not until recently recognized his "other half" energy.

New science, new philosophical theory, and new freedom to explore traditional belief systems have uncovered the basically androgynous nature of our species.

Understanding the Female Energy has become a giant challenge to our continued upward and forward evolutionary movement. The Male Energy has dominated the past five thousand years of our history. The pendulum is swinging back away from that predominance. As we make the gradual transition to develop a more balanced society, women must examine how to keep the best traits of Feminine Energy. Men must become acquainted with their latent Feminine Energy. Each of the sexes can help the other to uncover and use talents and possibilities lying hidden for centuries.

The use of the Silver crystal in aiding the revolution has been insured by the Female Energy as it expresses itself through inventors and artists, the true clairvoyants in any age. Silver jewelry, telescopes, reflectors, mirrors, film processing, silver table utensils, are all continually within our physical electromagnetic field, influencing us subliminally. There are increasing scientific applications of Silver crystals, because intuition and invention are Feminine Energy. The scientist (inventor) labors with Masculine-Energy mathematics, but the intuition or *idea* is Feminine Energy working within the human in either gender.

The Moon's silver ray is equated with abundant growth, embracing romantic love, not with war and/or violence. Police statistics, however, show an increase in problems during the full Moon. Emotions run high during these extrastrong days of full reflection. Emotional instability has traditionally been equated with Feminine Energy. The crimes of violence committed during these times seem to be when the Emotional Body is stirred within everyone; however, the violent reaction is higher in males. Men have not had experience or training in how to express their Female Energy *appropriately*.

The use of Silver in making the transition is at our fingertips. We have, provided for us by our Mother Earth, a material with which to balance our inner energies. Silver, being the greatest conductor of electric-magnetic impulses, can be our love secret to being in balance with our lover.

Silver Meditation

Follow directions for all meditation exercises. Hold the Silver upon the:

Solar Plexus: Say aloud seven times—"This Silver crystal is transmitting a balance of magnetic-Earth energy to my emotions."

Heart: "This Silver is vibrating Moon-beauty to my Spirit for nurturing and peace."

Forehead: "Silver vibrations fill my mind with psychic intuition and energy."

Wear silver at the throat or heart level and on the right hand or arm (to balance the masculine side with Feminine Energy).

PART VI

FAMILY AND FRIENDS—
THE CONNECTING
CRYSTALS

Family and Friends

Two souls at war
Dueling in a single breast
To capture the heart.
But one mind will persuade both
To turn against the true foe.
The ego.

—Buddhist saying

We are experiencing a time when several of the outer, transpersonal planets are at the point of their path around the Sun when they pass more quickly. In plain language this means Saturn, Uranus, Neptune, and Pluto are at apogee, turning the farthest corner on their racetrack. They have been on the "long stretch," now they are preparing for the "home stretch." Terms from horse racing may draw an easier picture for you. This means their cosmic rays are affecting Earth for shorter periods and each planet is giving its energy almost simultaneously. What we on Earth experience is more intense lessons and fast changes into new situations.

Another analogy may be our educational process on Earth. We begin kindergarten, go through the long climb up through the grades. We have a graduation, which is like coming to the end of the first part of a race around a track. When we continue our schooling, college is much more concentrated, focused, intense, stressful. The last periods are tests, examinations; we are required to prove what we have learned. This is exactly what is happening as Universal Energy is directed toward Earth now. I find it exciting the way humans understand how to make words expressing cosmic truth. Think of the word *university*. Our physical schooling system of attending a "university" is the equivalent of what happens in the Universe. Right now we are experiencing a lot of learning in a short time. We might even say we are in a *time warp*.

The French and Japanese have developed superfast trains, another symbol for us to consider. When it's time to get on a fast train, make the decision and *get on!* Don't miss this train. The two most valuable examinations we must now make in order to graduate into the twenty-first century are, what to keep that is good from our old world, and what to use that is new along with it, for our new world.

Saturn, the green ray, is our teacher from the old world, giving us structure, form, tradition, stability, time-tested, and also old, breaking-down, antiquated relics of once-vital forms.

Uranus, the blue ray, is always bringing us new discoveries, surprises, upheavals, revolutions, overthrowing the "status quo" and also being slightly radical, eccentric, far out, too extreme, and maybe outrageous!

These two energies are at work during the 1990s moving together at the bend of the racetrack, focusing in Capricorn: business and careers (1989–1991); Aquarius, friends' dreams, universal understanding (1992–1995); and Pisces (1995–1998), which deals with the mass mind, subconscious, and large groups. By the time these planets reach the constellation of Aries, which represents spring, new beginnings, rebirth, we will celebrate the year 2000, the beginning of the twenty-first century of this epoch of human history. It is exciting, but don't take it too seriously. Remember, we can chart our history back at least one and a half million years. Humans have experienced these same cosmic cycles many times before. We have had vast, intelligent, scientifically and technologically developed civilizations before in China, Egypt, Mexico, Central America, and Peru. We still don't know how accurate our group memory is concerning Atlantis before Egypt, or Lemuria before Atlantis!

We do know, however, the planets have a definite path and their travels affect Earth, always. *All ways.*

The Earth crystals that reflect the blue and green rays from Saturn and Uranus are combinations of these rays. The Azurite-Malachite-Chrysocolla aggregate and the new crystal Larimar are the best examples. I find it marvelous they each contain, on occasion, a streak of red.

These crystals and their love secrets can help direct the cosmic energies into our private and personal lives. The universal transformation cannot take place until the intimate personal change occurs.

Larimar—
For Love in the Family

Divine love has met and always will meet every human need.

—Mary Baker Eddy (1821–1910)
Founder, Christian Science

CHEMICAL COMPOSITION: $NaCa_2Si_3O_8(OH)$ (blue pecto-lite)
CRYSTAL SYSTEM: Triclinic, compact radiate masses of thin acicular crystals; globular masses
COLOR: Blue and green and white—some red veins
HARDNESS: 5–6 on Mohs' scale
PLANET AND COLOR RAY: Saturn, Uranus—Green, Blue
LOVE QUOTIENT: Healing family relationships

Larimar is truly a great gift from our Mother Earth to help us make our transition into a New Age. I find it very fitting that it was first brought to public notice by a member of the Peace Corps, a volunteer in Santo Domingo in 1974. New discoveries are credited to the planet Uranus, which also emits the blue ray. I believe there are no accidents. In 1974 the planet was traveling through the constellation of Libra. This group of stars affects our relationships with the significant others in our lives. Libra rules marriage and partnerships. The glyph or symbol for Libra is the scales of justice or balance. The rays from Libra affect everyone on Earth to search for balance in relationships.

Pectolite had been found in a few places before this, but the colors were white to gray. These were in Italy, Scotland, and the U.S. The blue pectolite was a great discovery.

The newest information and history of this crystal was recently published in the winter 1989 issue of *Gems and Gemology*. The first mention of Larimar as a gemstone was by Joel Arem in his gem encyclopedia of 1977.

The Dominican Republic is the eastern portion of the island of Hispaniola. Larimar is found southwest of the capital, Santo Domingo. At this time the mines are from a single volcanic deposit. All mineral rights belong to the government. L.A.G. Vega, a lawyer, owned a portion of the land where it was found. He formed a corporation with Miguel Mendez in 1975 and they originally called the stone Travelina.

Mendez shortly gave the blue crystal another nickname after his daughter, Lari, combined with the Spanish word for sea, which is *mar*. *Larimar* has become the trade name used consistently since 1975.

The country has coffee plantations and fishing to support inhabitants, so mining is done sporadically. It is not a rich country and has not been funded to purchase modern mining equipment. Everything is done by hand with picks and shovels. The mines occasionally flood or money runs out and production comes to a halt. The miners have formed a co-op, but almost all have other jobs and do not mine consistently. This means the price of Larimar is determined by how much is available. It is not inexpensive. Like Sugilite, another New Age crystal, it is still rather rare.

When it is cut and polished into ring, pendant, or bracelet stones, it sometimes resembles Turquoise. You will be able to tell the difference, however, by the brilliant shine, and the pattern of blue, white, and green. Look closely. On occasion there will be a streak of red Hematite (iron) in the pattern. If you want a simple meditation stone to hold, small tumbled stones are less expensive—but not as pretty!

There are two synthetic glass, man-made stones that could be mistaken for Larimar. They are Victoria stone and Imori stone (manufactured in Japan). Both of these stones are more vivid and a darker blue.

There are several qualities of Larimar, determined by color, pattern, and crystal hardness or lack of interior fractures. The cutting or carving grade is, of course, the best quality. All have the same metaphysical vibration and application.

I wish to thank Charles Mark of Ft. Lauderdale, Florida, for his generous help in supplying me with articles of information. He provided samples of Larimar for my research with clients. He imports the new crystal for distribution in the U.S.

THE PSYCHIC LOVE QUALITIES

The most satisfying part of my crystal therapy work has been the outcome of experiments to prove how each one of us *knows* deep down inside what we need to heal ourselves. When so many of my clients with the same basic complaint choose Larimar as their "medicine stone," it really means we are all intuitive (or we have all been a crystal!).

The visual patterns of Larimar are unique as they radiate out from the center of the form; no two are alike. The mixture of the various crystals of natrolite, chalcocite, Hematite, manganese, and pectolite are manifesting into one composite of a rhythmic pattern in blue-green. These vibrations blend into one *family*. As in our Earth family, there are many interactions.

The occasional inclusion of a red vein of Hematite in Larimar is pertinent to the love secret of this stone. Hematite is iron, an element found in healthy blood. The possibility exists that this version of Larimar would increase the cooperation and willingness to love between persons of a "blood" family. We have heard so many times an old expression used when two in a family are at odds for years: "There is bad blood between them." This expression is reserved for blood relatives. If this type of Larimar is chosen by a client, many cases have shown a need to heal a close blood relationship, to have a reconciliation.

This combination of elements could represent the total family of the children of Mother Earth. The blue, green, and white of our home planet paints a glorious portrait in space. We have only been able to see our

Mother Earth in full form since our first explorations with cameras in space a short thirty years ago.

Our hearts and our heads were turned around slowly by the creeping realization that we were taking our Mother Earth for granted. We have been misusing her and overworking her for several hundred years. When we had that first look at her in all of her precious total beauty, held in a pattern with all the other planets in our galaxy, we felt the "stuff" called love, which surrounds everything.

Once we began to realize that we were her children, the seeds of reconciliation were planted in our minds. The cycles are inevitable and we must decide to reunite as one family. Every one of us *knows* this *now*.

All through this writing of *Crystal Love Secrets* it has been repeated: everything is related to everything. We must begin to make peace within ourselves to make peace on Earth. We must begin to practice family love within our own family before the family of humans can have a coming together.

I hope you notice I include myself in the "we" because I want to learn a higher way of loving my family, too.

Family disagreements are common and widespread, nothing new, everyone experiences this sometimes. The New Age is coming to teach us to hold fast to the basic rules of successful relationships: (1) openness, (2) trust, (3) respect.

1. If you and I have a conflict, to prove that I am living and acting in a new way, I must be willing to talk to you, not to lie, and to be open to hearing what you say to me.
2. I have to trust myself to tell the truth. I have to trust that you will hear me and be fair.

3. I have to respect you as a mirror, showing me the parts of myself I do not recognize.

The family includes everyone connected through blood, marriage, or adoption. The mate and the mate's relatives are included whether or not there is a marriage certificate.

Often family conflict is an undercurrent of poison because no words are ever spoken. No one trusts themselves or the family *enough* to bring things into the open. Many sickening emotions and years are wasted because no one is willing to be open or vulnerable. Failing to have respect for the Spirit of a fellow human is more common with our family than with strangers. The Crystal Love Secret is to *have* no secrets. We are all in this together.

> Love is a force . . . it is not a result; it is a cause. It is not a product; it produces, it is a power, like money or steam or electricity. It is valueless unless you can give something else by means of it.

> **—Anne Morrow Lindbergh**
> *Locked Rooms and Open Doors*

Let all of us begin now to consider changing our "mind-set" toward that group or certain someone in our family (or friends) who has kept anger and strife alive and deadly to our health and happiness. Let us reconcile our Earth family.

The Larimar Meditation

Follow the procedure for all crystal active meditation exercises. Place the crystal upon:

Solar Plexus: Repeat two minutes—"This Larimar is vibrating to help my inner child make peace with my family (or personal name)."

Heart: "This crystal is vibrating to help my Spirit recognize the Spirit of————, who is playing a role for me."

Forehead: "The blue/green ray of Larimar is penetrating my Mental Body to erase old hurts and opinions."

There is no harvest for the heart alone;
the seed of love must be eternally resown.

—Anne Morrow Lindbergh
"Second Sowing"

Azurite-Malachite-Chrysocolla Aggregate for Friendship

Treat your friends as you do your pictures, and place them in their best light.

—Jennie Jerome Churchill
1854–1921

CHEMICAL COMPOSITION: Azurite: $Cu_3(OH)_2(CO_3)_2$ (basic copper carbonate)
CRYSTAL SYSTEM: Monoclinic, short or dense earthy aggregates
COLOR: Dark blue
HARDNESS: $3\frac{1}{2}$–4 on Mohs' scale
MALACHITE: $Cu_2CO_3(OH)_2$ (basic copper carbonate)
CRYSTAL SYSTEM: Same as Azurite
COLOR: Three-toned green
HARDNESS: Same as Azurite
PLANETS AND COLOR RAYS: Saturn, Uranus—Green, Blue
LOVE QUOTIENT: New thoughts for old relationships

Azurite-Malachite-Chrysocolla are formed by carbonated-water action on copper compounds or copper solutions upon limestones. It is most commonly found in Azurite-Malachite or Chrysocolla amorphous aggregate or Chalcedony Quartz forms. When drusy (baby) Quartz crystals form on top of Chrysocolla-Azurite aggregate, it is called Gem Silica.

The most well-known sources in the United States are Bisbee and Morenci, Arizona; Kelly, New Mexico; and around copper deposits found in Michigan and Pennsylvania. Found alone, the Azurite crystallizes in spherical aggregates in Chile, Russia, and around Chessy, France.

In the ancient Roman writings by Pliny, it was called Caeruleum. It has also been written of as Lapis Linguis, not to be confused with Lapis Lazuli.

Artists have used it to crush into powder and mix with oil for paints.

Cleopatra and Egyptian women used the powder to paint their eyelids.

There are also stones coming from Israel and the Middle East with mixed blue and green that are called Eliat stones. In appearance they look very similar.

PSYCHIC HEALING QUALITIES

Edgar Cayce, the most famous psychic in the U.S. of this century, gave several readings to persons seeking his advice in which he recommended this gem.

A survey of psychic readings concerning gem-crystals

published in 1977 listed readings about Azurite from Paul Soloman and Tracy Johnson as well as Cayce.

According to Soloman the stone was considered of great power in ancient Egypt. The use of the gem was shrouded in mystery as only the high priestesses were allowed the sacred information. Soloman recommends it be used to stimulate visual impulses and to clarify dreams.

Tracy Johnson suggests it would assist in helping us to communicate with ourselves. It will stimulate psychic awareness. It could be taped to the forehead during sleep or meditation to clarify dreams or visualizations.

Michael's Gemstone Dictionary, channeled by J. P. Van Hulle in 1986, is based on the teachings of an entity written of as appearing to a group in San Francisco for several years in the midseventies. The qualities afforded to Azurite by this group are communication enhancement and softening of stubbornness.

Katrina Raphaell, a nurse operating a healing center in Taos, New Mexico, had channeled the information in her book *Crystal Enlightenment* that Azurite moves subconscious thoughts into the conscious mind. Placed on any area of the physical body where energy is blocked, it will open the flow again.

Doris Hodges first published information she had researched in 1961, calling her book *Healing Stones*. She refers to the ancient name as Lapis Lingua (Chrysocolla). She gives them equal properties of healing and communication within the wave length beyond the Earth plane. She also mentions the borax present in Chrysocolla-Malachite. The stones were carried to fight off the cholera plaguing the ancient miners.

In 1976, Julia Lorusso and Joel Glick channeled their book *Healing Stoned*. Azurite is said to be coming into its power to replace the Sapphire reflecting the blue ray for the New Age. The healing qualities are listed as being able to change diseased tissue "like a radioactive isotope." In the future they feel Azurite will affect humans to develop the "sixth and seventh senses."

FINDINGS FROM MY PRACTICE

When displaying a tray of "healing crystals" to clients, they are asked to handle all the stones in the tray. When there is a preference for Azurite-Malachite-Chrysocolla, there is frequently unfinished business within the blood family of the client, or a definite rift in a close platonic friendship.

LOVE QUOTIENT

The blue ray, green ray, and aqua ray transmitted by this aggregate crystal stone are the messages from Uranus, Saturn, and an unknown source. They appear to encourage new thought (Uranus) concerning an old structure (Saturn) that has been the family unit and/or significant friends.

For those who choose to stay close to the family circle, to focus primary interaction with parents, brothers, sisters, cousins, aunts, uncles, or grown children, there is a special need for expanding awareness.

For those who choose to shift this energy onto friendships, the same needs will surface. There appears to be the tendency in human relationships to continue to "act out" our feelings toward our family members with new people we call friends.

Some recent discoveries of Azurite aggregate include a fourth substance called Red Jasper. This appears to be a visual trigger for clients who are specifically involved in emotional situations with their hidden anger. It increases their desire to negotiate a happy settlement.

Carole King sings to all of us who crave good friendly outcomes to misunderstandings in the lyrics to "You've Got a Friend."

No matter how we cut it, we are judged by the company we keep. Friendship is a necessary and intricate part of learning to be a fully functioning human. There are many old, trite sayings concerning the company we keep, such as, "birds of a feather flock together." The basic emotion that drives a person will attract other persons with the same vibration in their solar plexus. Angry young men find others like themselves and form gangs. People who like to sing usually get together in choruses, choirs, or as musical entertainers. Folks who like to move around have many brief friendships. People with roots may have fewer relationships, which last for years, and can be either stimulating or incredibly boring.

Lonely people make friends with animals or impersonal humans such as bus drivers or store clerks. Friendship is imperative in some form. The human life must express and partake of some level of the "stuff" that holds it all together called love. Intimate or distant, friendship is the next best thing to passion.

It is difficult to distinguish friendship from our family ties because often our relatives are our best friends also. In this treatise the Azurite-Malachite and Larimar are interchangeable for family or friends. However, Larimar seems to be chosen more often by clients who have specific family things to resolve.

The following are experimental affirmations that we are using at the present time. If there are any responses that you the reader can add to our meditation exercises, please write to us with your experiences. We are all in this together and we welcome all information.

Azurite-Malachite-Chrysocolla Aggregate Meditation

Follow the procedure for all crystal meditations. Place the crystal upon:

Solar Plexus: Say aloud seven times—"This Azurite is vibrating to allow my true feelings for my family (or friend) to arise." (Use their names here if you wish.)

Heart: "This Azurite is vibrating to activate my Spirit body to handle this situation with my (member of family or friend and use his or her name)."

Forehead: "This Azurite is vibrating to allow my Mental Body to send messages of healing and peace to my (friend or family and use his or her name)."

After this active meditation you will be stimulated to feel and think differently. Please keep a notebook or a cassette recorder handy. Make some notation every day, for at least twenty-eight days.

When you make a record of the thoughts or feelings that come to the surface during your meditation exercise, please begin each sentence with your own name! Pretend that you are taking dictation from the Universal Intelligence.

If you prefer, you may use a cassette recorder and simply speak these messages aloud.

After twenty-eight days of doing this exercise you will have many new realizations about yourself. You will now be prepared for efficient self-direction.

PART VII

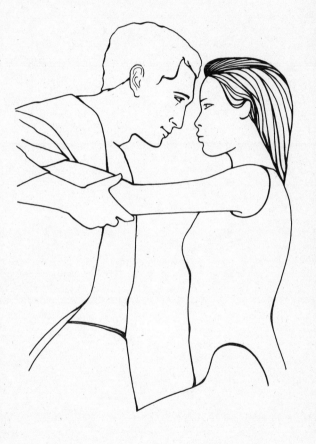

PASSION STONES

Passion Stones

> If we are unable to make passion a relationship of duration surviving the destructions and erosions of daily life, it still does not divest passion of its power to transform, transfigure, and transmute.
>
> **—Anaïs Nin**

Love, passion, and proper channeling of the creative/sexual Kundalini energy is still a challenge to the human race.

The giving we do in a state of passion offers total surrender of the self, much as Christ gave on the cross. The misunderstanding and misuse of the sexual creative power is the most mysterious to us. We can only experience the fulfillment of unity when we totally surrender our will to control another.

The death of selfish or purely material desire must

occur within all of us to be reborn as a spiritual desire for creative, caring love.

Conventional fears and inhibitions, self-consciousness, or judgment are lost in our passion. What we gain, whether in sexual or other creative expressions, is that elated, pure, and creative state of being known as self-satisfaction (not to be confused with the counterfeit emotion of conceit).

The element of fire in our lives produces a physical and emotional heat. It also produces light. The fire element is necessary in the everyday life of each individual as it manifests the will to live vibrating from the red ray of the planet Mars and the burgundy ray of Pluto.

The red ray is a primary color. It creates a primal, instinctual response in each of us to survive and to re-create ourselves so that our vibration remains active in the Universe through our children and future generations.

The red ray of fire also ignites a flame of passion that must be in a state of explosion for the burst of energy that creates either a new physical being on Earth or a new vision, thought, or action. The energy of the red ray affirms new life. The season of spring begins with Aries, ruled by the planet Mars, a time bursting forth with blossoms and leaves. Impregnation of the blossoms is done by the bees as their response to the Mars energy. "Busy as a bee" is an apt description of the positive Mars energy. All of the plant and animal kingdoms respond to the vibrations of Mars during this cycle of re-creating themselves.

The burgundy vibration of Pluto is in operation with Mars for many months when the human reproductive cycle begins. The burgundy ray is the deep, dark red of sexual surrender. It is the dying of the self, the allowing of vulnerability, and the transformation of independence to attachment through coupling, cooperation, and cocreation.

Orgasm is called the little death because the male offers a portion of his life force. The female sacrifices her freedom as a self-directed, independent single unit. The dark fire of sexual passion transforms both into spiritually driven, cocreating forces.

Through their lovemaking they experience a moment of oneness, a transforming act that changes them both forever. Their molecules have been mixed. Their Emotional bodies are intertwined, but so are the Spiritual and Mental bodies that exist in the aura surrounding their physical selves.

They may each forget or purposely put away from memory the occasion of their completion. However, it continues to exist as a change in the electromagnetic vibratory field that surrounds each.

If the outcome is positive, the individuals show signs of rejuvenation because there was an equal energy exchange. If the outcome is not balanced, each person is diminished. With the planetary burgundy ray of Pluto, there is no such thing as neutral reaction. It will transform, positively or negatively.

Eastern religions that infiltrated the Western world make millions of dollars teaching Americans to kill their desire. Americans feel guilty for being so creative, productive, and prosperous, yet we support or feed most of the countries that are professing the Eastern path to spiritual bliss. Their program of expecting nothing, desiring nothing, and doing nothing has produced nothing. The red and burgundy rays have stimulated only their sexual desires because the single most apparent result of their creative desire has been overpopulation.

Most of us think of passion in terms of animal lust, of loosening our straitjacket of controlled emotions to an unbridled outpouring of physical expression.

But passion is also the action of an individual directed toward any creative function. The desire of a poet to create reaches a vibrational rate of passion. The outpouring of a painter, sculptor, composer, inventor, writer, architect, etc., equals sexual passion's vibrational rate. In all instances it becomes a giving and a receiving. In order to receive, we must first give. This is an indisputable law of the Universe.

In the present age we have seen a pronounced emphasis on diseases of the life-giving organs resulting from the abuse of creative forces. The spread of AIDS and herpes has already begun to change some minds about promiscuity. The ancient knowledge and philosophies of Tantric Yoga and the Kundalini forces all deal with the transformation of the sexual urge toward physical union with another into the creative, spiritual union with the Universal Mind, Creator, God.

The Fire Opal from Mexico, being clear and pure and red, corresponds in every vibration to true passion. If this Opal is used in meditation, it will stimulate both the sexual and mental creative passions, discriminating between the two and directing the energy into the intended perfect balance.

There are various disturbances of the regenerative systems in women that can be attributed to negative mind-set that comes from imbalance. Feeling restricted often causes the pain that accompanies women's monthly cycle. Domination by another person, or the attempt to dominate someone else, can cause constriction and pain near the ovaries.

Sterility can be caused by hatred, fear, or anxiety. The fallopian tubes may close tightly when there is some hidden hostility toward the mate. This same symptom can occur if strong parental threats concerning sex are carried over into marital relationships. These are examples of how the invisible bodies are affecting the physical activities. On the surface, these problems appear to be distinctly medical. When crystals are used in daily exercises, the Emotional Body and the Mental Body are treated.

In the male, impotence can often be traced to childhood feelings of hostility toward the female, usually the mother. The prostate problems suffered by men can sometimes be traced to infidelity, either within the marriage or a close relationship. Sometimes the triangle is not reality but rather a mind function, such as occurs when a father-daughter relationship or a mother-son affection is so strong it negates the other parent.

There are crystals that will balance the chemicals of the yin-yang principle that have far-reaching effects on anyone using them sincerely. Time spent concentrating upon the vibration of the Red Garnet would bring about the perfect comprehension of the individual using it, relating to their male-female perfection within. For a man, his inner woman would develop, making his associations with the other half of the world population harmonious and pleasing. For a woman, her inner man would develop, vastly improving all her relationships and her understanding of her counterparts.

The Garnet transmits the rays of Pluto into our bodies through the "power center of life." That is a thinking area of the actual mind system located in the generative organs. The use of the generative organs during our past and present evolution has been strictly on a material-physical level. We were commanded to create more of ourselves and to populate the Earth.

Pluto's ray-waves will transform that strictly physical life-giving power center into a spiritual life-giving power center. We will learn the interaction of true love that gives life itself meaning.

The vibration arising from the passion crystal of this sexual geometry is the ability to raise love from the erotic level to the sensitive heart level. In the case of anyone who is "waiting" for love, this vibration will raise their awareness to the love that already exists. With a stimulated heart, they will be able to recognize and respond to that higher aspect of love—not discounting the sexual, but elevating the spirit of each. Continually to wish that my parents were different in their love for me or that my children were different in their love for me or that my lover were different in his love for me is to constantly negate the love that *does exist* from them. To be waiting constantly in expectation for that one great love to envelop us and overcome all our disappointments is like holding our breath for a lifetime. It will only make us one of the "living" dead.

The Ruby stimulates the heart, the heart thinks on its own. When this "mind in the heart" is stimulated, devotion activates a new love understanding.

The Ruby examined in this new look at crystals with love is the Star Ruby. This crystal is becoming more prevalent at this special time in history also. At the world's largest gem and mineral show in Tucson, Arizona, in 1988, 1989, and 1990, there were many more Star Rubies offered than I have ever experienced at any previous time or place. I believe Mother Earth is giving us another Crystal Love Secret.

Star Ruby—
Six Points of Passion

Not from me the cold, calm kiss of a virgin's bloodless love!

—Ella Wheeler Wilcox
1855–1919

CHEMICAL COMPOSITION: A_2O_3 (aluminum oxide) contains Rutile (titanium crystals, TiO_2)
CRYSTAL SYSTEM: Hexagonal (trigonal), flat-ended, six-sided rhombohedrons or plates
COLOR: Silky, dark bloodred; polished *en cabochon* shows star
HARDNESS: 9½ on the Mohs' scale
PLANETS AND COLOR RAYS: Mars, Moon, Sun—Red, Silver, Multiray
LOVE QUOTIENT: Passion in six ways

The Ruby is from the same "root" gem as the Sapphire, called corundum, derived from the Sanskrit *kuruvinda*.

The bright, clear red to pink color is caused by the element chromium replacing the aluminum of the Sapphire. Chromium causes a bright red fluorescence in the precious Ruby. A bit of ferric iron sometimes adds a slight orange cast to the red, or a slight amount of aluminum may give the red a small purplish glint.

Rubies are second in value only to Diamonds, being 9½ on the Mohs' scale of 1 to 10 in hardness. There are so few Rubies unflawed in anything over five carats that anything larger is more valuable than a Diamond of equal quality and size. The finest Rubies occur near Mogok, Burma, in crystals up to two inches in length. Cambodia, Thailand, Celon, India, Tanzania, and Australia are all sources. The latest finds have been in Norway and in the Ural Mountains of Russia. Small, pink cut Rubies are made from the pebbles gathered in streambeds of the Orient. Very few raw specimens ever leave the country of origin, as gem-quality stones are immediately faceted for greater value.

The Ruby replaces the lack of self-esteem that can cause all kinds of self-destructive behavior with the vibration that teaches the holder he is valuable and deserving of life, to the greatest heights of abundance. The Ruby will bring to its owners a sense of excitement within themselves that gives purpose to living. This is the very essence of our Creators within us.

The Life Force or Vital Energy resides in the sacral region and must be coaxed upward through the solar plexus to the heart. The stimulation of the solar plexus is the function of the adrenal glands, accomplished by emotional thought.

Our emotions govern every function of our bodies. The negative emotional thought that can damage our body through overstimulation of the adrenal glands is fear. When the Ruby is used with knowledge by the holder, fear is removed because it cannot remain in the same body with love. To truly love the Self is to be rid of all guilt and fear, with the knowledge that we are capable of the same creativity and goodness as our Creator. Believing this, and affirming it while contemplating the Ruby, restores the full potential of purpose, will, and creativity to life. When these three emotions that govern the Universe are healthy in people, they experience renewed interest in all facets of life, love, and passion. A belief in the positive outcome of every endeavor will then grow. Helen Keller understood and responded to this when she said, "Life is either a fantastic adventure or it is nothing."

The Star Ruby is a most exciting stone when polished correctly. It is not meant to be cut in facets like a Diamond, but to be shaped with a rounded, smooth dome. When this is accomplished, the Rutile (titanium) needle-like crystals inside the stone reflect light into the six-sided geometry of the Ruby. This produces a miracle called asterism (astral plane, astrology, asteroid, etc.), which we see as a silver, six-pointed star. As we move the stone around in the light, the star moves also.

As a rough crystal these Rubies appear dull and greasy. Humans have learned how to bring out of hiding this love secret of nature.

In the U.S., Rubies with asterism are sometimes found in North and South Carolina, Alabama, Georgia, or Montana.

There are many synthetic Star Rubies available because some years ago a scientist named Linde learned how to produce them by growing crystals in the laboratory. Any jeweler recognizes a "Lindy Star" because it is too perfect, and a lighter red than the ones produced naturally by Earth. The Lindy Star is expensive also. Do not be misled.

The Star Rubies I purchased in Tucson were not terribly expensive because they were not the most exquisite. The red is very dark, but as long as the star is visible, one knows the Rutile (titanium) is present, and the vibration can be measured.

LOVE AND PASSION SECRETS

The crystals within this crystal hold a key to the message it sends to us. Titanium is a metallic crystal named for one of the moons of Jupiter. In Greek mythology, the god Titan was a giant of great strength and power. Titanium is used with steel in aircraft and satellites. It has come to prominence in this new age, yet is named after a god of antiquity. Why have so many new metallic substances been named for the planets? (Uranium-Uranus, plutonium-Pluto, etc.) Why did the scientists name the planets after mythological gods? Aren't myths just ancient fairy tales? *Are they?* Or is Dr. Carl Jung right about myth? Is Joseph Campbell correct in his lifetime investigations worldwide of all native myths? Their findings show that all cultures and all races have the *same* myths. Their conclusions are that mythmaking is the human superconscious knowing of metaphysical, unseen *truth*. We all know how the Universe works because we are all *part* of it.

In myth, Titan represents strength and power, larger than life. Titanium Rutile crystals in the Star Ruby represent the first point of passion-strength. There is nothing weak about passion. There is no such thing as a little bit of passion, just as there is no such thing as partially pregnant. Passion is not a measured thing. We are either passionate or not.

I love people with a sense of humor; I want more humor in my life. I've always taken things too seriously, so I'm told. I like people who have a daring passion for humor, such as Phyllis Diller. In 1966 she wrote a book, *Phyllis Diller's Housekeeping Hints*. Her passionate advice to lovers was "Never go to bed mad. Stay up and fight!" "Oh, goodness no," you say, "that's not loving." But it is, because loving consists of the strength to continue communication all the way through a disagreement, until the passion of anger subsides.

One of the greatest lessons I have learned from a Taurus Rising lover is the physical stamina of the Bull (Taurus) to continue talking on and on into the night with a quest for resolution. I am learning to accept that his marvelous sexual stamina has its dark side! Just as we all are like a coin, our heads cannot be separated from our tails!

> The steel for the finest swords is thrust into the fire ten thousand times.
>
> **—Kung Fu saying**

The second ray of the Star Ruby is commitment. In order for any one of history's great humans to become great, they had to be passionate! They believed in their mission and were committed to it. Nothing took them away from their path for long.

Florence Nightingale was a committed and passionate

healer. She went into battle and tackled the gigantic task of patching up and nursing back to wholeness complete armies of men.

Mother Teresa is a passionate, committed advocate, feeding the poor and homeless. Her life is totally committed.

In a loving relationship we have a mission, an ideal, no different from the mission of the first prime minister of India who was a Feminine Energy, Indira Gandhi, or the first female to rule the Philippines, Corazon Aquino. Margaret Thatcher, former prime minister of Great Britain, and Violeta Chamorro, the newly elected president of Nicaragua, have dedicated their lives to a political idea and they are committed to their mission. The mission we have to produce a loving relationship is commitment to the *relationship*. It is a separate entity unto itself.

The third ray of the Star Ruby is courage. Passion takes courage, true passion *makes* courage. Joseph Campbell uses a phrase that seems to characterize this very well. "Libido over credo"; opening of the heart to another, even when the law is against it, or the religious belief denies it. The courage to love in the face of all obstacles is the courage of going through the fire of public opinion. We can all remember when the first marriages took place between Catholics and Protestants; then Catholics married Jews! Our parents and grandparents were outraged, and many families broke apart. The next step brought even more denial, anger, and pain when whites married Asians or blacks. "Libido over credo" was the flame of passion displayed as courage, against all odds. They were *heroes*, and we enjoy the freedom to choose a loving relationship with anyone on

Earth! We take this for granted. Our freedom was purchased with their strength, commitment, and courage.

The fourth ray of the star is consistency: to do the same things in the same way every day without fail, and to a high standard. This at first sounds rather boring or monotonous. However, excellence requires consistency. Two examples: (1) When we go to a restaurant to buy a meal, *we* decide if the place is going to be successful. If their food and service are *consistently* good, we will return. If the things we liked the first time are *consistent* on the second trip, we begin to trust. When the customers find consistent high standards, the owner is a success. (2) When an athlete wants to be a champion, he or she sets up a routine of practice. The same exercises are done at the same time each day. The winner wins because "practice makes perfect." The consistency trains brain and muscle to act automatically.

The fifth ray of the Ruby Star is cocreating. In a committed, strong, courageous, consistent effort toward building a relationship, the partners need to be focused on contributing to the thing they are building. When two people agree to work together, it is an agreement for each one to contribute equally in his own best-talented way to get the job done. Our Stone Age ancestors figured this one out a million years ago. The division of responsibilities between Male and Female Energy was sufficiently honored by each to bring us along this far.

The evolution toward more consciousness than just surviving has put pressure on humanity to move the emphasis from instinctual survival (the lowest primal chakra center in the genitals) up the body to the solar plexus (personal feelings of self-emotion) and now toward the heart (spiritual quest for at-onement).

Just merely dividing the labor between partners is not enough for the survival of the partnership. Now our Spirit cries out for understanding and affection, sympathy, empathy, kindness, caring, similar desires, a goal together. We are no longer required to pool our labor to survive. We can survive alone, without a partner.

The catch is this: Without the polarity of yin and yang, it is not possible to get the spark. No electricity! In studying the lives of persons we as a human family consider to be great among us, there are few, very few, who have left anything of value. Of those few, most all had the interaction of energy exchange with an opposite-sex person. Creativity needs a cocreator. Artists, musicians, poets, writers, politicians, religious leaders, leaders in battle, conquerors, philosophers, have been shown throughout history as having an opposite-sex person as a cocreator somewhere in the background. The ones who never married (such as popes, priests, or nuns) were not necessarily celibate. Many are listed as unattached by legal marriage (such as Michelangelo, Auguste Rodin, or Jesus) yet had a constant female companion.

The Designing Creative Force in the Universe is a dual entity and we are programed to be cocreators. In a successful relationship, both horses are pulling the same wagon, headed for the same destination. One may rest while the other strains, one may lead while the other follows, taking equal turns, each trusting the other will pull. Each horse may be thinking of different green pastures for periods of rest and reward. Each may have different memories of his or her past, but the task at hand is cocreating the journey.

The sixth ray of the Star as a point of passion is completion. Just as in a passionate period of lovemaking the completion is the explosion of the orgasm, so in relationship building are there levels of completion.

When humans have loving sexual encounters, this in itself is the completion of true passion. Physical completion such as climax for both parties may not take place. The affection, touching, commingling, of their invisible Emotional bodies on the molecular level is what the Spirit Body craves. Just to be an acceptable part of another—to come together—to feel unseparated, is our human desire to go back to our source, expressed in the concrete physical form of the Earth level of being. Most contemporary spiritually inclined philosophers say plainly, humans want to go back to their beloved Creator and mistake this urge for what they can find as a substitute on Earth, which is searching for a mate.

Psychologists and mind scientists put it into earthy terms and say each person is searching to find replacement of a mother or father. The definition of a mate is like that of a parent: "Someone who accepts me unconditionally, who will nourish, console, and protect me."

Whatever we choose to call this urge, it is the force within each human for completion, because we feel incomplete.

When we practice completion in our relationship, we bring both good projects and bad experiences to an end. The couple together decides what is the outcome they desire on any project, set up a plan of action, a projected time of completion, and go forward. They may have to rethink or renegotiate along the way. The alternative may be to abandon the project.

This can cover a broad spectrum between cooking dinner, landscaping the yard, taking a vacation, building a business, or the big project of building a monogamous significant relationship.

Renegotiation and/or abandonment of the project is sometimes a viable and justified way of completion. Forgiving and forgetting is completion of each stumbling block along the way. Complete and banish old debts, bad memories, and unfulfilled desires or dreams. Completion is fulfilling. Completion feels good.

Completion can also be what one partner gives to the "relationship entity" to fulfill a gap, because the other person cannot. Each person in contributing to the entity has his or her own special talents. In a truly satisfactory partnership, the talents of both are analyzed, and participation proceeds by "who does what best!" Each partner completes the other partner.

Completion of a relationship may never take place. It may go on indefinitely in this lifetime or many lifetimes, but renegotiation can change the form. Dissolution as live-in lovers can change to social friendship or vice versa. Death of a partner can change the form of the relationship from partner to invisible helper.

Passionate loving relationships can be helped by Star Ruby. Try this twenty-eight-day active meditation exercise.

Star Ruby Meditation

Follow the methods of all other crystal meditations. Hold the Star Ruby against your body at the:

Solar Plexus: Say aloud seven times—"This Star Ruby is vibrating to bring me courage and strength in passionate loving."

Heart: "This crystal is bringing cosmic help for my commitment and consistency in relationships."

Forehead: "This Ruby is transmitting the red ray of cocreating and completion in my relationships."

Red Garnet
for Sexual Arousal

Minutes pass in silence. . . . It is those few minutes that pass after we make love that are most mysterious to me, uncanny.

—Joyce Carol Oates
The Wheel of Love, 1967

CHEMICAL COMPOSITION: $Fe_3Al_2(SiO_4)_3$ (silicate iron)
CRYSTAL SYSTEM: Cubic or isometric—crystals have multiple faces from four to twenty-four; they appear man-cut
COLOR: Dark red
HARDNESS: $7-7\frac{1}{2}$ on Mohs' scale
PLANET AND COLOR RAY: Pluto—Burgundy
LOVE QUOTIENT: Sexual-spiritual balance

The Garnet is an uncanny crystal! The geometric perfection of a dodecahedron (twelve sides), octohedron (eight sides), and the other multiples of four this precise crystal uses to crystallize itself are such a wondrous tribute to the Designing Creative Force in the Universe.

Garnets are found in Canada and in Alaska, Colorado, Connecticut, Idaho, and Michigan. The best gems are from India, Africa, and Madagascar. The most precious crystals have been found in Hungary.

Garnet crystals are found in less than pea size up to . . . amazing! I have one from Idaho the size of a baseball with twelve faces.

The elements that cause the color and structure of this natural phenomenon are aluminum (feminine Moon ray) and iron (masculine red Mars ray). The dark red Garnet will also have inclusions that present a six-rayed star sometimes. The burgundy ray of Pluto is the basic vibration of the Garnet, which makes the Star Garnet almost black-red.

The planet Pluto, Mars, and the Moon vibrations entering and transmitting this burgundy ray through the Garnet directly affects the lowest chakra of the energy body; it is the root of life. The underworld, the dark recesses of inner Earth of caves, caverns, and subterranean passages is a world of mystery and adventure.

To an emerging Earthling in any society from our cave-dwelling ancestors to the present, *sex* is a mysterious, compelling, fearsome, delicious, desirable, sinful, holy quest for fulfillment. When we eventually experience the sexual connection with another human, sometimes it is disappointing.

Sex seems to be evolving as a "human expression"; the need to procreate more Earthlings is long past. Now the act of sexual contact between two humans is in a state of transformation. The Goddess energy returning to Earth has given those in female form more courage to ask for personal satisfaction and pleasure. The words *love, romance*, and *intimacy* have come into our vocabulary and sometimes into our experience. Sex just isn't sex anymore, it is a quest for self-fulfillment, body, mind, and spirit.

> Women complain about sex more often than men. Their gripes fall into two categories: (1) not enough, (2) too much.

> **—Ann Landers**
> 1968

I remember the only time my inhibited, merchant, Southern Baptist, Leo-birthday father ever said anything close to funny. I overheard him saying, "Business is like sex. When it's good, it's wonderful, and when it's bad, it's still pretty good."

The Male Energy has a somewhat more liberal or generous view of the physical act than the Female Energy wants to accept. Those of us who have chosen to come back to Earth during this sexual revolution have had a chance to exploit the plain, cold act of sex as a tension release. Guess what? It didn't relieve any tension at all; we created more. More crimes of sexual violence have occurred, including murder, than ever before in history recorded. Now, *killing* is the only thing we can do to relieve our tension!

We have committed crimes upon ourselves and our fellow Earthlings by living without passion, without romance, without intimacy, without love. The sexual act alone will no longer fulfill our desire. We are in a state of sexual, spiritual transformation. To be sexually aroused is not enough.

The planet Pluto has been in the constellation of stars

called Scorpio since 1984. Both planet and stars rule sex and the unseen forces of nature. Scorpio rules occult wisdom, which simply means facts and practices that are known by a select few people on Earth at any given time.

The Art of Sexual Ecstasy (J. P. Tarcher, 1990) by Margo Anand is a comprehensive guide in spiritual sex by a former student of Osho Rajneesh. She said: "We need a planetary sexual healing to transcend the separation between flesh and spirit, which has been implemented for centuries by Christianity and other fundamental religions."

LOVE QUOTIENT

The Plutonian burgundy ray transmitted by the Red Garnet is a transforming vibration. Both Male and Female energies must wake up the lower chakra and move the basic, primitive energy of sexuality up through the body. In ancient Hindu yogic practices this sexual energy is called the Kundalini. It is pictured as a serpent, coiled and waiting at the base of our spine. If we abandon it there, despised, we wither like a sour prune. We cannot condemn that creative energy as sinful or bad. If we use it only at that level, a low level, unsatisfying physical exercise is all we get out of sex. A good workout at the gym would do us more good! Having sex without raising the Kundalini energy up through the body to the heart and eventually the head (hypothalamus) is a starvation diet for our Spirit. Use the Red Garnet to raise Sexual Energy.

We call sex lovemaking. I don't believe we can "make" love. I tend to agree with Kahlil Gibran, the poet. Love is an entity, a force that comes to us when we are found worthy. Having sex does not make love come to us.

In my previous book, *Crystal Healing Secrets*, the chapter on Red Garnet speaks to the sexually dysfunctional men and women who are angry and punishing themselves or their mates. Sex is often used as a tool of hate and anger or control. It is not automatically a sign of love or respect. Sex is the last thing that needs to take place in a new relationship. Spirit-satisfying sex follows this path: *friendship, romance, intimacy* (psychological, emotional, intellectual), and finally *sex*. Arouse your Sexual Energy and bring it up to "high sex." When we have the wisdom and Self-love to follow this path, *sex* is always an expression of love. If the one you want to be with cannot wait for the sweet walk down this path, let them take the shortcuts with someone else. You have lost nothing. It is always your choice. Choose spiritually satisfying sex—"Just say no."

There is currently a war against drugs being fought by the U.S. government. It has chosen the slogan "Just say no." Now it is time to use this slogan whenever the idea of "sex without love" enters the scene. It is destructive and causes guilt, anger, self-disgust, and misplaced anger at the other person. The Red Garnet can restructure your will.

Many associations that begin with high hopes that love will "develop" leave us surprised when things go wrong. The Red Garnet will also help to remember past lives, past loves, with this same person in our present incarnation. Remembering how we interacted in the past can explain the karmic debts we may have to the other now.

(Karma is the philosophy of reincarnation, which believes we must relive a lesson until we get it right.)

The Red Garnet can help to solve our mysteries of love. Try it in a twenty-eight-day active meditation exercise.

Red Garnet Meditation for High Sex

Follow the methods for all other crystal meditations in this book! Hold the Red Garnet on the:

Solar Plexus: Say aloud seven times—"This Red Garnet is focusing the cosmic rays of Pluto to my Desire Body to raise my Sexual Energy."

Heart: "This crystal is vibrating to pull the Sexual Energy up into my Spirit place."

Forehead: "This Garnet is opening up my memory to understand my sexual-spiritual lessons."

Mexican Fire Opal

Whoever loves true life will love true love.

—**Elizabeth Barrett Browning**
1806–1861

CHEMICAL COMPOSITION: $SiO_2 \bullet nH_2O$
CRYSTAL SYSTEM: Amorphous, still under investigation
COLOR: Bright, clear, transparent red to orange
HARDNESS: $4\frac{1}{2}$–$5\frac{1}{2}$ on Mohs' scale
PLANET AND COLOR RAYS: Mars, Vulcan—Red, Multiray
LOVE QUOTIENT: Passion and creativity

As you might have guessed, this red, transparent Opal is nothing like the multicolored Opal from Australia. The major and best deposits are found in Mexico. It is also found in Brazil, Guatemala, Honduras, U.S., Western Australia, and Turkey. Glass imitations are also being sold to unwary buyers.

Sometimes it may be called Sun Opal or even Sunflower Opal. Like all other Opals it is best displayed by using a domed, oval, round, polished shape called cabochon by lapidaries. It must be set properly in jewelry as it is sensitive to stress.

The pure red ray of Mars is clearly transmitted by this clear red crystal. The Masculine Energy of Mars is a thrust of forward, bold energy. This energy can be needed and used by men or women especially while making physically affectionate embraces and sexual activity expressing love.

There seem to be a number of excuses or reasons why some humans are unable to express love in sexual exchange. I have many clients both male and female of many ages who confess to a complete disappointment in physical love expression.

The major issue of *giving* love has been discussed thoroughly in this book. The ability to give love depends on our abundantly full cup of the love we give ourselves. However, if we need that extra push to overcome inhibitions, drilled into our brain computer by years of parental or societal *rules* against sexuality, Fire Opal will help.

The vibration of the crystal helps to release the endorphins in the brain that act as a tranquilizing, pleasure-increasing aphrodisiac. Pure pleasure is what we dream of, an unusual and difficult-to-explain state of being. The dream and the search have a tendency to put too much pressure on the outcome. The Fire Opal can stimulate and slow the pleasure. It can help to quiet the nagging and demands of our "monkey brain."

The distractions we feel in moments of romantic closeness that tend to take away the pleasure of the moment can be dissolved in advance by wearing and meditating with the Fire Opal. The pure passionate pleasure of giving and receiving the right "stuff" we call love, which flows through two people as they mix their invisible "aura" bodies and their physical bodies, is a blessing and a "right" of every living thing.

The pure passionate energy of the Fire Opal has no dark intention, no purposeful destructive or violent energy. It is pure, straightforward, adventuresome, exploration energy. The Fire Opal energy can be pictured as a young spirit, an innocent man, setting forth to find new horizons, an unspoiled, brave, curious, and strong Spirit. It is passion and zest for life in a fresh package.

> Liszt said to me today that God alone deserves to be loved. It may be true, but when one has loved a man, it is very different to love God.
>
> **—George Sand**
> Female author and lover of Chopin

Our sensual nature has been repressed in the name of moral law for two thousand years. It was in *divine order* as everything is. Now we are making the transition from the chaotic dichotomy of love or sin—to *love* understood. The last dying energies of the violent sexual conquest (one and a half million years is a hard habit to break) may be with us a long time yet. It will be determined by the ability of humanity to focus our minds in such a strong way as to fill the morphic field of thoughts surrounding Earth with ideas to teach all peoples who meditate. The reason we must sit in silence after each active meditation exercise is to *receive* information from that morphic field, or as Dr. Carl Jung called it, the Universal Unconscious.

One of the reasons we repeat positive affirmations of love during our active meditation exercises is to contribute positive information to the Cosmic Data Bank, morphic field, Universal Unconscious.

When 51 percent of all Spirits living on Earth receive these thoughts on love, this will be the critical mass needed to tip the scales. In order to receive the feelings as well as the *ideas* of pure spiritual passion in physical sexual love, we must allow our senses to explore what has been forbidden by religion.

The red ray of the Cosmos is called the builder, the energy that *does* things. The green ray is opposite and preserves what the red ray has built.

The Fire Opal is a fire-starter and is not to be confused with constancy. Passion cannot be constant; it is too exhausting to experience a fiery energy twenty-four hours a day. This crystal must be considered a short-term "medicine." When this crystal is chosen, I suggest the client wear it and use it only until the successful feelings of innocent sexual passion come. If the client has no relationship, this crystal will bring the sexual animal magnetism up to an attracting level. It will help to show a level of personal excitement to those around, so as to excite their interest in getting more energy exchange.

This crystal is a pure, clear vibration that speaks to our passionate little child and power animal in their most natural state. It has no vibration of violence or darkness. Sexual arousal and passionate, affectionate feelings of coming together with another person is a normal desire and state of being, healthy among all humans.

> In most issues of sexuality we know what we are *against*. A wholistic view requires that we know what we are *for*, and manifest that knowing in our attitudes and behavior.

> **—Louis R. Batzler, Ph.D.**

I have cassette tapes of affirmations that I require some clients to use daily while falling asleep at night. These are statements repeated to convince the subconscious (tough, dictator, parent side) how sexuality is good and we deserve good sexual relationships. If you will use the Fire Opal consistently for at least twenty-eight days, you will find in your own note-taking phrases you can use to make your own cassette of "permission to passion."

Fire Opal Meditation

Follow procedures for all crystal meditations in this book. Place the crystal on:

Solar Plexus: Say aloud seven times—"This Fire Opal is attracting the red ray of passion into my Desire Body."

Heart: "This red crystal is waking up my Spirit to recognize passion is good."

Forehead: "This crystal is a tool from Mother Earth to help me understand pure, creative, loving passion."

PART VIII

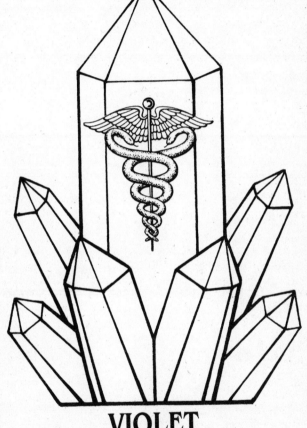

VIOLET
TRANSFORMATION
CRYSTALS

Violet Transformation Crystals

> No love is real without a unity of Eros and agape. Agape without Eros is obedience to moral law . . . without longing, reunion. Eros without agape is chaotic desire.
>
> **—Paul Tillich**

I have a confession to make; I am biased and prejudiced in favor of the violet ray! Many folks studying metaphysics today are saying the Earth is being totally enveloped by the violet ray.

In my early training in psychology, using the theories of Dr. Max Lüscher (*The Lüscher Color Test*, 1948), I discovered his findings on the color violet to be viable. In my own case, I did not want to admit the personality description of violet was so accurate.

Violet is the *first choice* color of a large number of preadolescent children. A desire for physical objects and surroundings of violet frequently proved the emotional, psychological state of a client to be overly idealistic. It is chosen not only by idealists but by artists and those sensitive to aesthetic beauty. The shades of violet, from pale orchid, lavender, through purple and ultraviolet, denote an emotional, psychological preference for non-physical reality—such as nature spirits and spirit guides, the vibrations of joy from a sunset rather than the crop a sunny summer produces. The negative side of this personality could be described as illogical, impractical, immature, unrealistic, air-head! Many of the worlds great artists, musicians, philosophers, and visionaries were described by their contemporaries as exactly thus!

I have vacillated between red, yellow, and violet all of my remembered life. The violet finally overcame the others in the midseventies when I followed the path of idealism out of the business world into the inner world of "mind" through psychology as total way of life. The influence of the violet ray was always hovering over me, and most of my work has been devoted to a search for a way to use art and beauty in a way to heal myself and others psychologically.

When I was introduced to Dr. Max Lüscher's work using color as an emotional indicator in psychological analysis, I was also studying another scientist's work. Dr. "Dinshah" had introduced the theories of healing with colored light. Dinshah P. Ghadiali (1873–1966) was a native of Bombay, India, graduated from Bombay University, and was eventually associated with electricity as an engineer. He met Thomas Edison and Nikola Tesla in 1896 when he was on a lecture tour in the U.S. to inform of his discoveries on radioactivity and X rays. In 1900 he founded the Electro-Medical Hall in Ajmer, India. There, teaching and healing using color, electromagnetism, mental science, and traditional medicine, he was especially successful on bubonic plague and other "incurables."

The scientific findings of these two researchers have never really been given sufficient recognition. There are many other persons and dedicated healers who have added research and professional-healing testimony to the invisible effect of cosmic colored rays and vibrations. They have proven these rays can be *directed* and *focused* to make physical and emotional changes in life. Please read the bibliography to find further writings.

The violet ray appears to hold much significance in my life and in those of many persons now studying metaphysics. It could be that a number of us have come back to Earth now (as a Group Soul) to make some significant changes in the understanding of *body, mind, spirit* connections to a formula for successful living.

Though I do not necessarily accept or condone all of their teachings, there is one Special Entity who has been recognized as an emissary of the violet ray.

The Summit Lighthouse, Summit University Press, has published channeled material concerning St. Germaine, the patron saint of all healers. A series of verses are attributed to St. Germaine as a means of healing by the spoken word. This theory of sound and healing is recognized by all religions, i.e., chanting, singing, instruments of music: organ, piano, harp, flute, and earliest sounds of drums.

The combination of vibrational healing by colored light and sound of the spoken word is basically an original metaphysical practice of the earliest Christian cathedrals, filled with colored-glass windows and chanting monks. Why do you think the shape of the building was so important with the specially constructed geometric vaulted ceilings? I spent eighteen months in Europe lying on the floors of cathedrals, photographing their ingeniously devised acoustics in the ceilings. All designed to *change* the vibrations for the worshipers, to make them *feel* better.

I hope you can now see why it is so important to repeat and chant an affirmation at the same time we are using the crystals to attract the colored-light vibration. It's slang definition would be in fact to give you a "double whammy"!

The violet ray enveloping Earth is a possible explanation for the voluminous amounts of communication taking place now in the forms of published, printed materials, books, cassettes in audio and video, magazines and newspapers, radio and television via satellite!

The violet ray is from Mercury. Mercury is the messenger of the gods; the staff of Mercury is the symbol for healing, the caduceus. This symbol is represented by the two serpents (male and female—electromagnetic) entwined in balance around the staff. The staff is a symbol for the spine, and the serpents represent balanced energy rising from the genitals to the top of the staff, which has wings. The wings represent angelic mind or higher thinking. The medical profession, which most despises such things as crystal therapy, chose this ancient metaphysical archetype as their model and reminder of true healing. The energy must be raised up through the body, through the mind, and into the Spirit to be whole, or holistic.

All healing and all healers are subject to the violet ray. Because I have dedicated my life to healing myself and passing on anything I learn to others, I believe this last group of crystals of transformation to be most important in learning the Crystal Love Secrets.

Amethyst— Healer, Forgiveness

I am forgiveness acting here
Casting out all doubt and fear
Setting me forever free, with wings of
   cosmic victory.

—Decrees of St. Germaine
Summit University Press

CHEMICAL COMPOSITION: $SiO_2(Mn?)$ (tektosilicate ion)
CRYSTAL SYSTEM: Hexagonal (trigonal)
COLOR: Pale lavender to dark purple, clear, transparent
HARDNESS: 7½ on Mohs' scale
PLANET AND COLOR RAY: Mercury—Violet
LOVE QUOTIENT: Healing, forgiveness

The complete history, myths, and magic of Amethyst are covered in my previous book, *Crystal Healing Secrets*. The healing qualities and methods are also explained. The Amethyst is versatile and can be used by anyone for any ailment. It is specifically controlling the upper chest and throat, speaking and breathing apparatus.

This writing concerns the secrets of love, and how they can be disclosed to us by using the Amethyst crystal to direct the violet cosmic ray from Mercury, the planet of communication.

One of the biggest stumbling blocks to love is the refusal to forgive and forget. Mercury rules the mind of humans and therefore is one of the planets that affects our ability to remember. In the process of loving there are many things we need to remember and just as many we need to forget. Forgiveness is one of the most important healing processes humans can accomplish in their quest to learn to love. To speak the words aloud to ourselves is the beginning of the act of forgiving. The first step in the act is to change the mind.

We build up a list of positive, complimentary things in our mental computer for each person in our lives. We also tabulate the things we find unattractive or even maddening. We take offense at certain actions or words and draw conclusions focusing on the worst connotations. We may even have such low self-esteem or be paranoid to such a degree that we actually imagine an intended effort to hurt us, coming from another. We may be angry over something and therefore perceive the other person as angry. There are many ways to concoct a rift in relationships, or to find our feelings hurt and to hold a grudge against someone. Unforgiveness festers like dirt in a wound. It won't heal until it is opened up and cleaned out!

When my clients are suffering (yes, *we* suffer from not forgiving others) because their love has been canceled by unforgiveness, they often choose Amethyst.

One of my clients had many relationships that seemed

to end because she felt the other person was not emotionally involved or was too detached. After some analysis done through a past-life psychic reading and a memory regression in this life, she found a long line of imagined betrayals from others.

In this life she blamed her father for being so distant and uninvolved with her life. She constantly chose lovers who appeared to be detached or uncommunicative. Her healing and enlightenment came when she used an Amethyst crystal in meditation exercises, speaking aloud how she was forgiving her father (deceased) for not being the kind of father she wanted. She also forgave herself for holding this grudge over imagined betrayal for so long.

She spoke aloud the names of all the men she had punished because she was angry with her father and asked each of them to forgive her. She forgave them for not being the kind of emotionally involved and affectionate men she wanted as lovers.

She continued to use the Amethyst for several years (also wearing it as an amulet), repeating the eight lines of the decrees of St. Germaine on forgiveness. She eventually was able to *change her mind*, eliminating the old thought patterns. She attracted an affectionate, emotionally involved relationship that is ongoing. There were intermediate relationships, and each one was a learning experience in communication.

LOVE QUOTIENT

Communication, the spoken word, is a great part of relating, and forgiving. To be free in speaking to a new relationship concerning our hopes and fears is of utmost importance. Being able to tell another person what we want can be a great victory over hoping they will "guess" or "read our mind." The voice, the ability to speak, comes from our *power center*, the throat chakra.

Telling another of the qualities we treasure in their actions toward us is a positive love builder. Speaking the healing words *I love you* every day, over and over, can never become trite because it comes from our place of power.

When there has been a misunderstanding or a quarrel, it is imperative to come into forgiveness as soon as possible. Speak the words aloud to yourself. Forgive *yourself* and the other. It takes two to tangle.

In most cases of unforgiveness, the anger is really self-anger, directed toward another, and not recognized.

The violet ray of Mercury the messenger and healer directed with Amethyst can change your mind and heal the hearts in love. Speak the words and forgive.

Amethyst Meditation

Follow the precedure for all crystal meditations. Hold the Amethyst against the:

Solar Plexus: Say aloud seven times—"This Amethyst is vibrating to reach my Emotional Body with understanding."

Heart: "This violet crystal is transmitting the forgiving rays of healing to my Spirit."

Forehead: "This crystal is helping me to change my mind, to speak the loving word *forgiveness*."

Sugilite— Transforming Love

I am changing all my garments,
Old ones for the bright new day:
With the sun of understanding
I am shining all the way.

—Decrees of St. Germaine
Summit University Press

CHEMICAL COMPOSITION: $(K,Na)(NaFe_3+)_2(LiFe_3+)$
$Si_{12}O_{30}$
CRYSTAL SYSTEM: Hexagonal
COLOR: Purple, magenta, burgundy
HARDNESS: $6\frac{1}{2}$ on Mohs' scale
PLANET AND COLOR RAY: Pluto—Burgundy; Space—
Black; Mercury—Violet
LOVE QUOTIENT: Transforming fear to love

The discovery of the planet Pluto in our solar system in
1930 may have signaled our Mother Earth to expose a

new crystal for our use. Pluto is known to astrologers as the planet of transformation, or in more direct terms, "death and rebirth."

A new crystal was discovered in Japan in 1944, not long before the explosions that changed the course of that nation forever. The Japanese people had a "death and rebirth." The crystalline-structured mineral was named after the distinguished petrologist Kenichi Sugi.

I find no other mention of the mineral until the mid-seventies. Mysteriously, a small group of Middle Eastern jewelers set up a corporation to market small polished pieces designed into Gold and Diamond jewelry. They trademarked the name for the stone as Royal Azel. It was only marketed in fine jewelry stores. Their supply must have been mined out, because the jewelry was not replaced and soon sold out of existence.

In the early 1980s, another find of the beautiful violet stone was a joyous surprise to amateur miners in South Africa. In their search for large Quartz crystals, the Sugilite was uncovered. Nesting together for thousands of years were some of the largest Quartz crystals ever found on Earth, and precious beds of powerful purple magic began to release their influence to all who beheld them. In a typical wave of spiritual New Age thought, the stone was called Luvulite (Love-u-lite).

As the stone is also found occasionally containing streaks of blue, brown, black, or even a peach color, it can be very exotic. The most recognizable and preferred is a bright violet, purple, magenta color. It is seldom seen as crystals as it grows into masses like Lapis Lazuli, Jade, or Turquoise.

The International Mineralogical Association, Commission of New Mineral Names, has given honor to the original discoverer. The crystalline glory is officially named Sugilite.

Only two purple stones are now available that are strong enough and priced right to be used as healing crystals. Sugilite and Amethyst are transmitting the New Age messages.

LOVE QUOTIENT

The consensus of metaphysicians seems to be that Earth has progressed into the violet ray of the Aquarian Age. This violet crystal along with the Amethyst seems to be effective in healing and activating our surrender to the transformations we make in our daily attitudes and actions.

Wearing or meditating with the Sugilite has been reported to bring a relief from the fear and anxiety of drastic change (otherwise known as transformation).

"Chaos precedes transformation" was the scientific revelation of chemist Illya Progeni, who received a Nobel Prize for science in 1978.

In these historic times of great change, both in physical Mother Earth and our own personal lives, we experience an undercurrent of anxiety! Predictions by scientologists and meteorologists of Earth's destruction are read and heard daily. The ozone layer, rain forests, nuclear testing and waste, accidental explosions, volcanic eruptions, fires, earthquakes, and political rebellions are all part of our subconscious fears.

In our personal careers and relationships we find men

and women changing roles. The divorce rate is high, forcing fathers to nurture their children on alternate weekends, buy groceries, cook, and make a home of their own. Mothers must now leave the nest, go out into the world of competition, and use their masculine qualities of logic and assertiveness. Men are no longer responsible for women and vice versa.

Religions and education are foundering.

The most important death and transformation brought about by the changes taking place on Earth is the death of the Negative Ego, that is, our selfish desires to focus on satisfying only our physical self. To have money, position, power, and freedom is not enough. We know at last, we cannot survive without trusting, affectionate companionship and love.

We desperately want to transform our fears of giving up our Negative Ego, our autonomy, control, and willful desires to satisfy our Self.

We see the need to change, we feel the changes happening all around Earth, and we are uneasy. We don't know what to expect next! We may know intellectually that everything will work out, it always does . . . but the Emotional Body, inner child, power animal, is not convinced . . . we are afraid.

We are afraid to trust, afraid to give love unless we have an ironclad contract that it will be returned (how absurd). We are even fearful of anyone who loves us too soon or too much (they can't be real)! The fact is, some folks are just more willing, able, and unafraid to *express* love sooner. Does that make them stupid and us smart? It simply shows us how fearful and untrusting we are of the binding forces in the Universe that carry these messages of love.

These changes feel like chaos. The underlying discontent is the result of giving up the old, safe ways in order to achieve soul evolution.

The burgundy ray from the planet Pluto and the violet ray from the planet Mercury are captured by the New Age crystal Sugilite. The resulting vibration affects the human psyche and the invisible Emotional Body. It acts as your antenna and transmitter to send and receive messages of safety as well as the knowledge that we have been transforming for millions of years.

The Earth has experienced many cataclysms but never dies. The incarnating spirit of each of us may have lived a thousand lives but never dies. There is no death, only transformation.

To soothe the "chaos" that may be felt during these times, try using Sugilite in a way that feels comfortable to you. Sugilite is for surrender, to let go, get into the flow. Love conquers fear.

Sugilite Meditation

Follow the procedure for all crystal meditations in this book. Hold the Sugilite against the:

Solar Plexus: Repeat aloud seven times—"This Sugilite is vibrating to calm the fears of my inner child."

Heart: "This purple crystal is bringing the violet ray to transform my heart, to surrender my control, and trust in change."

Forehead: "This part of Mother Earth is my connection to safely let the old ways go, to be born again, with love."

Kunzite

CHEMICAL COMPOSITION: $LiAlSi_2O_6$ (lithium aluminum silicate)
CRYSTAL SYSTEM: Monoclinic
COLOR: Pale orchid, lavender, pink
HARDNESS: 6–7 on Mohs' scale
PLANETS AND COLOR RAY: Mars, Pluto, and Mercury— Red, Violet
LOVE QUOTIENT: Giving and receiving unconditional love

When this crystal of the pale pink/lilac, almost fluorescent color was discovered in the late 1800s in southern California, Indian children were playing with it. Crystallography was a mature science; however, the finding of the X ray made it possible to identify each new crystal by its interior structure. The expert at the time was G. F. Kunz from Tiffany's in New York. The crystals were sent to him for identification in 1902. Later the International Mineral Naming Committee called the wonderful stones after him, adding *ite* to the end of his name, as is the custom in mineral naming.

Since that time three other major deposits have been

found in Madagascar, Africa, and Brazil. The larger crystals have been forming for perhaps millions of years. Other natives of these lands may have used them for religious rituals or healings in times past.

The fact that we, in our time of great worldwide transformation, have discovered this wonderful gift from our Mother Earth is no accident. When the farthest-out planet in our solar system appeared, we called it Pluto after the mythological Greek god of the underworld. It represented *transformation* or naturally occurring "death and rebirth." Our world was just beginning the great upheaval of evolution to a higher level when the discovery was made. Pluto's rays are transmitted by Kunzite.

It has been evident through my research that discovery of a new crystal coincides with a new planet! The crystal is called forth by the planetary rays and transmits to Earthlings the direct power and messages it represents.

Since Pluto's discovery the world has been torn apart by war (death) and reborn again with new wealth, technology, information, and nations. Backward, underdeveloped lands and people are now in the forefront of progressive activities.

Kunzite appears to be one of the crystals that is transmitting the Plutonian, indigo, burgundy ray to us as a symbol of steadfast and constant support by the Universe.

There are two other planets, Mars (red ray) and Mercury (violet ray), that are focused by Kunzite. The violet ray of healing by the spoken word and the red ray of active desire and action are combined with transformation. When healing action and renewal are focused energies, the result is a feeling of satisfaction.

The physical substance in Kunzite is lithium. This is a natural form of a tranquilizing drug extracted from the matrix where Kunzite is found. These are gifts to us from the Designing Creative Force in the Universe, through our Mother Earth. We are always provided with everything we need to be prosperous, creative, and calm. The lithium in the crystal is mood-balancing.

When my research with Kunzite began, few people had ever seen the crystal. With the increase of new publications all around Earth, and the movement of the planet Saturn into the group of stars named Capricorn, more emphasis has been placed on spreading the word, and the crystals. Why? Because Saturn and Capricorn rule rocks, minerals, and crystals, all of which make up the crust of the Earth. Saturn is a major instigator of our present concern over our neglect and ecological destruction of Earth. We are waking up to the need for repair. Kunzite teaches us to love Earth.

What can a Kunzite crystal possibly have to do with unconditional love? What's all this talk about destruction and renewal? How does a tranquilizing element such as lithium affect my understanding of love?

LOVE QUOTIENT

The Kunzite encourages us by directly attracting, receiving, and transmitting invisible cosmic rays for specific vibrational messages of healing through the spoken word, as well as for desired action toward making a transformation. In the areas of our personal lives, with relationships, career, and inner-growth struggles happening simultaneously, Kunzite can be a natural tranquilizer.

Some nights I have actually gone to sleep with a large Kunzite crystal lying on my heart, and as I lay there, I felt the peace of the Universe come over me. I knew that I was connected to, and part of, the Designing Creative Force in the Universe.

The tranquil feeling of "unconditional" love, which comes surging through the Universe, is sent to every person, plant, and animal regardless of where it is found, whether on this or other planets. As the vibrations wash over us, they seem to diminish the anxiety felt as changes take place. The Kunzite attracts and channels those rays of unconditional love so Earth beings are made more aware of their own special place in the Universe.

My clients have told me that in using the Kunzite crystal for the twenty-eight-day affirmation exercises as I suggest, their feelings of love for themselves and all life increase. They experience a calm and peaceful acceptance of the magnitude of unconditional love, which surrounds us, realizing that it is all a matter of acceptance, all a matter of perspective.

The clear and beautiful orchid-pink crystal can bring peace and safety to your Emotional, Mental, and Spiritual bodies if used for a few minutes a day on the solar plexus, heart, and forehead. Soon your spirit will feel a lift, and you can be filled enough to pass it on!

This desire to experience love coming to ourselves without conditions is a consistent dream. Our Earth life begins with parents giving us conditions and limits. We will be acceptable to them (loved by them?) as long as we meet their conditions. This is not unreasonable, as we need to become acquainted with this new game (Earth Plane) our Spirit is playing. Our parents (or substitutes) are here to explain the rules of the game. In some cases their perceptions may be unrealistic because of their experiences or their parents' misconceptions of the rules. Many families pass down to generation after generation twisted views of the rules of the game. Some examples of this would be:

1. The Mafia or Cosa Nostra families whose business is organized crime.
2. Families who never work and always live on welfare.
3. Families who always engage in fighting for nationalistic territorial boundaries or religious beliefs, such as in Ireland and the Middle East.

In such cases there is no concept and no question of unconditional love. The incoming child is taught a different set of rules.

It seems that parents must give us our beginning set of conditions as best they understand. I believe we have free will as a Universal Spirit and as such choose the parents and conditions of our reentry onto the Earth Plane. I do not believe there are any accidents.

Quantum physics is now beginning to research a new theory called chaos, which at first glance appears to have no order. Scientific and other phenomena appear to be totally random and chaotic. The advent of computers, however, makes our observation and calculation abilities vast and fast beyond all past possibilities. This enables science to prove mathematically that chaos is not chaotic but in fact eventually predictable *when we can see the larger picture*.

The point to this discovery of how the Universe is actually in *divine order* is the fact that our lives may seem chaotic, that love on this Earth Plane may seem conditional, but the larger picture of each life shows order. The overall story or drama of each individual is written by the Spirit before reentry and acted out line for line until the desired lesson is learned. The Designing Creative Force in the Universe observes the drama with unconditional love.

The Kunzite crystal, by transmitting transforming planetary rays directly into our human "light body," helps to make us more aware of the benevolent attitude that surrounds us. It helps us to discover how we set up our own conditions and rules for the Earth Plane Game. It helps us to understand that we can choose to be our own parent. The Kunzite vibration encourages us to realize that another person may not be acting out the same story-lesson as we. Maybe their spirit has chosen to learn another strategy in the Earth Plane Game. Maybe the reason we feel so judgmental when we observe someone else's actions as being negative or destructive is because we learned the same lesson ourselves through pain.

Our tendency is to forget the atmosphere of space is *love*. We get into the Earth Plane Game to learn this game, and we must become tangible, physical flesh. We lose our freedom of vaporous, cloudlike, astral travel. We lose our memory of past lives on other planets or on this planet. We become a dense body, a dense mind, very limited. The secret of the game, and the real trick is *the magical, universal, creative, eternal spirit* that we really are is down there inside of this flesh-and-bone, limited Earth body! We can contact, engage, and use our Spirit.

Most humans spend seventy or so Earth years each time they take another crack at the game. It seems we use most of that time attempting to *wake up* and remember what we are doing here.

Approximately 90 percent of the clients I see are concerned about not being able to decide what their true occupation "should" be. They feel lost as to a personal goal. This includes men and women in executive, high-salaried positions who appear to their contemporaries as "having it made"!

There is a growing anxiety, an undercurrent of unrest among the more experienced (more times in the Earth Plane Game) Spirits living now, because they *have* become more conscious, more awake. They are responding to the movements of the major planets that are sending energy to Earth. The energies are being focused through constellations of stars that have specific evolutionary powers in certain areas of each life. The pressure is on everyone on Earth to wake up and realize that Earth is a part of the universal plan. It isn't floating alone. It is part of the machinery, and we are sabotaging the whole machine when we let one cog go bad.

The Kunzite crystal attracts and focuses these rays to help us look past the chaos of our own little drama to see the overall picture and to understand that we are each personally responsible to maintain our portion of space. It is up to all of us to clean up our acts, to get rid of our own pollution, to use smog-control devices in order to keep the psychological atmosphere pure. Of course our physical world reflects our mental and emotional world.

The Kunzite crystal helps each of us receive the pure, fresh, abundant supply of the "stuff" that holds the Universes together. Love without any conditions allow us to go in any direction we choose, even if we destroy ourselves. The unconditional love of the Universe restores our sanity! We wake up to the realization that we are our own parents. We are responsible for whatever we experience. The knowing we receive from the Kunzite vibration is: A mistake in judgment does not condemn us forever.

We may temporarily forget the script or the lines in our drama. We may do a scene extemporaneously, just make it up as we go. Eventually we can see that it was really meant to be, it wasn't random chance or chaos.

By meditating daily with Kunzite and wearing it as an amulet, we become more aware of the loving atmosphere of space and less fearful. We stop being such harsh self-critics, which allows us to be less judgmental of others. We begin to realize that we must accept our fellows as ourselves. We also accept and understand how another person may be living a different self-written lesson plan than our own. How can we presume to make a judgment when we do not know the plot?

Everyone can benefit from having and using a Kunzite crystal. It is important to personal peace of mind not to be so judgmental of others. I believe as each human on Earth is able to produce this personal behavior of peace of mind, the dream of peace on Earth will automatically occur.

> We are one in all and all in one.
> There are no men but only the great.
> WE. One, indivisible and forever.

> **—Ayn Rand**
> *Anthem*

LOST LOVE

When we feel that we have lost a beloved person from our physical presence through separation or death, we feel we have lost love. Of all the emotions we can experience on the Earth Plane, lost love is the most excruciating pain. All of our invisible bodies and our physical body suffer severe agony. A great many of my clients are in the process of overcoming what they perceive to be "lost love." Some are in the first stages, the most intense feelings of loss. Others are in the void, not in pain, but simply unfeeling, dull, hopeless, or angry. The third group is in recovery. They are determined to recover their ability to love.

The Kunzite crystal is most helpful when this true desire comes alive. I have made a list of statements to be said aloud when using a Kunzite to speed the recuperation from the disease that overtakes us when we think or fear that we have actually lost "love."

These phrases can be used under any circumstances. When anyone leaves his or her body and we believe they have died, we misunderstand. We forget that we are free Spirits and as such can come and go throughout the Universe at will. The Spirit of a loved one can be contacted. Forgiveness and release can be accomplished.

In matters of dissolution or separation, when we carry the anger or sadness or self-pity too long, we halt our own growth and progress. We also send negative vibrations to all around us. Others sense these obnoxious energies and begin to stay away from us. This makes us more lonely and we feel even more separated from *love*!

We also send these stifling vibrations to the "significant

others"; we are giving off dangerous, poisonous emissions, we are polluting their atmosphere long distance! I have known jilted lovers so angry they can cause radio and television interference for miles between themselves and the lost lover! This is destructive energy and it kills everything in its path, including the sender. These energies running rampant emerge as *war* or violence somewhere on the planet. Do not allow yourself to be a party to this destruction.

I have recorded these phrases of encouragement and healing on a cassette, and I listen to it while falling asleep. Thoughts more readily enter the subconscious mind when we are in the hypnogogic state. I have experimented with clients to see how recovery can be speeded up or enhanced by listening. I have had them try the affirmations without the Kunzite and with the Kunzite. Kunzite is atomic, much more powerful, and it works faster.

If you are experiencing any feeling of lost love for *any* reason, consider getting this tape, or recording your own tape by reading the following phrases out of this book onto a cassette. Remember to read each sentence aloud three times.

Possibly you will want to do a shorter meditation each day by holding the crystal on the three areas prescribed always. If that is easier for you, then read over all the sentences and choose *one for each area*. Say it at least seven times while holding the Kunzite on the body area. These sentences repeated while holding the Kunzite on the three major areas are magnified, focused, positive energy. This is time and effort spent in your own healing. The Universe rewards your efforts with "sweet medicine." When you begin this exercise meditation affirmation hold the crystal on your solar plexus the first day. This area is where your little child inside lives. This child is the one who is experiencing over again the feeling of separation, who needs comforting.

On the second day, hold the crystal over your heart. This is where your Spirit lives. Your Spirit needs to be reawakened, to remember where it originated, and how it is a part of the Great Spirit, which nurtures it.

On the third day hold your Kunzite crystal on your forehead during the affirmations. This is the home of your Mental Body. The brain is full of false beliefs about the Self and about love. It needs to be reprogramed. The old canals need to be filled in and new highways built for love to travel easily in the Earth mind.

Trust this process, repeat it anytime you feel your emotions becoming negative. Repeat the phrases that stick in your mind. The ones that you remember are the most important because you have an emotional attachment to the ideas they express.

If you are with other people when the negative emotions begin to roll in, take out your crystal and hold it. Let the Kunzite talk to you of how you are loved. Focus on the people who are with you, secretly point the crystal toward them, and notice everything about them. Let the crystal be a channel for your love to flow toward them. Remember that they have also walked your path, they have been in your shoes; everyone has at some time.

Every day that you do the exercise, after the first three days, hold the crystal at any of the power points we have used: Emotional Body, Spiritual Body, or Mental Body. Just do it the way that feels best at the time. Your superconscious knowing will tell you for that day; trust yourself.

You may do this without the Kunzite; it will still help you. A Quartz could be substituted as it will hold whatever it hears. If you use no crystal at all, it will help you. The crystal makes it faster and stronger.

Are you ready to begin? We are saying each line 3 times.

1. I forgive my loved one for not doing everything in our relationship the way I wanted him (her) to do.
2. I forgive myself for everything I did not do the way I wanted to do it in this relationship.
3. I have not lost my love, I still have love inside of me.
4. This person I love is not gone, their spirit will be with me forever.
5. The pains I'm feeling are "growing pains"; each time I let myself love, I grow.
6. When I was a young child, I felt this pain each time my mother figure left me, but I had to grow!
7. I wrote this separation into my own life script so I could move ahead in learning more.
8. This special one I love is also growing and learning more. I will not hold them back.
9. We have agreed to play these roles for each other because we love each other.
10. There is no death, only transformation. This relationship is changing form.
11. The vibration of my body was changed by this relationship; it is higher and better now.
12. The aching that I feel is my body telling me to wake up and let love flow through.
13. The love of the whole universe can push through my blocks if I let the river flow!
14. The love I have inside me can be directed to my little inner child now.

15. I comfort, kiss, and hold my inner child now. I am my own loving parent.
16. This relationship was a great learning experience.
17. Each relationship in my life is like a mirror. I have a chance to see what I like or deny about myself.
18. Every time I bring the love inside me out to share with another, I learn and grow.
19. The other person will also learn and grow because I am his (her) mirror.
20. I will let myself love again soon because blocking the flow causes my pain.
21. I am not afraid to love again because I trust myself.
22. I can love anyone I choose, I am free to love; I do not demand they love me.
23. Love comes to me from every direction; I will not expect it from only one person.
24. I have so much love to give, I cannot funnel it into only one person.
25. I begin every day by letting my love flow through me. Loving myself is healing myself.
26. The more I take care of my inner child with Self-love, the more love I have to share with others.
27. I have not lost the person I love, I have released their Spirit to its destiny.
28. I am a better lover now than I have ever been. Every time I love, I do it better and better.

These 28 affirmations add up to a #1 vibration.

$$(2 + 8 = 10) : (1 + 0) = 1$$

New beginnings = I can have a fresh start.

APPENDIX A

Crystal Structures and Hardness

Each of the approximately 3000 crystals that have been identified is a member of one of these seven geometric families:

GENERAL APPEARANCE	EXAMPLES	SYSTEM
Blocky, ball-like, similar appearance from many points of view		ISOMETRIC
Squarish cross sections, crystals often long, sometimes very long and slender to acicular		TETRAGONAL

Hexagonal or triangular cross sections, some-times nearly round. Commonly short to long prismatic, columnar

 **HEXAGONAL**

Rectangular or diamond-shaped cross sections, stubby to short prismatic

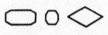 **ORTHORHOMBIC**

Blocky or stubby crystals with tipped faces which match only on opposite ends of crystals

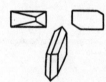 **MONOCLINIC**

Knife-edged, wafer-like crystals, only opposite faces match. Absence of right angles on faces or edges

 **TRICLINIC**

The trigonal system using the same pattern as the hexagonal system. The main axis, however, has threefold symmetry only

 TRIGONAL

SCALE OF HARDNESS

The classification of all gems, minerals and crystals as to their hardness (durability), or susceptibility to breakage, is called the Mohs' Scale of Hardness. It is based on a classification of over 2000 examples, and was developed by German mineralogist Friedrich Mohs in 1812. The English translation came in 1820.

The softest mineral found, Talc, is 1 on the scale. The hardest on Earth, Diamond, is 10. All other minerals fall in between. (Please note: I recommend using crystals that measure a hardness of 4 or more.)

Here is a scale of selected crystals, many of them examined in *Crystal Healing Secrets* and *Crystal Love Secrets*:

1: Talc

2: Sulphur, Ulexite, Alabaster

3–3½: Chrysocolla, Calcite, Celestite, Flourite

4–4½: Pearl, Coral, Azurite, Malachite, Rhodochrosite, Apophyllite

5: Kyanite, Lepidolite, Smithsonite, Dioptase, Apatite

5½: Glass, Obsidian (glass), Moldavite (glass)

5–6: Turquoise, Lapis Lazuli, Sodalite, Rhodonite

5½–6½: Opal, Hematite

6–6½: Rutile (Titanium), Pyrite, Moonstone, Aventurine

6–7: Kunzite, Larimar, Labradorite

6½–7: Tanzanite, Peridot, Jasper, Jade, Chrysoprase, Chalcedony, Agate, Sugilite

7: Tiger's-Eye, Rose Quartz, Smokey Quartz, Clear Quartz, Cintrine, Amethyst

7–7½: Tourmaline, Garnet

7½–8: Emerald, Aquamarine, Morganite

8: Topaz, Spinel

8½: Alexandrite

9: Ruby, Sapphire (Corundum)

10: Diamond

APPENDIX B

Emerald City

Dorothy, who wanted to go home, the tin man, who wanted a heart, the scarecrow, who wanted a brain, and the lion, who lacked courage, searched together for Emerald City. These four believed that the Wizard of Oz, who lived in Emerald City, had the power to grant their self-satisfying desires. After a long and arduous journey, this group discovered the Wizard was a nice person, but a fake. The moral of the story was twofold:

▲ No one could do it for them
▲ They already possessed within themselves the qualities they desired

THIS IS THE DRIVING MESSAGE OF THE NEW AGE EMERALD CITY!

Emerald City is conceived as a supportive community staffed by dedicated, talented, spiritually aware workers and teachers. Residence in the complex will be available for staff, but not required.

Vacation time for working people could be a healing time for the body, mind, and spirit. The nature communion available with outdoor activities, sun, and water would be enhanced by the most natural landscaping and design possible.

Emerald City is visualized as combining several successful ideas already working:

▲ Findhorn, a community for spiritual learning with everyone working together in partnership with nature—located in Scotland.

▲ Disneyland where fantasy is made real and usable.

▲ La Costa, California, where people can vacation and temporarily experience the commune.

▲ The Golden Door in southern California where the vacationer gets very individual treatment but is expected to experience group regimen.

Emerald City has no need to be separated by distance from the population. It can be isolated from worldly noise and distraction by its own environment. The flow of people will be directed by landscape design and grounds layout to give everyone a feeling of privacy in nature.

A distinct feeling of other-worldness will be promoted. The attitude of separation from the busy world will be included in the architecture and overall layout. Spaces for commercial offices, shops, and overnight accommodations will be camouflaged as imaginatively as possible. The basic aim is to provide a total environment for rejuvenation.

There may be certain areas designed to resemble the interior of a spaceship—or a primitive Indian village. Using the concepts of Walt Disney, Emerald City can bring all manner of joy and awakening to a group that may never find any other orthodox avenue to understanding. The subliminal messages, plus overt activities, must have a lasting effect upon any visitor.

Plans for Emerald City include a spiritual spa, retreat, reeducation, vacation, recreation, commercial shopping, restaurants, theater, New Age private school for children, and holistic New Age health care. The concept is unique in that it serves the local surrounding community as well as visitors from other states and countries.

Whether a person comes to attend self-realization classes, self-actualization seminars, metaphysical arts, the health and workout spa, or to purchase personal vibration clothing or jewelry, the emphasis is on his or her growth.

Opportunities will be available for research in several areas, including medicine, human potential, nutrition, and gardening. Eventually food and decorative plants will all be cultivated on the premises.

Everyone connected in any way with Emerald City will have a deep desire for spiritual understanding. The basis for Emerald City's existence is to provide a better life for all concerned. Eventually there will be an Emerald City within every major city in the world.

Take a few minutes to meditate about where you fit into this marvelous concept.

Emerald City is a commercial enterprise—a "win-win" entity. If you are of like mind and desire to participate in this unique and dramatic metaphysical adventure— to assist in growing needs for endowments—you may contact me. Benefactors will be drawn to the development of Emerald City—a nucleus of realistic and objective metaphysicians are already fully committed to get Emerald City going.

FOR MORE SPECIFICS, SEND NAME AND ADDRESS TO: Brett Bravo, 742 N. Granados, Solana Beach, CA 92075 or telephone 619-755-1530.

HERE'S TO YOUR PROSPEROUS FUTURE!

APPENDIX C

1991 Emerald City Update

Since Warner Books distributed *Crystal Healing Secrets* worldwide in 1988, I have received a constant stream of letters. It has been a great validation to know how many others from every country have had the same vision and burning desire to work in a place like Emerald City. All have wanted more information or a way to help bring it into physical manifestation. I am grateful to know how much mind energy is working together toward a miracle.

Since I first received the vision and instructions to "hold the vision" but not to attempt any old-fashioned physical work, I have been thoroughly tested! I like to work (Sun and four planets in Virgo in the sixth house) and I like to do things *now*! I have Aries rising with Uranus there at birth and my Moon is in Aquarius—I'm impatient. I never dreamed it would take so long.

I have been totally discouraged many times. I have looked out into space, shaken my fist, and said, "Okay, you all"—my spirit guides—"if I'm really supposed to do this, if I'm really not crazy, give me a sign or I'm going to quit!" At first I was only joking, but to my surprise, the next day a greeting card arrived, unsigned. It had twelve little cartoon people in yellow rain hats and coats, standing in a lifeboat, with rain pouring down on the ocean. The caption was "We are all in this together!"

I was so shocked, I couldn't believe it because I have a sign in my home that we have used as the mantra chant or slogan for Emerald City—you guessed it! "We Are All in This Together."

Since then, I have had all manner of "signs." Each time I ask my Guides for confirmation, some stranger, without knowing of Emerald City, says something I know could only come from an insider. Once, the only donation ever received arrived without a name or return address. I framed the five-dollar bill to remind myself of the subtle ways in which the invisible helpers let me know I should continue holding the vision.

It may be the time will be right when the two influential planets of this decade, Uranus and Saturn, move into Aquarius. That constellation rules Universal Understanding, friends, hopes, wishes, and the imaginative, inspirational, electrical New Age!

Hold the vision with me. Pass the word; mail copies of the description of Emerald City; become one of the critical mass of 51 percent. The investors will appear. It will be magic. We can do it.

BIBLIOGRAPHY

BOOKS AND DISSERTATIONS

Alexander, Thea. *2150* A.D. New York: Warner Books, 1976.

Anand, Margo. *The Art of Sexual Ecstasy.* Los Angeles: J. P. Tarcher, 1990.

Arem, Joel. *Gems and Jewelry.* New York: Bantam Books, 1983.

Arroyo, Stephen. *Astrology, Karma & Transformation.* Reno, Nevada: C.R.C.S. Publ., 1978.

———. *Astrology, Psychology, & the Four Elements.* Davis, Ca.: C.R.C.S. Publ., 1978.

Berne, Eric, M.D. *Sex in Human Loving.* New York: Simon & Schuster, 1970.

Bolen, Jean Shinoda, M.D. *Goddess in Everywoman.* San Francisco: Harper & Row, 1984.

Botwin, Carol, with Jerome L. Fine, Ph.D. *The Love Crisis.* Garden City, NY: Doubleday & Co., Inc., 1979.

Bradshaw, John. *Bradshaw on: The Family.* Pampano Beach, Fl.: Health Comm., 1988.

Branden, Nathaniel. *The Psychology of Romantic Love.* New York: Bantam Books, 1983.

Bravo, Brett. *Crystal Healing Secrets.* New York: Warner Books, 1988.

Brodie, Fawn M. *Thomas Jefferson: An Intimate History.* New York: Bantam Books, 1981.

Buscaglia, Leo, Ph.D. *Living, Loving & Learning.* New York: Holt, Rinehart & Winston, 1982.

Capra, Fritjof. *The Tao of Physics.* Boston: Shambhala Publications, 1983.

Cayce, Edgar. *Twenty-Two Gems, Stones, and Metals.* Virginia Beach, Va.: Edgar Cayce Publishing Co., 1960.

Chardin, Teilhard de. *The Phenomenon of Man.* New York: Harper & Row, 1965.

Cunningham, Scott. *Cunningham's Encyclopedia of Crystal, Gem & Metal Magic.* St. Paul, Minn.: Llewellyn Publ., 1988.

De Angelis, Barbara, Ph.D. *How to Make Love All the Time.* New York: Rawson Associates, 1987.

Dinshah, Darius. *The Spectrochrome System.* Malaga, N.J.: Dinshah Health Society, 1979.

Durfee, Cliff. *Feel Alive With Love, Have a Heart Talk.* San Diego, Ca.: Live Love Laugh, 1979.

Evola, Julius. *The Metaphysics of Sex.* New York: Inner Traditions International, 1983.

Fortune, Dion. *Esoteric Philosophy of Love and Marriage.* New York: Samuel Weiser, Inc., 1979.

Gems, Stones, & Metals for Healing & Attunement: A Survey of Psychic Readings. Phoenix, Ariz.: Heritage Publications, 1977.

Gibran, Kahlil. *The Prophet.* New York: Alfred A. Knopf, 1964.

Goodman, Linda. *Linda Goodman's Love Signs.* New York: Harper & Row, 1978.

Goodman, Marris C. *Astrology and Sexual Analysis.* New York: Fleet Press Corp., 1972.

Gowan, John Curtis. *Enveloped in Glory*. Westlake Village, Ca.: John Curtis Gowan, 1982.

Greene, Liz. *Relating*. New York: Samuel Weiser, Inc., 1978.

Harris, Thomas A., M.D. *I'm OK—You're OK*. New York: Avon Books, 1973.

Hendrix, Harville, Ph.D. *Getting the Love You Want*. New York: Henry Holt & Co., 1988.

Hodges, Doris M. *Healing Stones*. Perry, Iowa: Pyramid Publishers, 1982.

Johnson, Robert A. *"We," Understanding the Psychology of Romantic Love*. San Francisco: Harper & Row, 1983.

Joy, W. Brugh, M.D. *Joy's Way*. Los Angeles, Ca.: J. P. Tarcher, Inc., 1979.

Keyes, Ken, Jr. *A Conscious Person's Guide to Relationships*. Coos Bay, Oreg.: Living Love Publications, 1979.

Krantzler, Mel. *Creative Divorce*. New York: Signet, 1975.

Lair, Jess, Ph.D. *"Ain't I a Wonder . . . And Ain't You a Wonder, Too!"* New York: Fawcett Crest, 1977.

Lamsa, George M., translator. *The Holy Bible from Ancient Eastern Manuscripts*. Nashville, Tenn.: NJ Holman Co., 1933.

Lerner, Harriet Goldhor. *The Dance of Intimacy*. New York: Harper & Row, 1988.

Long, Max Freedom. *Introduction to Huna*. Jerome, Ariz.: Luminary Press, 1975.

Lorusso, Julia, and Joel Glick. *Healing Stoned*. Albuquerque, N.M.: Brotherhood of Life, 1983.

Lowen, Alexander, M.D. *Love and Orgasm*. New York: Signet, 1965.

Miners, Scott. *A Spiritual Approach to Male/Female Relations*. Wheaton, Ill.: Theosophical Publishing House, 1984.

Morris, Desmond. *Intimate Behaviour*. New York: Bantam Books, 1977.

Moss, Thelma, Ph.D. *The Body Electric*. Los Angeles, Ca.: J. P. Tarcher, 1979.

Norwood, Robin. *Women Who Love Too Much*. New York: Pocket Books, 1985.

Ouspensky, P. D. *The Psychology of Man's Possible Evolution*. New York: Random House, 1974.

Partnow, Elaine. *The Quotable Woman*. Garden City, N.Y.: Anchor Books, 1978.

Peck, M. Scott, M.D. *The Road Less Traveled*. New York: Simon & Schuster, 1978.

Perera, Sylvia Brinton. *Descent to the Goddess*. Toronto, Canada: Inner City Books, 1981.

Pietropinto, Anthony, M.D., and Jacqueline Simenauer. *Beyond the Male Myth*. New York: Signet, 1977.

Ponder, Catherine. *The Dynamic Laws of Healing*. Marine del Rey, Ca.: DeVorss & Co., 1966.

———. *The Prospering Power of Love*. Lee's Summit, Mo.: Unity Books, 1966.

Prophet, Mark and Elizabeth. *The Science of the Spoken Word*. Colorado Springs, Colo.: The Summit Lighthouse, 1974.

Rainey, Dennis and Barbara. *Building Your Mate's Self-esteem*. San Bernardino, Ca.: Here's Life Publishers, 1986.

Rajneesh, Bhagwan Shree. *I Am the Gate*. New York: Harper & Row, 1977.

Raphaell, Katrina. *Crystal Enlightenment*. New York: Aurora Press, 1986.

———. *Crystal Healing*. New York: Aurora Press, 1987.

Ray, Sondra. *Loving Relationships*. Berkeley, Ca.: Celestial Arts, 1980.

Reed, Richard and Janet. *How to Create Love in Your Life*. Encino, Ca.: Prasad Press.

Richardson, Wally, and Lenora Huett. *Spiritual Value of Gem Stones*. Marina del Rey, Ca.: DeVorss & Co., 1980.

Saint-Exupéry, Antoine de. *The Little Prince*. New York: Harcourt Brace Jovanovich, 1971.

Schaef, Anne Wilson. *Escape From Intimacy*. New York: Harper & Row, 1989.

Scheid, Robert. *Beyond the Love Game*. Berkeley, Ca.: Celestial Arts, 1980.

Schulman, Martin. *Karmic Astrology*. New York: Samuel Weiser, Inc., 1975.

Schumann, Walter. *Gemstones of the World*. New York: Sterling Publishing Co., 1979.

Simenauer, Jacqueline, and David Carroll. *Singles, the New Americans*. New York: Simon & Schuster, 1982.

Sinkankas, John. *Mineralogy*. New York: Van Nostrand Reinhold Co., 1964.

Steiner, Rudolph. *Love and Its Meaning in the World*. Hudson, N.Y.: Anthroposophic Press, 1990.

Stone, Merlin. *When God Was a Woman*. New York: Harcourt Brace Jovanovich, 1976.

Thorsten, Geraldine. *God Herself, the Feminine Roots of Astrology*. Garden City, N.Y.: Doubleday & Co., 1980.

Van Hulle, J. P. *Michael's Gemstone Dictionary*. Orinda, Ca.: Michael Educational Foundation, 1986.

Viorst, Judith. *Necessary Losses*. New York: Ballantine Books, 1986.

Vissell, Barry, M.D., and Joyce Vissell, RN, MS. *The Shared Heart*. Aptos, Ca.: Ramira Publishing, 1984.

Wheelis, Allen. *How People Change*. New York: Harper & Row, 1973.

Women Pro & Con. Mount Vernon, N.Y.: The Peter Pauper Press, 1958.

Woolger, Jennifer Barker and Roger J. *The Wounded Goddesses Within*. New York: Ballantine Books, 1989.

Yarbro, Chelsea Quinn. *Messages from Michael*. New York: Berkley Books, 1984.

Zukav, Gary. *The Dancing Wu Li Masters.* New York: Morrow, 1979.

Zyir, Dhara Star, and Marilyn Painter. *Love's Awakening.* Kansas City, Mo.: Uni ☆ Sun, 1987.

JOURNAL ARTICLES, CONFERENCES, AUDIOTAPES

Journal Articles

AHP Perspective: "In Quest of the Mythical Mate." Ellyn Bader & Peter T. Pearson. June 1989. "Sex in the Forbidden Zone." Peter Rutter. Dec. 1989. "Love's Executioner." Irvin D. Yalom. Dec. 1989.

Birth into Light (newsletter): "Awakening Your Light Body." Orin & DaBen. May/July 1990.

Body, Mind & Spirit: "How to Master Relationships." Dick Sutphen. Mar./Apr. 1988.

Challenge: "How Do We Create Empowering Relationships?" Milt & Lynda Lafair. Summer 1989.

Dell Horoscope: "Pluto: The Great Transformer." Herbert Kugel. Nov. 1988. "Sun-Sign Encounters in the Office." Esther C. Seltzer. Sept. 1988. "Destiny Times Two." Richard Nolle. Mar. 1990.

Discover: "Diamond Vision." Paul Hoffman. May 1989.

Holistic Life Magazine: "Human Sexuality and Wellness." Louis Richard Batzler, Ph.D. Fall 1984.

The Light Connection: "You Can Have the Relationship You Desire!" Cyndi Wells. Feb. 1989. " 'If You Really Loved Me . . .' The Dilemma of Loving." Paul & Layne Cutright. July 1988. "Love, Sex, Loneliness & Relating." Richard Lee Van Der Voort, M.A. May

1988. "From *Lifemates:* The Love Fitness Program for a Lasting Relationship." Harold Bloomfield, M.D. & Sirah Vettese, Ph.D. June 1990.

Magical Blend: "Releasing Sex from the Obligation to Make Us Feel Better." Robert Augustus Masters. Oct. 1989. "Reflections on Love." Marcel Vogel. May 1988.

McCall's: "The Process of Falling Out of Love." 1983.

Montecito Life: "Ways of Living." Dr. Larry Decker. April 7, 1988.

New Age: "Unlimited Partners." Frank & Sharan Barnett. Mar./Apr. 1989.

New Frontier: "Bioelectric Energy Love." Wilhelm Reich, M.D. May 1990.

New Realities: "An Open Life." Joseph Campbell. Mar./Apr. 1989.

New Woman: Men and Obsessional Love. Robin Norwood. Feb. 1988. *Why Men Fight Differently Than Women.* Steve Berman. Feb. 1985.

Omni: "The Importance of Hugging." Howard Bloom. June 1988.

Psychology Today: "Heart & Soul." T. George Harris. Jan./Feb. 1989. "How Do You Build Intimacy in an Age of Divorce?" Caryl S. Avery. May 1989.

Science of Mind: "A Revised Look at Intimate Relationships." Ronald S. Miller. Nov. 1985.

Success!: "Make Love Not War." Dr. Srully Blotnick. 1989.

Visions: "Love." Lazaris. Mar. 1990.

Vogue: "Falling in Love." Barbara Ehrenreich & Deirdre English. July 1988.

Conferences

"Bringing Out the Best in Our Relationships With Others." Brother Premamory. Self-realization Fellowship. 1983.

"Getting Well." Simonton, Dr. Carl. 1988 Conference.

"Healthy Pleasures." Robert Ornstein, Ph.D., David Sobel, M.D., Margaret Kemeny, Ph.D., Shelly Taylor, Ph.D., Gary Emery, Ph.D. March 4, 1990.

"Men/Women: Can We Be Friends?" Rhonda Morris, M.A. & Andrea Glass, B.A.

"The Secrets of a Great Relationship." Manny & Rhonda. L.A. Loving Relationships Trainings. 1986.

"Toward a New Sexual Reality." Dr. Bob Fischer. 1982.

Audiotapes

Bravo, Brett. "Affirmations to Heal an Evolving Relationship." Emerald City Productions, 1988.

Bravo, Brett. "Affirmations to Heal the Inner Child." Emerald City Productions, 1990.

Konikov, Barry. "Relationship Reprograming" (self-hypnosis). Potentials Unlimited.

May, Rollo, Ph.D. "The Devil & Creativity." AHP, Washington, D.C. July 1988.

Ray, Sondra. "Your Ideal Loving Relationship." Loving Relationships Trainings, 1977.

INDEX